THE MUSIC GUIDE TO ITALY

ELAINE BRODY
CLAIRE BROOK

THE MUSIC GUIDE TO ITALY

Dodd, Mead & Company
New York

1   2   3   4   5   6   7   8   9   10

Library of Congress Cataloging in Publication Data
Brody, Elaine.
    The music guide to Italy.

    Includes index.
    1. Music—Italy—Directories. I. Brook, Claire, joint author. II. Title.
ML21.B783   780'.25'45   78-6846
ISBN 0-396-07436-7

Preface

This book, conceived in frustration, was born into a world besieged by unprecedented economic problems. It was originally planned as one mammoth volume covering eighteen European countries, but like so many grandiose projects, has fallen victim to our current recession. The result is a series of self-contained fragments—each book treating a specific country or area and each one available at a negotiable price. However, this necessary compromise has moved us far from our original intention.

How did it all start?

We both travel as much as our professional responsibilities will allow. We are both trained musicians married to men whose work requires them to spend some part of each year in Europe and we try to accompany them whenever possible. Too often, however, we have found ourselves in the right city at the wrong time or—worse still—in the right city at the right time without being aware of it until it was too late.

Often when faced with the delightful prospect of a few weeks abroad, we have been astonished at how difficult it is to acquire sufficient information to make these visits as fruitful as possible. The musical traveler has no central source of data on a multitude of questions practical, historical, or theoretical. There are those who want to be sure that if they are in Bayreuth on a Tuesday, they can visit the theater even though there is no performance; others may try for weeks to isolate the moment when the Musée d'Instruments of the Paris Conservatory receives visitors and allows them to play the instruments on display; the curious amateur may wish to locate the Brahms House in Baden-Baden, while others may have heard that there is an interesting music festival in Fishguard without being able to guess exactly where it is and when it is held. Graduate students seeking to avail themselves of the resources of the Gesellschaft der Musikfreunde in Vienna will be grateful for precise information concerning the visiting hours and credentials requirements; the opera lover enjoying a performance at La Scala would have to be aware of the proximity of La Scala Theater Museum in order to explore it during an intermission. The young scholar arriving in Rome on a two weeks' summer leave, only to find that all the libraries are closed and there is no one within miles to provide a bit of assistance, could have been forewarned had schedules been available to him. And so on and so on and so on.

The idea for the *Music Guide* came to us in recognition of the need for a handbook which could provide to the widest range of people—from the musical dilettante to the highly motivated specialist—a compendium of information of a practical nature. The idea seemed so straightforward and obvious that we could not understand why such a guide did not already exist. Once we had embarked on the project, we understood only too well; it had not already been done because it was utterly impossible!!!

But we are getting a bit ahead of ourselves. The *Guide,* once we began to classify and organize the areas for investigations, began to shape itself. Certain editorial decisions concerning the geographical limitations of this volume had to be made arbitrarily. In addition, we would not know just how to treat individual cities until enough information had been gathered to determine the extent of the musical activity and resources in each place. Questionnaires were prepared in five languages for five categories. With the invaluable cooperation of the official cultural offices in each of the eighteen countries we had decided to discuss, we amassed lists of places and people that formed the basis of a large initial mailing. So the process of information-gathering began. As the responses came in, most of our questions concerning inclusion, exclusion, format, and style were answered. The results are to be found in the volumes that follow.

Within each country, the physical, political, and musical organizations indigenous to that nation determined the ordering of the material. In some instances, a chapter consists of a series of short essays on individual cities; in others where there is only one important urban center, additional information applying to cities outside that center is provided by categories: i.e., miscellaneous opera houses and concert halls, libraries, conservatories, etc. We have taken it upon ourselves to enter the lists editorially by making evaluative judgments.

In addition to decisions of qualitative merit, we have had to take cognizance of length and usefulness. We have tried to maintain a reasonable level of consistency in approach and depth of information. Although we sent the same questionnaires to each country, the responses were incredibly uneven. In some cases information was unavailable because we received no replies and it was impossible to pursue the matter personally. In other instances one of us did the necessary legwork to ferret out answers when the official sources were uncooperative. Very often, however, we received invaluable help from many of the Music Information Centers (CeBeDeM in Brussels, Donemus in Amsterdam, the Music Information Centers of Finland and Sweden, to mention but a few) as well as from individuals whose professional affiliations enabled them to provide us with precise details in addition to general information.

Subject to geographical variations, the information we have prepared is organized under the following general headings: Opera Houses and Concert Halls; Libraries and Museums; Conservatories and Schools; Musical Landmarks; Musical Organizations; Business of Music; Miscellaneous. At the conclusion, there is a section devoted to Festivals and Competitions.

Opera Houses and Concert Halls: we have tried to include the information necessary for the reader's use in determining season, program, and hours of performances. Although we mention some churches in which concerts usually take place, we have not attempted to be overly comprehensive, since almost every church will house the odd public concert from time to time and this does not automatically qualify it as a site for musical entertainment. There has been an increasingly prevalent tendency to present concerts, opera, and chamber music in castles, courtyards, parks, and gardens. The reader is therefore advised to consult a local newspaper or concert guide, which will be indicated at the beginning of most city segments, for details of the unusual events taking place in the unexpected places.

Libraries and Museums: to facilitate practical reference to specific collections, we have attempted to give library and museum names in their original languages. We wish to acknowledge here and now our gratitude for the scholarship and generosity of Rita Benton, whose *Directory of Music Research Libraries* constituted the basic foundation of our investigations in this category. (Hence Ben. 1, 2, etc. found in our volumes refer to Dr. Benton's numbering system.) We are particularly grateful to Dr. Benton for permission to see the third volume of this important work while it was still in manuscript. For more detailed information about the institutions mentioned in this present volume, please consult her book. Where our questionnaires contained information at odds with hers, we assumed that we had the more recent data.

For the most recent and most comprehensive coverage of archives, collections, libraries, and museums, consult the cumulative index (vols. I-V, 1967–1971) of RILM (acronym for the *International Repertory of Music Literature*), an absolutely essential reference work available at most libraries.

Established in 1966 by the International Musicological Society and the International Association of Music Libraries to attempt to deal with the explosion in musicological documentation by international cooperation and modern technology, *RILM,* a quarterly publication of abstracts of books, articles, essays, reviews, dissertations, catalogues, iconographies, etc. is available in the USA through the International RILM Center, City University of New York, 33 West 42nd Street, New York 10036. European subscriptions are available from RILM Distributor for Europe, Bärenreiter Verlag Heinrich-Schütz-Allee 31–37, D-3500 Kassel-Wilhelmshöhe, West Germany.

Institutes of Musicology are to be found under different headings according to their function within the host country. In France, for example, the Institute is part of the university and is found under Schools and Conservatories. In Spain, it is a library and publishing organization and will appear under Libraries.

Schools and Conservatories: we have had to eliminate ruthlessly all but the major musical institutions in the interest of keeping this book portable. Because course offerings and degree requirements differ from country to country, we have eschewed program descriptions and instead supplied an address from which the interested reader may obtain further information. Summer courses are included in this section, except where they are clearly allied with a festival, in which case they can be located through a cross reference. A cautionary word: those planning to attend seminars or master classes in European universities should bear in mind that no housing arrangements are made by the university. The administration will supply the names of private persons who take in boarders, but these arrangements should be made well in advance of arrival. A list of organizations with special services for the English-speaking student abroad can be found in the Appendix.

Musical Landmarks: after an enthusiastic beginning, it became apparent that it would not be possible to include every commemorative plaque and graveyard that concerned a musician or musical event without rivaling the telephone directory in size. Therefore, we have usually restricted ourselves to establishments which are open to the public but do not qualify as museums. Occasionally the address of such a place seems to differ in alternate descriptions of the same place. This is invariably due to the fact that building compounds may have entrances on several streets. Where a mailing address is at variance with the public entrance, we have indicated both.

Musical organizations of international significance have been mentioned and, in some exceptional instances, described in detail. The same criteria were applied to commercial musical establishments.

The concluding section, that devoted to Festivals, Competitions, and Periodicals, brings together a body of material never before found between the covers of a single volume. Because we did not wish to build immediate obsolescence into the book, we have not supplied exact dates or typical programs for Festivals and Competitions. Instead, we have sought to give an accurate name and address to which the reader might address himself for that information. We did attempt, wherever possible, to provide descriptive as well as factual material on the more colorful festivals.

There is always a question, where co-authorship is concerned, about the division of labor in any particular project. We are sure that others have arranged their mode of cooperation in a variety of ways. Once the operational procedures had been established by mutual decision, we found it expedient and practical to divide our work on a geographical basis. Therefore, Elaine Brody supervised the research and wrote up the materials on Germany and Austria, Belgium, the Netherlands, Spain, Portugal, Switzerland, Luxembourg, and Monaco; Claire Brook did the same for Great Britain, France, Italy, and the four Scandinavian countries: Denmark, Finland, Norway, and Sweden.

The problems inherent in this kind of compendium are legion. Having to depend on the cooperation of hundreds of functionaries from

secretaries to cultural ministers—disinterested at one extreme and overly
zealous at the other—as well as on our own researching techniques and
efforts, has resulted in somewhat uneven coverage with somewhat
variable accuracy quotient. Although we have visited almost every one
of the cities discussed in depth and many of those covered more cur-
sorily, we have not attended all the festivals nor have we physically
investigated all the libraries, institutes, and museums. It has been utterly
impossible to check all of our sources personally. We have tried to
circumvent this lapse from scholarly grace by choosing our sources as
carefully as we could.

Three years after we began this Herculean task, we halted the
gathering, collating, checking, writing. It would not be accurate to say
that we "finished," for we are both only too aware of the fact that we
have barely skimmed the surface of the material. But our manuscript
had already become five times the length contracted for, and other
duties called. In those three years we had the good fortune to work with
a group of exceptional people—exceptional not only because of their
extraordinary sense of responsibility and selfless dedication to their
nation's music, but also for the care and precision with which they
answered our questions. We would like to thank the following people—
and to apologize to those whom we have inevitably and inadvertently
overlooked: John Amis (London), Dr. R. Angermüller (Salzburg), the
Comtesse de Chambure (Paris), Ulla Christiansen (New York), Hans
Conradin (Zurich), Adrienne Doignies-Musters (Brussels), Ady Egleston
(New York), Dr. Georg Feder (Cologne), Marna Feldt (New York), Jean
and Mimi Ferrard (Brussels), Prof. Kurt von Fischer (Zurich), Claire
Van Gelder (Paris and Brussels), Dr. Jörn Göres (Dusseldorf), Marlene
Haag (Salzburg), Prof. Edmund Haines (New York), Ernesto Halffter
(Madrid), Dr. Hilde Hellmann (Vienna), Per-Anders Hellquist (Stock-
holm), Maurice Huisman (Brussels), Antonio Iglesias (Madrid), Dr.
Erwin Jacobi (Zurich), Jean Jenkins (London), Newell Jenkins (Giglio
and New York), Prof. Rudolf Klein (Vienna), Kåre Kolberg (Oslo), Dr.
Johanna Kral (Vienna), Dr. Gunnar Larsson (Stockholm), Albert
Vander Linden (Brussels), Anders Lönn (Stockholm), Per Olaf Lundahl
(Stockholm), René de Maeyer (Brussels), Matilde Medina y Crespo
(Madrid), Per Onsum (Oslo), Dr. Alfons Ott (Munich), Pierluigi Petro-
belli (Parma), Henry Pleasants (London), Andrew Porter (New York
and London), Sheila Porter (New York and London), Anders Ramsay
(Stockholm), Albi Rosenthal (London), Dag Schjelderup-Ebbe (Oslo),

Torben Schousboe (Copenhagen), Jarmo Sermilä (Helsinki), Sheila Solomon (London), Anna van Steenbergen (Brussels), Jean Touzelet (Paris), Edmund Tracey (London), Tatu Tuohikorpi (New York and Helsinki), Renaat Verbruggen (Antwerp), Linde Vogel (New York), William Weaver (Monte San Savino), Henry Weinberg (Florence and New York).

We would also like to acknowledge the invaluable help we received from the team of graduate students and research assistants who have supplied so much of the energy and muscle for this project. They include: Asya Berger, Louise Basbas, Lisa Mann Burke, Pamela Curzon, Hinda Keller Farber, Anne Gross, Peter Kazaras, Debbie Moskowitz, and Barbara Petersen.

And, finally, we two very liberated women would like to thank our husbands for their encouragement, patience, and touching faith that sooner or later we would emerge from behind the mountains of colored questionnaires better people for having written the *Music Guide*.

ELAINE BRODY
CLAIRE BROOK

Contents

Cities Briefly Noted   115

THE MUSIC GUIDE TO ITALY

Introduction

From chants to chance—from Ambrose to Berio—the history of Italian music is a long and illustrious one. Much has been surmised and more conjectured about Greco-Roman music as far back as the singing of Etruscan herdsmen in the eighth century B.C.; but only with the decline of the Roman Empire and the codification of Christian chant do we begin to have a clearly documented and well-defined record of musical development. Although the final evolution of the so-called Gregorian chant took place outside of Italy, there can be no doubt as to Rome's fundamental contribution to its existence. By the Middle Ages, however, Italy was completely outranked by France, where polyphony reigned supreme until the end of the thirteenth century.

Melody and melodic invention, which seem to have been and continue to be the birthright of the Italian composer, came into fashion with the compositions of Francesco Landini (1325–97), an early exponent of the *bel canto* style. The spontaneous flowing melodies that were so characteristic of Italian music in the fourteenth century, bore little resemblance to the highly complex polyphonic music, texturally and rhythmically sophisticated, which was then current in France. Eventually, however, that melodic genius was wedded to at least three native dance forms, resulting in the very popular, complicated, and highly polished hybrid versions of the madrigal, the *caccia*, and the *ballata*.

The fifteenth century saw the complete triumph of the Franco-Flemish school in Italian art and church music. In popular music the indigenous products thrived, and a spate of new forms like the *frottola*,

1

the *"canti Carnascialeschi,"* and the *ricercari* appeared on the musical horizon. In the sixteenth century, these native forms, touched by the ever-present polyphonic genius imported from the North, resulted in the incomparable masterpieces of Andrea Gabrieli (c. 1510–96) of Venice, Luca Marenzio (d. 1599) of Rome, and Carlo Gesualdo (c. 1560–1613) of Naples. Rome became the center of religious music, all activity revolving around the virtuosity of Giovanni Pierluigi da Palestrina (1525–94); while in Venice the younger Gabrieli, Giovanni (c. 1555–1612), was reaching for new levels of perfection in writing for the great organs of San Marco.

We must dart back and forth across the face of Italy in order to trace the high points of musical chronology even in the sketchiest way. And with the understanding that all kinds of music continued to exist simultaneously, we will touch lightly on those apogees of musical development in each of the periods by which we commonly describe recent history.

The Baroque era in Italy saw the establishment of a body of ideas and new vocabulary which remain in good part with us today: the *Camerata*, the *concerto grosso, monody, oratorio, sinfonia, cantata,* and *opera* are some of the new words for the new concepts. Composers whose works are the mainstay of our current repertory flourished: Scarlatti, Vivaldi, Pergolesi, and, above them all, Claudio Monteverdi (1567–1643), the figure who stands at the point of transition to the modern world.

Opera, which was born in Florence, midwived by the group who called themselves the Camerata, became a national preoccupation during the seventeenth century. The roster of native composers whose works filled the rapidly proliferating opera houses throughout the country contained a substantial percentage of mediocrities and a fair sprinkling of nonentities. However, the genius of one such as Monteverdi, who, in *Orfeo* (Mantua, 1607) treated of the human passions, allowed the text to dominate the music, and supplied the necessary contrasts with solos, duets, dances, and ensembles, provided the necessary excitement and stimulus to keep the interest in opera at nearly fever pitch.

Italian church music, which was moving on a parallel course with opera as the seventeenth century gave way to the eighteenth, was brought to a new peak of perfection and lyricism by the young Neapolitan Giovanni Battista Pergolesi (1710–36) in his *Stabat Mater*. Instrumental chamber music, bolstered by the masterful achievements of the great violin makers of Cremona, gained preeminence throughout Europe. From the sonatas of Corelli (1653–1713) to the concertos of Vivaldi (c. 1678–1741) and Tartini (1692–1713), the development of a strong instrumental tradition to keep pace with the ever-increasing vocal one, continued energetically.

The emergence of a new and brilliant opera style in the early eighteenth century—a style almost literally called forth by the poet Pietro Metastasio (1698–1782), whose dramas were set to music over and over during his lifetime—firmly established Italy as the unchallenged leader of opera in Europe and opera as the unchallenged favorite form of music in Italy. *Opera seria,* as we have come to call it, aimed for universal appeal in dealing with human, rather than godlike or religious emotions. The format that gradually evolved was of three acts in which recitatives alternated with set arias. The names that come to mind as the earliest exponents of this new stylistic direction are Tommaso Traetta (1727–79) in Parma, and Johann Christian Bach, then of Milan. The *opera buffa* evolved early in the same century out of the tradition of presenting short comic interludes or *intermezzi* between the acts of a serious opera. The same Pergolesi already mentioned was one of the first masters of this form, others being Giovanni Paisiello (1740–1816) and, of course, the incomparable Mozart.

By the nineteenth century, when the national preoccupation with opera had achieved the proportions of a national sport, instrumental music had dropped very much into the background as the giants of Italian music drama began to march across the opera stage: Gioacchino Rossini (1792–1868), endowed with an immense gift for melody and an instinct for stage effects, wrote thirty–two operas, including the famous *Barber of Seville* (premiered in Rome, 1816); Gaetano Donizetti (1797–1848), among whose seventy operas can be found *Lucia di Lammermoor* and *Don Pasquale*; Vincenzo Bellini (1801–35), whose unmistakable melodic style and refinement may be heard today in opera houses the world over in *Norma* and *La Somnambula*; and finally, Giuseppe Verdi (1813–1901), probably Italy's most ringing answer to Richard Wagner and the reigning genius of the Italian musical stage. To choose only a few of his operas as illustrative of his finest achievements requires almost arbitrary and random judgments, but surely *Il Trovatore, Rigoletto, La Traviata, Aida, Don Carlo, Otello,* and *Falstaff* fulfill the twin criteria of popularity and greatness.

The importance of Verdi in Italian music cannot and must not be underestimated. The lasting imprint of his image on the Italian audiences as well as on the composers who followed him has yet adequately to be gauged. However, interest in instrumental music returned in the early 1900s and composers like Busoni (1866-1924), Respighi (1879-1936), and Casella (1883-1947) led the way for the more adventurous and contemporary works of Goffredo Petrassi (b. 1904) and Luigi Dallapiccola (1904-75), to mention but two of the leading members of the older generation of modern Italian composers.

What position does music occupy in present-day Italy? As we proceed to attempt a description of those institutions that have been set up to reinforce and perpetuate the rich musical traditions of this country, we should bear in mind the simple historical fact that Italy has not known a protracted period of peace and democratic growth until very recently, and even that has been under less than ideal internal conditions.

With the gradual decline of the impresario system in the twentieth century, especially as it applied to opera, it became apparent that another way of subsidizing musical theater had to be found. As early as 1921, La Scala in Milan was receiving some degree of publicly financed support from the government. The Rome Opera also received some assistance in order to maintain a regular season in the face of rising costs and inflated prices. During the Fascist regime, attempts were made to regularize musical life, but with little positive result. The Italians, it should be noted, by their very nature are not easily "regularized."

After World War II, legislation was enacted concerning the physical institutions of music. A decree was issued that operatic activities and other forms of musical performance be considered of public interest because they contributed to cultural and social progress. Hence the government took steps to assure the protection and development of these activities. A central Music Commission was established within the Ministry of Tourism and Entertainment to deal with all the problems of musical subsidy. A sound plan—on paper, at least.

Eleven *enti autonomi* (autonomous or independent corporations that were, in fact, state theaters run by self-governing boards) were officially designated: the Communales of Bologna, Florence, and Genoa; La Scala of Milan, the San Carlo of Naples, the Verdi of Trieste, the Massimo of Palermo, the Rome Opera, the Regio of Turin, the Fenice of Venice, and the Arena of Verona. Two organizations were later added: the Istituzione dei Concerti e del Teatro Lirico of Cagliari and the

Accademia Nazionale Santa Cecilia of Rome. These houses were subsidized by the government with an annual stipend, approved a year in advance and usually amounting to one-half of what they needed to survive. In 1975, they were transformed into *istituzioni nazionali*, to be governed by a national commission and their regional governments jointly. This attempt at decentralization was designed to bring music to audiences outside the large cities. In addition, the law allots special sums to fifteen "established" theaters, which, although they are not nationally owned, have historical and artistic merit and provide the musical life around the provincial city in which they are located. These established theaters are the Petruzelli of Bari, the Bellini of Catania, the Ponchielli of Cremona, the Comunales of Ferrara, Modena, and Treviso, the Grande of Brescia, the Sociales of Como, Mantua, and Rovigo, the Coccia of Novara, the Regio of Parma, the Municipales of Piacenza and Reggio Emilia, and the Verdi of Pisa.

There are, in addition, at least forty-two opera houses throughout Italy that are neither state nor established theaters which give regular annual seasons of opera.

What of the works performed there and the forces who do the performing? There are official incentives organized for the production of works by Italian composers. In addition, six concert-promoting groups receive special grants from the government for the purpose of increasing and broadening the scope of musical activities. Competitions, experimental productions, and special events of all kinds are given careful attention. In most Italian provincial cities there is at least one "Friends of Music" organization which sponsors chamber music, solo recitals, lectures, or discussions. There are the official tourist services, which seek to exploit every possibility that can be called a festival—ranging from one- or two-day affairs to a weekly concert series.

Festivals exist in almost every town, village, and hamlet in Italy. There are also many professional organizations that attempt to impose a standard of achievement and minimal excellence on the musical activities of the country. They are national and international, musical, scholarly, or fraternal, and they all, without exception, attempt with sincerity and high purpose infinitely more than they can achieve. Amateur performing groups are not a native Italian product. There are some choral societies, a few chamber music playing organizations, but the main thrust in this country is most assuredly for spectator as opposed to participatory music activity.

Italy has fourteen national conservatories and nineteen "equalized" institutes. The latter are considered to be on the same level as the former except that they function in less-populated areas. They also lay no claim to the ancient traditions and rich libraries that belong to conservatories such as the Santa Cecilia in Rome, the Luigi Cherubini in Florence, the Benedetto Marcello in Venice, etc. The equalized institutes were originally subsidized locally for the benefit of the music students who could not go to a big city conservatory, and in order to serve as the focal point for local musical activities. Today the instruction is standardized by decree regulating the functioning of the educational system, and the same diploma may be issued by either kind of school. Admission to all Italian conservatories, incidentally, is open to foreigners as well as Italian citizens, provided the necessary documentation is provided. This information may be obtained from the Italian consulate in the country from which the applicant originates.

In the libraries and archives of the conservatories, music schools, churches, monasteries, seminaries, and public institutions, the vast and incredibly rich accumulations of centuries of music are now at last undergoing careful scrutiny and cataloging. The Ufficio Richerche Musicale (Office of Musical Research), was set up for this purpose and is funded by the Ministry of Education and the National Council for Research. It is based at the Biblioteca Nazionale Braidense in Milan and will at last make available to students, scholars, and performers from all over the world the essential information concerning the contents and provenances of many of the most important musical collections in existence, which have, until now, been shrouded in mystery, dust, and confusion.

Statistics issued by the government on concert and opera attendance in Italy are impressive and detailed. Modern music organizations, encouraged by the official attitude toward supporting native artistic efforts, and the excellent work done by the RAI (see p. 24), exist in fair abundance in all the major urban centers. The Italian contemporary music scene is well represented at all international events by composers of the impressive stature of Luciano Berio (b. 1925) and Luigi Nono (b. 1924). They serve to perpetuate the image of the Italian as the most natively musical person in the Western world.

So it is with some affectionate amusement and not a little cynicism that one must acknowledge, after the most cursory examination of those carefully amassed and lovingly compiled statistics, and after the briefest of glances at the disastrous attendance records of even slightly adventurous musical productions, that, blessed with an illustrious musical tradition, a blandly approving but insufficiently funded governmental agency, and a firmly entrenched musical establishment dominated by the operatic star system, the Italian music lover loves Verdi, looks at Verdi, and listens to Verdi. Everything else is make-believe.

NATIONAL HOLIDAYS

January	1	New Year's Day
	6	Epiphany
February	11	Anniversary of the Concordat with the Vatican
March	*	Easter Monday
April	25	Liberation Day
May	1	May Day
	*	Ascension Day
June	2	Republic Day
	*	Corpus Christi
	29	National Holiday
August	15	Assumption Day
November	1	All Saints Day
	4	Victory Day
December	8	Immaculate Conception
	25	Christmas
	26	St. Stephen's Day

* = movable

ROME (Lazio)   Tel. prefix: (06)

For centuries Rome, the Eternal City, has been a shrine to those who have come to look upon its wondrous splendors—the ruins of another age; the churches, palaces, and architectural masterpieces; the creations of centuries of geniuses. All these still remain, and added to them the latterday pilgrim will find the winding streets and dark alleys, the tiresome suburbs, the chic shops, and the incessant sound of traffic hallmarks of the contemporary city. With the Vatican at its heart, Italy's capital on the banks of the River Tiber is a thriving and vital metropolis where the monuments of the past coexist with the monstrosities of the present.

Legend has it that Rome was founded in 753 B.C. by Romulus and Remus, the twin sons of Mars; fact shows that the city had much more plebian origins as a fortified marketplace of the Latium. The village thrived for some three centuries, evolving into the Roman Republic by 509 B.C. For another five hundred years or so, Rome served as a model of sound, social balance and political equality and power. The influence of this republic continued for yet another five centuries until it virtually disappeared. It was the Catholic Church that rescued the city from total obscurity when Charlemagne, self-appointed Defender of the Faith was proclaimed Emperor of the Holy Roman Empire by Pope Leo III in 800 A.D., on Vatican Hill before the tomb of St. Peter.

From then until the present, the Church has provided the single strongest influence on the character of the city, its history, and musical life. The great composers who lived and worked in Rome were, certainly until the beginning of the eighteenth century, in the employ of the Church and reflected its prevailing humor.

The physical appearance of Rome is unique: originally built on seven hills, it retains the visible traces of all of its greatest periods in history, side by side. There are Etruscan huts dating from 900 to 800 B.C.; the massive fortress on the Capitol and the temples of Jupiter and Juno stand close by the marble columns of the Forum and the public buildings of the Palatine; the wonders of Renaissance Rome, a facade by Michelangelo, a church by Bramante, or a colonnade by Bernini; and the Baroque villas, fountains, and gardens attest to the living glories of this multi-faceted city. Rome is a very large city. Sprawling over 62,000 acres (not counting Vatican City), inhabited by some two million citizens, it is the capital of modern-day Italy. Wherever the Roman visitor goes, he will find the 1911 monument honoring King Victor Emmanuel II blocking his way and his view. This enormous white wedding cake has its uses; for one thing, it serves admirably as a direction-finder.

Vatican City, which has existed as a separate sovereign state since 1870, sits on 108 acres on the west bank of the Tiber River, surrounded by a high wide wall. The mini-state has its own power plant, post office, and radio station, which transmits in fourteen languages twice a day. Saint Peter's stands at its center. The residential sections of Rome—its seventeen *quartieri*—stretch around the ancient Aurelian Wall and continue to grow at an impressive rate, testifying to the city's vitality and ability to survive in today's civilization.

The music life of Rome is an active one. There is opera both in the winter and summer. There is also a respectable, if not especially distinguished, concert season which has more of an international than regional character. Major performing artists and groups may be heard in Rome with reasonable frequency. The heart of the academic or conservatory life in Rome is the Accademia di Santa Cecilia. It is interesting to note that the first real school of music as we know it, was the Schola Cantorum, founded by Pope Gregory I in Rome in 600 A.D. It was not until the sixteenth century that conservatories as such began to flourish in Italy. Originally the conservatories were found in orphanages where, under the supervision of first-rate instructors, most of the practicing musicians were educated. This situation continued until the eighteenth century. Today, every major Italian city has a conservatory modeled on the one in Paris, offering training of a practical and theoretical nature.

Guides and Services

This Week in Rome
Via Toscana 30.   Tel.: 46 54 92
This very useful little booklet, which comes out in English every Friday, may be found at newsstands and at all major hotels. It contains concert and opera schedules, as well as movie programs, art exhibitions, lectures, and a wide range of useful information for the visitor in Rome.

The following organizations supply information to the visitor in Rome. They will be very helpful in such matters as ticket purchases or current schedules:

International Cultural Information Center
Via Mario dei Fiori 42.   Tel.: 678 57 47

Associazione Italiana Autonome Soggiorno, Cura e Turismo
Via Lucrezio Caro 12.   Tel.: 38 51 96

Ente Provinciale per il Turismo
Via Parigi 11.   Tel.: 46 18 51

Unione Nazionale fra gli Enti Provinciali per il Turismo
Via Magenta 5.   Tel.: 495 73 83

Opera Houses and Concert Halls

Teatro dell' Opera
Via Viminale.

Mailing Address: Via Firenze 63, Rome 00184.   Tel.: 46 36 41
Public Entrance: Piazza Beniamino Gigli.
Season: November through June; opera from winter until spring; concerts from
autumn to winter. Ballet at irregular intervals. Summer season of opera
held at the Baths of Caracalla (see p. 172). Concerts of instrumental music
by the opera composer being featured each week are held in the foyer of the
opera house for the benefit of the season subscribers and students.
Box Office: Piazza Beniamino Gigli.   Tel.: 46 17 55
Tickets are on sale four days before each performance.
Hours: weekdays from 9:30 AM to 1:00 PM; 5:00 PM to 7:00 PM. On
performance days, tickets are sold up to the hour of the performance; on
Sundays, the box office is open from 10:00 AM to 1:00 PM and from 3:00 PM
until the performance starts. Evening performances usually begin at 7:00
PM and matinees at 4:00 PM. No standing room.
Seating Capacity: 2,200.
Customary Dress: evening dress advisory only for opening night of the season.
The theater, originally called the Teatro Costanzi, after Domenico Costanzi, a
rich builder who commissioned its construction, was designed by Achille
Sfondrini and opened in 1880 with a performance of Rossini's *Semiramide.* There
were 104 boxes in three tiers and two galleries, accommodating 2,293 spectators,
but the stage was dreadfully small and the front plaza outside unbearably
crowded. It was here that Toscanini made his Italian debut in 1892 and where
many important Verdi and Mascagni works were premiered.
    Under the direction of Costanzi's son, the Teatro went through a period in
which operettas and equestrian circuses were featured. From 1911 to 1925,
Emma Carelli directed the house; many new operas were given, but nothing of
lasting importance. Finally, in 1926, the theater was acquired by the city of
Rome, closed for two years of renovation under the supervision of the architect
Marcello Piacentini, and renamed the Reggio Teatro dell'Opera. It reopened in
1928 with Boito's *Nerone* and sported a new plaza on the Via Viminale, as well as
a stage that was 6,500 feet square and movable. Subsequently, the word Reggio
was dropped from its name. The Teatro dell'Opera was one of the first Italian
opera houses to abandon the rapidly declining impresario system of the
nineteenth century and to assume the status of *ente autonome,* a publicly financed,
state-supported theater. Since 1975, it has been designated an *istituzione
nazionale.*

Accademia Nazionale di Santa Cecilia Auditoria (also called *Auditorio Pio*)
Via della Conciliazione 4.   Tel.: 654 10 44
Many of the large orchestral concerts featuring international soloists and guest
conductors are given in this hall, which is lent to the Accademia Nazionale di
Santa Cecilia by the Vatican.

Aula Magna dell'Antonianum (also called *Ateneo Antoniano*)
Via Merulana 124. Tel.: 757 47 27
Concert series of ORSAM (see p. 27) and major choral concerts.

Aula Magna dell'Università di Roma
Città Universiteria, Piazzale delle Scienze 5. Tel.: 495 72 34
Mailing Address: Concerto Organizzati dalla Istituzioni Universiteria dei Concerti, 00100 Rome.

Auditorium di Foro Italico
Lungatevere Diaz 26. Tel.: 38 7 81
Orchestral series on Saturdays by invitation only. Performances by the orchestra and soloists of RAI (see p. 24).

Oratorio del Gonfalone
Church of Santa Lucia al Gonfalone, Piazza di Tor Sanguigna 2.
Tel.: 65 59 52
A restored, deconsecrated church where much ancient music, primarily of a choral nature, is performed. But recitals given there as well.

Sala Accademica
Accademia Nazionale di Santa Cecilia, Via dei Greci 18. Tel.: 67 36 17
Outstanding hall for chamber music and solo recitals. Located in the conservatory building, it is connected to the Accademia Nazionale di Santa Cecilia.

Sala Casella
Via Flaminia 118. Tel.: 36 01 702
Concert hall frequently used by the Rome Philharmonic Academy (see p. 25).
Tickets for all concerts available at the concert hall box office.

Sala Monteverdi
Via Vittoria Colonna 1 (1st floor).
Chamber music concerts arranged by the Claudio Monteverdi Music Association.

Teatro Argentina
Largo di Torre Argentina. Tel.: 65 54 45
Built in 1731-2 for the Duke Giuseppe Szorza-Cesarini by the architect Giovanni Theodali, the Teatro Argentina was the scene of the premiere of Rossini's *Barbiere di Seviglia* in 1816, to the accompaniment of great booing by the audience. First performances of some Verdi operas fared better here, however. After 1946, it was used for some time as a concert hall for the Accademia di Santa Cecilia, but it is now used almost exclusively for plays.

Teatro delle Arti
Via Sicilia 59.   Tel.: 46 01 41
Used primarily for popular and semi-classic programs.

Teatro Castel Sant' Angelo (Sala per concerti e conferenze)
Lungotevere Castello 1.   Tel.: 65 45 036
Intimate theater, it is the site of concerts, operas, and ballets sponsored by the
Amici di Castel Sant' Angelo (see p. 25).

Teatro Olimpico
Piazza Gentile da Fabriano 17.   Tel.: 30 26 35
Box Office: in the lobby of the theater.   Tel.: 36 01 752; 39 62 635
Winter season of the Accademia Filarmonica Romana held here. Also occa-
sional chamber operas. Special reductions available to students.

YMCA Concert Hall
Piazza Indipendenza 23.

The following are a few Roman churches in which public concerts take place:
   Chiesa del Gesù, Piazza del Gesù.
   Chiesa dei Santi Cosma e Damano, Via dei Fori Imperiali.
   Chiesa di San Carlo al Corso, Via del Corso.
   Basilica di Santa Cecilia in Trastevere, Piazza di Santa Cecilia.
   Chiesa di Santa Maria della Merced, Viale Regina Margherita angolo Via
      Vasento.
   Chiesa dei Santi Giovanni e Paolo, Piazza Santi Giovanni e Paolo.
   Chiesa dei Santi Apostoli, Piazza dei Santi Apostoli.
   Basilica di Santa Sabina, Via di Santa Sabina on the Aventine.
   Chiesa di Sant' Anastasia, Via di San Teodoro.
   Chiesa di San Pio X, Via Frigeri-Balduna.
   Chiesa di Santa Maria in Aracoeli, Piazza dell'Aracoeli.

A few locations of summer concerts in Rome:
   Basilica di Massenzio, Via dei Fori Imperiali. Outdoor concerts.
   Thermae di Caracalla, Via della Termi di Caracalla. Summer opera
      season. See p. 172.
   Piazza del Campidoglio, Basilica Bagenso. Private gardens, castles, and
      cloisters.

Libraries and Museums

Accademia di Francia (Académie de France), Biblioteca [Ben. 302]
Villa Medici, Viale Trinita dei Monti.   Tel.: 68 83 81; 68 90 30; 678 26 67
Hours: 9:00 AM to 11:00 AM on Wednesdays all year except for annual closing in
August. No admission fee. Written request for admission to the library of
music is necessary.
Description of the Collection: works on history of music and musicians, on musical
technique; scores, especially of French music from the eighteenth century
to the present. Total collection ca. 12,000 vols.
The Academy was founded in 1666 by Louis XIV to allow young French artists
to study in Rome. In 1803 it was moved to the Villa Medici, a building dating
back to 1514. Today, only the gardens are open to the public.

Accademia Filarmonica Romana, Biblioteca [Ben. 303]
Casina del Valadier, Via Flaminia 118.   Tel.: 360 17 02; 360 28 78; 360 65 90
Description of the Collection: exclusively musical: ca. 6,000 printed and ms. vols;
5,000 letters and other documents; many eighteenth- and nineteenth-century editions.
The Accademia was founded in 1821 to promote the cultivation and practice of
musical art.

Archivio e Biblioteca Doria Pamphili [Ben. 305]
Via Santa Maria dell'Anima 30.   Tel.: 67 43 65
Hours: Tuesday, Friday, Saturday, and Sunday from 10:00 AM to 1:00 PM.
Description of the Collection: sixteenth- and seventeenth-century madrigal collections; works by Roman composers Feretti, Cori, Boccallino, etc. Late
eighteenth-century works: operas, symphonies, chamber music.
The Archive and Library, founded by Cardinal B. Pamphili (1653–1730) is one
of the few private collections still owned by Italian nobility. The archive in the
famous Palazzo Doria Pamphili at Via del Corso 304 has no musical works in it.
For further information concerning the collection and its disposition, write to
the Amministrazione Doria Pamphili, Piazza Grazioli 5, I-00168 Rome.

Archivio Storico Capitolino e Biblioteca Romana [Ben. 306]
Palazzo Borromini, Piazza della Chiesa Nuova 18.   Tel.: 55 26 62
Hours: Monday to Saturday from 9:00 AM to 1:00 PM. Closed in August.
Description of Collection: band music, nineteenth-century works of musical litera-
ture. Archives include *Atti della Camera capitolina* (sixteenth century) and
Urbano (from 1632), Anguillara, Boccapaduli, and Orsini. Documentation
on Rome and its environs.

Biblioteca Angelica [Ben. 307]

Piazza Sant'Agostino 8.   Tel.: 656 80 41

Hours: 8:30 AM to 1:30 PM daily except Wednesday and Friday. During summer
   months, open 4:30 to 7:30 PM as well. Borrowing service daily from 9:30 AM
   to 12:30 PM. Closed October 1–15.

Description of the Collection: opera libretti (bequest of Marchese Nicola Santan-
   gelo of Naples). Printed works of sixteenth to eighteenth centuries; manuscripts of eleventh to eighteenth centuries. Eleventh-century gradual from
   Bolognese school. When the Angelica was given to the state, the bulk of the
   music in the collection went to the Santa Cecilia Library (see p. 16), but a
   catalog is maintained at this library.

This is the oldest public library in Rome, founded in 1614 by Angelo Rocca, an
Augustinian bishop. It became state property in 1873.

Biblioteca Apostolica Vaticana [Ben. 308]

Città del Vaticano.   Tel.: 69 82, x.3323

(Entrance at the Porta Santa Anna and Cortile del Belvedere)

Hours: open daily from 9:00 AM to 2:00 PM, except holidays. Closed July
   15–September 15.

Credentials: card of admission required. Foreigners need letter of introduction
   from embassy official of their country.

Description of the Collection: The museum of the library contains ancient musical
   instruments. As to the collections, there are approximately seventeen, of
   which only three are entirely musical (Cappella Giulia; Cappella Li-
   beriano di Santa Maria Maggiore; and Cappella Sistina).

Biblioteca Casanatense [Ben. 309]

Via di Sant'Ignazio 52.   Tel.: 679 05 50

Hours: weekdays from 8:30 AM to 1:30 PM. On Tuesday, Thursday, and Friday,
   open continuously until 5:00 PM. Annual closing September 16–30. No
   admission fee. Identification documents required for admission.

Facilities: reading and reference areas. Microfilm reader. Copies possible.

Description of the Collection: one of the richest collections in Italy of Baroque
   manuscripts: arias, duets, chamber cantatas. Gino Baini collection. Choirbooks from Dominican convent of Santo Spirito in Siena.

The Library was founded in 1698 with the bequests of Cardinal Gerolamo
Casanate and became the property of the state in 1873.

Biblioteca del Pontificio Istituto di Musica Sacra [Ben. 325]

Piazza Sant'Agostino 20a.   Tel.: 654 04 22

Hours: open weekdays from 8:30 AM to 1:30 PM, and from 4:00 PM to 6:00 PM.
   Closed July through September. For permission to enter, apply to institute
   director.

Facilities: microfilm and microcard readers. Systematic catalogs.
Description of the Collection: exclusively musical collection of music, records, and microfilms. Standard reference works.
The library was founded in 1910 by Angelo De Santis and contains part of the collection of Santo Spirito in Saxia.

Biblioteca dell'Academia Nazionale dei Lincei e Corsiniana [Ben. 310]

Palazza Corsini, Via della Lungara 10.   Tel.: 656 18 66
Hours: open daily from 8:30 AM to 1:30 PM. Closed in August.
Description of the Collection: 432,000 printed volumes, including Oriental, Ethiopian, Rossiniana, librettos, rare books. Circulation limited to members and other libraries.
The library was founded in 1730 by Cardinal Corsini. His family added to the collection later, as did G. Chiti. The library became the property of the Academy in 1883.

Biblioteca dell'Archivio di Stato di Roma [Ben. 304]

Palazza della Sapienza, Corso Rinascimento 40.
                         Tel.: 65 52 34; 65 38 23; 56 41 23
Hours: opens daily at 8:00 AM; closes Wednesday and Saturday at 1:30 PM; other days at 4:30 PM. Closed during August.
Credentials: free admission to scholars upon presentation of a document of identity.
Facilities: can make microfilm and quick photocopies. No microreaders. Reading room.
Description of the Collection: specialized library for the study of Roman documents, especially those concerning the history of the Papal States. Since 1949, the collection has included the holdings of the Biblioteca Casanova. Rich bibliographical collection for archival study. Many manuscripts and prints of early music. Newspapers of the early nineteenth century. International archive inventories. The complete Pier Francesco Valentini collection.

Biblioteca dell'Istituto Nazionale di Archeologia e Storia dell'Arte [Ben. 321]

Sezione Musicale, Palazzo Venezia, Piazza Venezia 3.   Tel.: 68 17 67
Hours: daily 9:00 AM to 1:00 PM and 4:00 to 8:00 PM. Closed August 15–31.
Facilities: microfilm reader. Reference only.
Credentials: university or professional status necessary for admission.
Description of Collection: the music section includes theoretical treatises, early seventeenth-century cantatas, eighteenth-century editions. Separate theater section has a large collection of seventeenth- and eighteenth-century librettos. Separate dance collection. Each rubric separately catalogued. Library established in 1922.

Biblioteca dell'Istituto Storico Germanico [Ben. 322]
Sezione Storia della Musica, Palazzo Ginnasi, Largo di Santa Lucia Filippini 5.   Tel.: 623 30 11
Hours: Monday to Friday, 4:00 PM to 6:00 PM. Closed July 15–September 15.
Description of the Collection: a special file of doctoral dissertations concerning Italian music, from all countries. Sixteenth- to seventeenth-century editions of works by Zarlino, Vicentino. A general musicological library with a special emphasis on Italian music history. Founded in 1888 along with the Institute.

Biblioteca Musicale del Conservatorio di Musica Santa Cecilia [Ben. 316]
Via dei Greci 18.   Tel.: 678 45 52
Hours: daily from 9:00 AM to 1:00 PM. Closed in August.
Description of the Collection: 170,000 volumes; 30,000 libretti; 6,707 manuscripts. As the official repository of the Italian music publishing industry, the Santa Cecilia receives copies of all musical editions published in the country. It is the youngest major music library in Italy and was opened to the public in 1878.
The music collection is in two sections:
(1) Biblioteca Accademica o Scolastica: exclusively for the use of the students and professors since 1887. Many first and rare editions, eighteenth-century Italian vocal music, manuscripts. Collection of books on nineteenth-century teaching principles.
(2) Governativa: includes first collection of the Library, that of Alessandro Orsini. Also several other famous collections from private libraries. Huge libretto collection of V. Carotti. Church music.

Biblioteca Nazionale Centrale Vittorio Emanuele II [Ben. 312]
Viale Castro Pretorio.   Tel.: 49 89
Hours: Monday through Saturday, 9:00 AM to 1:00 PM, 4:00 PM to 8:00 PM.
Credentials: For entry, apply to the Ufficio Permessi.
Description of the Collection: music manuscripts in separate collection with inventory. Separate collection of libretti from eighteenth to twentieth century. Since 1886 this library receives a depository copy of everything printed in Italy. Musical compositions are transferred to Conservatorio Santa Cecilia, but books and reference works on music remain here. National Union Catalog. Discoteca (record library) for public use.

Biblioteca Romana annessa all'Archivio Storico Capitolino [Ben. 306]
Palazzo Borromini, Piazza della Chiesa Nuova 18.   Tel.: 65 26 62
Hours: Monday through Saturday 9:00 AM to 1:00 PM. Closed August.
Description of the Collection: nineteenth-century music literature. Large collection

of band transcriptions. Documentation on Rome and its surrounding plain. Does not circulate.

Biblioteca Romana A. Sarti
Piazza Accademia di San Luca 77. Tel.: 68 88 48
Hours: daily; closed in August.
Credentials: restricted to proven specialists.
Description of the Collection: primarily history of art with related theater and opera collections. Full runs of periodicals.

Biblioteca Teatrale del Burcardo
Via del Sudario 44. Tel.: 654 07 55
Hours: weekdays from 9:00 AM to 1:30 PM. Closed in August.
Credentials: no admission restrictions.
Description of the Collection: reference only. Includes many items for operatic stage, such as photos, prints, programs, posters, costumes, props, souvenirs, etc. Supported by the Società Italiana degli Autori ed Editori.

Biblioteca Universitaria Alessandrina [Ben. 313]
Palazzo del Rettorato, Piazzale delle Scienze 5, Città Universitaria.
Tel.: 495 12 09
Hours: daily, 9:00 AM to 2:00 PM. Evening hours: Monday to Friday, 8:00 to 11:00 PM. Closed Easter week, August 1–15.
Facilities: microfilm reader; makes copies. Special catalogs.
Description of the Collection: ca. 514,126 volumes and 356,221 pamphlets; 365 manuscripts and 659 incunabula; 6,880 letters and documents. Provincial depository. Has Union Catalog of all University of Rome libraries (of which there are fifty-two). Sixteenth- and eighteenth-century prints of theoretical works.
Opened to the public in 1670 primarily for the use of students and faculty of the Ateneo Romano, which became the University in 1870. Moved in 1935 to the present quarters.

Biblioteca Vallicelliana [Ben. 314]
Palazzo Borromini, Piazza della Chiesa Nuovo 18. Tel.: 654 26 71
Hours: 8:30 AM to 1:30 PM, Monday, Wednesday, and Friday. Also from 4:30 to 7:30 PM. Closed October 15 to 30.
Facilities: microfilm reader. Make film and slide copies. Special catalogs.
Only partially a music library, this began as a small reading library for the fathers of the Congregazione dell'Oratorio in the sixteenth century. At that time, the collection, founded by S. Filippo Neri, had a small nucleus of 2,000 or so prints and manuscripts. In the nineteenth century, the state took over the

entire Vallicelliana, including the library. The musical works passed to the Conservatorio Santa Cecilia, leaving only a few sixteenth- and seventeenth-century prints and the church music belonging to the priests who served the churches.

The British Council Library
Palazzo del Drago, Via IV Fontane 20.   Tel.: 65 26 71
Hours: daily from 10:00 AM to 1:00 PM; from 4:00 PM to 6:30 PM. Tuesdays until 8:00 PM. Closed Saturday afternoons and in August.
Credentials: passport or other official identification document.
Description of the Collection: all subjects relating to Britain with emphasis on English language literature. Periodicals.

Discoteca di Stato [Ben. 318]
Via dei Funari 31.   Tel.: 56 56 76
Description of the Collection: 65,000 records and 5,000 tapes. Recordings of current events, ethnic-linguistic works, theatrical pieces, as well as music of all types. Now issues recordings for purchase.

Museo Africano
Via Ulisse Aldrovandi 16.   Tel.: 87 37 12; 87 97 30
Hours: daily from 9:00 AM to 1:00 PM
Founded in 1914, the collection contains about eighty African musical instruments.

Museo degli Strumenti Musicali
Soprintendenza alle Gallerie di Roma I, Piazza San Croce in Gerusalemme 9a. This collection was brought into existence in 1964 with the amalgamation of several specialized collections. It is characterized by its broad coverage of instruments, ranging from antiquity to the present time. Incorporated within it is the collection of the tenor Evan Gorga, noted for the richness and variety of his instrumental holdings. The rooms are divided by centuries and periods, covering two floors.

Museo nazionale delle Arti e delle Tradizione Popolari
Piazza Marconi 8.   Tel.: 59 61 48
Hours: 9:00 AM to 2:00 PM, Tuesday to Saturday; 9:00 AM to 1:00 PM Sundays and holidays.
Facilities: guided tours, recorded and taped performances.
Description of the Collection: about one hundred folk instruments from various regions of Italy, including winds, strings and percussion of Paleo-Mediterranean origin. A section called "Music, Song, and Dance" displays the most popular instruments.

Museo Preistorico Etnografico "Luigi Pigorini" (Luigi Pigorini Prehistoric and Ethnographic Museum)
Via del Collegio Romano 26; Via Lincoln 1.   Tel.: 68 37 22; 591 07 02
Hours: 9:00 AM to 1:30 PM Tuesday through Saturday; 9:00 AM to 1:00 PM Sunday and holidays.
Facilities: guided tours, photographic services.
Description of the Collection: There are about 500 ethnographic musical instruments including prehistoric instruments, folk music instruments from Africa, Oceania, and America.

Museo Strumentale Antico e Moderno
Accademia nazionale di Santa Cecilia, Via Vittoria 6.   Tel.: 67 53 71
Hours: 9:00 AM to 1:00 PM Monday through Saturday.
Founded in 1899, the collection contains about 200 instruments, mostly stringed, but there are some wind and percussion as well. There is a section devoted exclusively to twentieth-century instruments.

Radiotelevisione Italiana, Biblioteca
Viale Mazzini 14.   Tel.: 38 7 81
The Library of the RAI is open to staff only during office hours.

United States Information Service
Via Veneto 62B.   Tel.: 46 74 481
Hours: Monday to Friday from 10:00 AM to 6:00 PM. Closed Saturdays and holidays.

Some of the most noteworthy church archives in Rome with important music collections are the Archivo di San Giovanni dei Fiorentini, the Archivio di San Giovanni in Laterno, the Archivio di San Luigi dei Francesi, the Archivio di Santa Maria in Trastevere, the Archivio di Santa Maria Maggiore, the Archivio di Santa Sabina, and the Archivio di Santo Spirito in Sassia. For more information, see Ben.

Conservatories and Schools

Accademia Nazionale di Santa Cecilia (National Academy of Saint Cecilia)
Via Vittoria 6.
One of the oldest musical organizations in the world, originally established in 1566 by Pierluigi da Palestrina under the sponsorship of Pius V. For details concerning its non-educative functions, see p. 25. It administers the Santa

Cecilia Conservatory (see below) and supports, on its premises, the following organizations: Instituto Italiano per la Storia della Musica (see p. 21); Centro Nazionale Studi per la Musica Popolare (see p. 27); and the Associazione Nazionale della Liuteria Aristica Italiana.

In addition, the National Academy pursues some independent didactic activity in the form of its Santa Cecilia Academy International Courses. These consist of post-graduate courses in composition, piano, violin, cello, ensemble playing and conducting; free courses for vocal concert interpretation for young Italian and foreign graduate students; courses in Italian literature for foreign students. For more information, write to the directorate at the address above.

Collegio di Musica della Farnesina
An annex to the Conservatory of Saint Cecilia (see below), this is the only resident school for music in Italy.

Conservatorio di Musica Santa Cecilia
Via dei Greci 18.   Tel.: 68 45 52

Teaching in national conservatories is divided into main and supplementary courses. The main courses, which are also called "schools," are in the subjects in which the students take their final diplomas; the supplementary courses serve to complete the student's general and vocational training. As an example, the School of Pianoforte is attended by students taking their diploma in pianoforte; the supplementary course in pianoforte is attended by those taking their diplomas in other subjects.

The main courses are subdivided into periods (lower and advanced or lower, intermediate, and advanced) varying in length according to the subject. The total length of the courses is as follows: School of Composition (harmony, counterpoint, fugue and composition), ten years; School of Polyphonic Vocal Composition, ten years; School of Orchestra Conducting, ten years; School of Organ and Organ Composition, ten years; School of Choir Music, seven years; School of Singing, five years; School of Pianoforte, ten years; Harp, nine years; Violin, ten years; Viola, Oboe, and Violoncello, ten years; Double Bass, Clarinet, Bassoon, seven years; Horn, Trumpet, Trombone, six years.

The supplementary courses include *solfeggio,* harmony, chamber music, acting, singing, history, aesthetics, Italian, history and geography, literature; religion; and physical training.

Students passing final examinations in each school are awarded the appropriate diploma; those who pass all examinations in the lower or middle period are awarded a study certificate. The description above applies to all twenty music conservatories in Italy. The individual schools, however, have individual strengths for which they are well known.

Foreign Students: Initial inquiries for admission to Italian conservatories should be made through the Italian embassy or the nearest Italian consulate. For admission requirements and applications, one may write to the Dirizione dei Corsi Superiori di Studi Musicali per Stranieri at the address above.

Founded under the name Congregazione di Maestri e Professori di Musica in Roma, the Conservatory was granted the title of Academy in 1839; in 1877, a Liceo Musicale opened in the building of the former Ursulines nunnery, which the Italian state had given to the Academy. In 1919, the Conservatory, as it stands today, achieved independent status and became a state school of music.

Foro Italico International College of Music
For male students of the Saint Cecilia Conservatory, both foreign and Italian. This department of the Conservatory can accommodate 100 students. Has its own library, concert and study facilities in the Foro Italico Park. Established jointly by the Board of Education and the Gioventù Italiana (Italian Youth Commission) following the tradition of the ancient colleges of Italian Conservatories. Scholarships are awarded annually on a competitive basis. Only students over 18 years of age are admitted to the program.

Accademia Musicale Eco di Roma C.S.M.
Via Pietro della Valle 13.   Tel.: 654 15 34
Instruction in *solfeggio,* theory, instruments, voice, etc.

Istituto Italiano per la Storia della Musica (IISM)
Accademia Nazionale di Santa Cecilia, Via Vittoria 6.   Tel.: 68 82 59
Opened on November 24, 1938, to encourage the study of Italian music history and the publication of important and rare editions.

Centro Romano della Chitarra
Corso Vittorio Emanuele II 294.   Tel.: 656 92 42

Scuola di Musica e Canto per Religiose
Associazione Italiana Santa Cecilia per Musica Sacra, Via della Scrofa 70.
                                                                Tel.: 654 05 61

Scuola di Musica F. Vergati
Via Velo 12.   Tel.: 77 60 66

Summer Schools

Centro Internazionale Studi Musicali (C.I.S.M.)
Segretaria C.I.S.M., Via San Lucio.

Dates: early May through mid-June.
Courses of Study: piano, violin, cello, and chamber music, as well as orchestral conducting. Scholarships offered on merit basis. Also sponsors summer school and festival in Taormina (see p. 176).

Centro Internazionale di Studi per la Diffusione della Musica Italiana
Via Vittoria 6.
Dates: July 20 to September 20. (First month in Venice, see p. 74)
Application Deadline: end of March.
Courses of Study: orchestral conducting, piano, vocal repertory, violin, flute, composition, organ, Italian opera.
Age limit: 35.

Rome Festival Orchestra
Director of Admissions, Summer Institute, Rome Festival Orchestra, 170 Broadway, Suite 201, New York, N.Y. 10038.
Courses of Study: master classes in violin, cello, bass, voice, piano, and classical guitar. Regular orchestral study, rehearsal, and performance.

Società Dante Alighieri
Segreteria, Piazza Firenze 27.   Tel.: 68 17 05
Dates: months of April, June, and July.
Courses of Study: history of music, Italian language.
Credits or Diplomas: certificate of attendance, study certificate.
Lodging Information: Ente Provinciale del Turismo, Via Parigi 11, Rome.

Musical Landmarks

Caffè Greco
Via Condotti 86.   Tel.: 678 25 54
First established in 1760, the Caffè Greco is open daily at 8:00 in the morning. Throughout the long day, this cafe caters to local patrons, foreign visitors, tourists eager to glimpse the place which Goethe, Byron, Shelley, Pope Leo XIII, and Ludwig of Bavaria were known to frequent. The cafe's paneled bar, complete with the inevitable shiny espresso machine, and replete with picture-covered walls and marble-topped tables, was declared a place of public interest in 1953. Nevertheless, the proprietors continue to serve coffee, alcoholic beverages, sandwiches, antipasto, and whipped-cream desserts. The musicians who contributed to the memorabilia and the nostalgia of this old-world establishment, include **Berlioz, Liszt, Bizet, Gounod, Wagner,** and **Toscanini.**

Church of Santa Maria in Vallicella
Via del Governo Vecchio 134. Tel.: 65 52 89
The prayer room, or oratorio, now belongs to the state. Enter through the door to the left of the main entrance. Accommodates concerts and conferences. The musical form, oratorio, was created in this room by Filippo Neri in the last years of the sixteenth century. On Sunday nights, the congregation (Congregazione dei Prei dell'Oratorio) would listen to the recital of a religious story, pray, and sing songs. This evolved into the art form brought to such eminence by **Handel** in his *Messiah*. **Pierluigi da Palestrina** became part of this circle.

Teatro Valle
Direzione, Viale Teatro Valle 23a. Tel.: 656 90 49
Season: October to May. Closed July to September.
Only drama is now presented in this 800-seat theater.

In 1727, this wooden building was erected by Domenico Valle, in the courtyard of the Palazzo Capranica, close to the Piazza Navona. In the nineteenth century, it became an important opera house. Premieres of **Rossini**'s *Cenerentola* (1817) took place here, as well as five works by **Donizetti**. About mid-century (1850 or so), it was turned into a theater for drama.

The Tosca Tour
For the dedicated opera buff, it is possible to visit each place designated as the precise location of an act in *La Tosca*, the opera by **Giacomo Puccini**, based on the drama by Victorien Sardou, with libretto by Luigi Illica and Giuseppe Giacosa.

The first act, as we know, takes place in the Church of Sant'Andrea della Valle (Corso Vittorio Emanuele behind the Teatro Argentina). The Attavanti Chapel is nearby, but the exact spot where Mario Cavadarossi set up his easel is not really known. The church is open to the public.

Act II takes place in Scarpia's apartment in the Farnese Palace. The Palazzo della Farnesina (Via della Lungara 230. Hours: daily from 10:00 AM to 1:00 PM. Closed on holidays) is today the home of the French embassy and a museum. Brilliant works by Peruzzi, Raphael, and Sebastiano del Piombo are on display in the regular collection. Although we do not know the exact room in which Scarpia was murdered, the general atmosphere of the palace will supply the true afficionado with interesting insights.

The third act takes place on a platform set on the wall of the Fortress Saint Angelo (Castel Sant'Angelo, Largo Castello. Hours: daily 9:30 AM to 4:00 PM; holidays 9:30 AM to 1:00 PM. Closed on Mondays). If the visitor mounts the stairs leading to the upper terrace, alongside the huge statue of St. Michael, he will see all of Rome at his feet. Perhaps it was here that the execution took place. In any case, it would certainly give Floria Tosca an excellent point of departure for her final, dramatic gesture.

Villa Medici

Viale Trinità dei Monti 1.   Tel.: 68 90 30

Since 1803, when the Grand Prix de Rome was established by the Institut de France, this villa has housed its winners for their sojourn in Rome. Among the illustrious residents in the villa were **Berlioz, Bizet,** and **Debussy,** who all lived as pensioners during their prize years. The villa may be inspected by visitors for a few hours during the week upon request to the director or his staff. Note, however, that one of the recent acts of the Ministry of Culture in France, subsequent to the uprisings of 1968 and the reforms it engendered, was to terminate the Prix de Rome as an archaic and irrelevant institution. It is not known, at present, to what use the villa will be put as the Académie de France à Rome.

Musical Organizations

Performing Groups

Coro Polifonico Romano

Auditorio del Gonfalone, Vicolo della Scimia 1/B.

Coro Polifonico Vallicelliano

Via F. D'Ovidio 10.

These two semiprofessional choral societies rehearse and perform regularly in Rome.

Orchestra Sinfonica dell' Accademia Nazionale di Santa Cecilia

Via Vittoria 6.

This is one of the two resident orchestras in Rome, which has been perigrinating in search of a home. Concerts are held in the Sala della Conciliazione, Teatro Argentina, etc.

Season: fall and winter programs of an international character. Approximately two concerts a week, with guest conductors in the summer season at the Basilica of Maxentius near the Forum. Chamber music concerts run concurrently with the symphony concerts.

Orchestra Sinfonica di Roma della Radiotelevisione Italiana (RAI Orchestra)

Via Asiago 10.

Every Saturday, from September through June, there is a concert by this orchestra transmitted over RAI. They perform in the RAI Auditorium at the Foro Italico in a large, ugly red stone compound of quasi-modern buildings.

Tickets may be obtained by writing for them, but they are hard to get and it's simpler if you know someone at the RAI. The radio in Italy is much less active on the contemporary music scene than elsewhere in Europe, but this orchestra does present the most interesting and varied programs emanating from Rome, and the group is of a very high performance calibre.

Professional, Official, and Concert Societies

Since Rome is the bureaucratic capital of Italy, there is a superabundance of acronymic organizations relating to music based here: AGIS, ANELS, ANIT, and ATIT—not to mention ENPALS, AIAC, ACT, and AMR. The particular province of each of these and other government organizations will be explained below as briefly as possible. In the main, the descriptions of private and public music organizations will give the reader an idea of the position that music occupies in Italian daily life.

Accademia Filarmonica Romana
Via Flaminia 118.   Tel.: 31 25 60
Originally founded in 1821, the organization sponsors a concert series of rather advanced, experimental music by the Italian avant garde composers. The winter season takes place at the Teatro Olimpico and the summer season at the Accademia Gardens.

Accademia Nazionale di Santa Cecilia
Via Vittoria 6.   Tel.: 67 53 71; 68 39 96; 679 03 89
One of the world's oldest organizations, the Accademia was established in 1566 by Pierluigi da Palestrina. In 1839, it received the title of Pontifical Academy, and in 1870, Royal Academy. It has held to its present function since 1955, when the aims of the organization were defined as the development of the art of music in all its branches. In addition to supervising the Conservatory, the Accademia confers membership and the title of Academician on worthy musicians; gives private and public concerts and recitals; awards medals; sponsors competitions, publications, lectures, and courses in musical culture; makes judgments and gives opinions; sets up funds to aid musicians; and establishes a research library (see p. 16). It is the parent organization to several subgroups variously listed above and below.

Associazione Amici di Castel Sant'Angelo
Castel Sant'Angelo, Largo Castello.   Tel.: 65 50 36
Sponsors the artistic season, including concerts, operas, and drama in a cozy theater in the Castello. Chamber music, symphonies, ballet, and choral music are offered, together with the most avant garde compositions performed by

young musicians. Founded in 1911 by students and patrons of the arts to restore the museum and recover works of art to offices, museums, art galleries, etc.

Associazione Cultura e Teatro (ACT)
Via della Pigna 13a.
A concert and theater organization which is registered in AIAC.

Associazione dei Teatri Italiani di Tradizione (ATIT)
Via di Villa Patrizi 10.
A society, apolitical but government-sponsored, that devotes itself to the support of, study of, and promotion of traditional theater, including, of course, musical theater. Founded in 1967, the Association has gathered together supporting statistics and made economic studies designed to aid in the dissemination of traditional theater.

Associazione Generale Italiana dello Spettacolo (AGIS)
Via di Villa Patrizi 10.
Government agency for the support and coordination of activity relating to the stage: theater, concerts, opera, ballet, etc.

Associazione Giovanile Musicale (AGIMUS)
Via dei Greci 18.   Tel.: 68 92 58
This Youth Music Association is one of the principal organizations devoted to the advancement of music among young people. The Italian equivalent of the Jeunesses Musicales, the organization publishes *Agimus* (see p. 197).

Associazione Italiana fra le Attività Concertistiche (AIAC)
Via di Villa Patrizi 10.
A government agency that serves to coordinate all concert activity throughout the country. Consists of member organizations who receive help and advice from the central office.

Associazione Musicale Romana
Via dei Banchi Vecchi 61.
Arranges concerts. Member of AIAC.

Associazione Nazionale Enti Lirici e Sinfonici (ANELS)
Via di Villa Patrizi 10.
An organization of all the major opera houses and symphony orchestras in the country. Devotes itself to solving union problems, exchange of information, and all other questions pertaining to the operation of a major musical organization.

Associazione Nazionale Bande Italiane Musicale Autonome (ANBIMA)
Via Marianna Dionigi 43.

Founded in 1956, this organization devotes itself to studying the questions of repertory, regulations, and standards in regard to all kinds of bands. Publishes *Risveglio Bandistico* (see p. 205).

Associazione Romana Amici della Musica (ARAM)
Via G. Medici 1a.
This organization came into being in 1971 for the purpose of bringing together the public, the concert organizations, and the RAI-TV to promote and initiate the diffusion of Italian musical culture. Publishes *Il Notizario ARAM*.

Centro Nazionale Studi di Musica Popolare (National Center for Folk-Music Studies)
Accademia Nazionale di Santa Cecilia, Via Vittoria 6.   Tel.: 68 89 02
Founded in 1948 for the study and gathering of Italian musical folklore, this center has documented the oral musical traditions throughout the country. In cooperation with L'Archivio Etnico-linguistico-musicale (AELM) of the Discoteca di Stato (see p. 18), they have amassed an archive that now consists of more than 15,000 documents. They publish a bulletin, *Studi e Ricerche*.

Cassa Nazionale Assistenza Musicisti (National Fund for Musicians' Assistance)
Via Vicenza 52.   Tel.: 49 04 67

Ente Nazionale Assistenza ai Lavoratori (ENAL)
Via Monte Giordano 369.
An organization established to provide working people with a series of musical activities that include competitions, an international guitar festival, a festival of alpine singing, a national conference of orchestras of plucked instruments, etc.

Federazione Italiana Musica Jazz
Piazza San Silvestro 13.

Istituzione Universitaria dei Concerti
Città Universitaria.
Season: October to May, following the academic calendar.
Presents an average of fifty concerts a season, or three each week. Presents lecture-recitals on specific subjects. Organizes meetings with other university groups, as well as record sessions, conferences. Private organization founded in 1946.

Organizzazione Romana Sviluppo Arte Musicale (ORSAM)
Via Cola di Rienzo 13.   Tel.: 38 37 06
Private organization founded in 1950 that sponsors important concerts in Orvieto, Spoleto, etc. Dedicated to the restoration of interest in classical vocal

polyphony and the raising of the status of folk music of a polyphonic nature, the group organizes festivals around a specific theme. Now has series, "Concerti Corali di primavera" (Spring Choral Concerts), at the Aula Magna (see p. 11).

Società Italiana Musica Contemporanea (SIMC)
Piazza Buenos Aires 20.
The Italian Society for Contemporary Music is the Italian member organization of the ISCM (International Society for Contemporary Music) and helps coordinate and disseminate new music performances throughout the country.

Sindicato Musicisti Italiani
Via di Villa Albani 8.
The national union of musicians of Italy, of which Goffredo Petrassi is president.

Società Italiana Autori Editori (SIAE)
Viale della Letteratura 30.
The general performing and mechanical reproduction rights society, equivalent to ASCAP or BMI in the United States.

Unione Società Corali Italiane (USCI)
Via Caltagirone 6.
An organization devoted to the promotion of choral music and the establishment of competitions in this area.

The Business of Music

A major city the size of Rome boasts a musical business life commensurate with its importance in all other areas. Although Milan is generally acknowledged to be the music-publishing center of Italy, there are many prominent firms with headquarters or, at the least, branches in the capital. We shall not attempt to list them all, nor the retail music shops, record stores, or instrument makers who thrive in this cosmopolitan city. We shall, instead, provide for the visitor, a small and useful list of some of the best examples of service and reliability in each of the categories mentioned.

Music Publishers

ARIS: Edizioni Musicali e Discografiche
    Via E. Pimentel 2.   Tel.: 31 19 79; 31 22 96
Edizione Musicale Curci
    Via Pasublo 2.   Tel.: 31 19 09; 31 19 19

Edizioni Musicale Giraffa Paola
    Via Montoggio 53.   Tel.: 628 29 09
Fans Edizioni Musicali
    Via Muggia 33.   Tel.: 38 18 65
Scogliera Edizioni Musicali
    Via Dardanelli 26.   Tel.: 359 81 16

Music Shops

Ceccherini
    Via Nazionale 248.   Tel.: 46 19 10
Centro Musicale Roma
    Via dei Prati Fiscali 196.   Tel.: 81 23 801
Euromusikal
    Viale IV Novembre 33, Castelfidardo (Arcana).   Tel.: (071) 7 80 55
Messaggerie Musicali
    Via del Corso 122.   Tel.: 68 81 97; 679 39 48
Musicarte
    Via F. Massimo 35/37.   Tel.: 38 39 38
Riccordi
    Via Battisti 120/c.   Tel.: 68 80 22
    Piazza Indipendenza.   Tel.: 475 16 87
    Via Corso 506.   Tel.: 68 92 71; 679 13 10
Chiappini (book and music antiquarian)
    Via Teatro Valle 38.   Tel.: 56 10 58

Record Shops

Disco Shop
    Piazzo della Radio 69.   Tel.: 55 17 01
Boutique del Disco (wholesale, retail, musical instruments, recording studio)
    Via Taranto 57 a/b.   Tel.: 75 42 27
Il Discofilo (imported records, tapes, accessories, stereos)
    Via Tosatti 19 (Piazza Talenti).   Tel.: 829 83 67
Città 2000
    Viale Parioli 94.   Tel.: 80 30 00
Scorpios Hi-Fi Discoteca
    Piazza della Balduina 47.   Tel.: 345 38 00
Discoteca Laziale
    Via Mamiani 60/a, presso Ferrovie Laziali.   Tel.: 73 40 20

Musical Instruments

Alfonsi (sales representative for all major makes of pianos)
    Via Giovanni Lanza 103.   Tel.: 73 62 59

Musical Centro "Hammond" Cherubini (electric organs, wind instruments)
Via Tiburtina 360/362. Tel.: 43 38 40; 43 34 45; 43 91 003
Centro Ciampi (new and used organs, lessons)
Via Cola di Rienzo 42. Tel.: 35 31 51
Ciampi Pianoforti (restoration, tuning, distribution of all major makes)
Via Vespasiano 34. Tel.: 35 36 70
Via Germanico 32. Tel.: 38 37 24
C. D'Amore Strumenti Musicale (pianos, organs, classical guitars, wind and percussion and brass instruments)
Via Principe Amedeo 52/54. Tel.: 46 14 63
Rossana D'Amico Strumenti Musicali (electric organs, guitars, wind instruments)
Lido di Ostia, Viale Vasco de Gama 97. Tel.: 669 63 58
Hortus Musicus (Italian recorder center)
Via Lima 9. Tel.: 85 17 47
Manno Urbano (band instruments and accessories)
Via Germanico 190. Tel.: 35 05 62; 35 25 34
Music Center di Gino Ferrari (organs, pianos, guitars, drums, and instruction)
Viale Somalia 186. Tel.: 831 23 08
La Chitarra Artigiana (guitar repair and construction; sales)
Viale Villa Pamphili 75/a. Tel.: 589 12 17
International Music S.R.L. (instruments)
Via la Spezia 133–7. Tel.: 77 45 80; 77 43 44
Sisme Strumenti Musicali (pianos, guitars, amplification)
Osimo Scale. Tel.: (071) 7 90 12/13

Concert Managers

Agenzia Internazionale Concerti Propaganda Musicale
Via Sicilia 154. Cable: PROMUSIC; Tel.: 46 52 26
Ann Summers Dossena Management Inc.
Via Mario de' Fiori 42. Cable: ANNSUMMERS; Tel.: 678 57 47
Simonetta Lippi
Via San Teodoro 18. Tel.: 68 44 37
Metropolitan Artists Management Corp.
CP 9034 Aurelio. Tel.: 33 62 61
WWMM—World Wide Music Management Organization, S.A.
Via Casseria 1. Cable: PENTAGRAM; Tel: 31 23 82

MILAN (Lombardy)   Tel. prefix: (02)

Milan is the modern "capital" of Italy. Notwithstanding both church and state, this city of 1,500,000 inhabitants exists wholeheartedly in the twentieth century. This does not preclude the fact that its architectural masterpieces, its art collections, and its historical monuments are the equal of any city in Italy. But the skyscraper spirit, the presence of international banking and commercial interests here more than anyplace else, the concentration of industry ranging from building trades to fashion, is reflected in the character of the Milanese, who is businesslike, somewhat proud, and not at all *dolce far niente*.

It should come as little surprise to learn that only Rome compares with Milan in the number of concerts and opera performances presented every year. The most ardent partisan of Rome will admit, however, that musical life in Milan is more sophisticated and varied. This may be due in part to the fact that Milan is the seat of the music publishing business and has, as a consequence, the greatest recourse to modern technology, contemporary techniques for dissemination, and money. La Scala dominates the scene. That domination has been unrelenting since the theater was opened in the late eighteenth century. Before that, the musical activities of Milan were based in the Duomo, from the end of the Treicento, when its construction began. This was especially true in the late fifteenth and early sixteenth centuries, when Franchino Gafori (or Gaffurio), theoretician, innovator, and friend of Leonardo da Vinci, directed the music at the cathedral. At the same time secular music was thriving at the Sforza court, where such composers as Agricola and Josquin des Prez were contriving musical entertainments for the cognoscenti. The contest between secular and sacred was inevitably resolved by history, but before it was, a very interesting intermingling of style, form, and intention continued in Milan.

During the eighteenth century, opera held sway in the city. Johann Christian Bach became house musician to Count Litta; Giovanni Baptistia Sammartini conducted outdoor concerts at the Castello Sforzisco; the Mozarts, father and son, spent three months observing the musical life and trying to get a commission (which Wolfgang eventually did. *Mitridate, Re di Ponto* was performed there at the Teatro Regio Ducale in 1770, to be followed in 1771 by *Ascanio in Alba* and, in 1772 by *Lucio Silla*). After the opening of La Scala, the history of music life in Milan reads like the programs of that house: Rossini, Bellini, Donizetti, Verdi, Puccini, and finally, Toscanini, who reintroduced the operas of Verdi during his tenure as director of the opera.

To this day, Verdi remains king. Although there are far fewer *prima assoluta*s than there were, the musical life of Milan is still focused on La Scala and the manners and mores of musical behavior in this cosmopolitan city continue to reflect the traditions and standards of that great establishment.

Guides and Services

Ente Provinciale per il Turismo
Via Marconi 1.   Tel.: 80 88 13; 80 06 59; 87 00 16; 87 04 16; 89 70 15
Information office at the Stazione Centrale.   Tel.: 20 32 05

Opera Houses and Concert Halls

Teatro alla Scala
Via Filodrammatici 2.   Tel.: 80 70 41
Public Entrance: Piazzo della Scala.
Season: The opera season runs from December through May; ballet, September; and symphony, from the end of September to mid-November, and from mid-May to the beginning of July. Annual closing from mid-July to the end of August. (For details of the summer season, see p. 167.)
Box Office: Piazza della Scala.   Tel.: 87 64 74
On the left side of the facade of La Scala, is the entrance to the old box office, called the *"botteghino".* Through this you go down to the new box office, which is below street level. During the performances, a window in the old box office is kept open for the sale of tickets.
Box office open daily, except Monday, from 10:00 AM to 1:00 PM and from 3:30 PM to 5:30 PM. On days of performance, it is open from 5:30 to 10:00 PM for the sale of tickets to that performance, only. Tickets may be reserved by mail when request is accompanied by postal money order.
Seating Capacity: 2,000.
Customary Dress: dark suit for all performances; full dress for opening nights and galas.
Ballet School: Via Verdi 3.   Tel.: 87 79 95
Gift Shop: Via Balducci 85.   Tel.: 37 00 73
The Teatro alla Scala was designed by Giuseppe Piermarini on the site of the demolished church of Santa Maria della Scala. The "solemn inauguration" of the new house took place on the evening of August 3, 1778, with a performance of Antonio Salieri's *Europa Riconosciuta,* composed especially for the occasion. The facade of the new theater did not meet with universal acclaim. However, the Milanese of the time were unanimous in their praise of the elegance and beauty of the auditorium with its daring and majestic proscenium.
    Many renovations and alterations took place before the theater was rebuilt after World War II. In 1807, for example, the ceiling decor was redone and the stage enlarged; in 1891, the standing room was eliminated on the orchestra level; in 1907, a fifth tier of boxes was transformed into a gallery and the orchestra was lowered to create "the mystic gulf" or pit required by Wagnerian

opera; in 1921 the boxes were decorated in red damask, as they are today, and the stage apron, which had previously extended as far as the proscenium boxes, was moved back to make way for radical modernization of the stage. In 1935 the foyer was redecorated, and in 1938 the stage was equipped with bridges and stage wagons.

In the spring of 1945, work was begun to restore the war-battered La Scala to its former glory. The roof was rebuilt in iron, the architectural proportions of the house were reproduced according to the plans of Piermarini and Sanquirico, the decorated ceiling was reproduced according to the drawings of 1879, the sixty candelabras and the great crystal chandelier were restored, and the inimitable acoustics of this *bel canto* house revived. For the reopening, Toscanini, who had not conducted in Italy since 1930, returned on May 11, 1946, to perform a concert of music by Rossini, Verdi, Boito, and Puccini.

Today La Scala has a new lighting plant, a new entrance and foyer, new rehearsal rooms and dressing rooms for soloists and technical personnel. The first house to become an *ente autonomo* (in 1921) and now an *istituzione nazionale,* it enjoys a special status by law. The wise balance of popular and lesser-known operas, old and modern, characterize the careful programming one regularly finds here. The addition of Piccola Scala, for the performance of chamber operas, experimental operas, and works created for theaters of a more intimate nature, serves to broaden the range of performance possibilities even further. The name La Scala remains to this day synonymous with the very best in musical and operatic traditions throughout the world.

Teatro Piccola Scala
Via Filodrammatici.
Season: January through June.
Seating capacity: 600.
Five or six of the operas on the regular season program of La Scala are given in this diminutive theater. Inaugurated on December 26, 1955, with a performance of *Il Matrimonio Segreto* by Cimarosa, the activities of the Piccola Scala today include chamber music concerts, experimental theater productions, and stimulating congresses.

Angelicum
Piazza San Angelo 2.   Tel.: 63 27 48
Founded in 1930, this theater has been the locale of many important revivals of little-known eighteenth-century concert works. Since 1942, it has been used primarily for a winter chamber music series.

Aula Magna del Politecnico
Piazza Leonardo Da Vinci 32.   Tel.: 29 21 01
The Ente Concerti del Politecnico hold regular season concerts here.

Teatro Nuovo
Corso Matteotti 18/20.   Tel.: 70 00 86
Now a cinema, the concerts of the Ente dei Pomeriggi Musicali (see p. 41) are
held here on Saturdays at 4:00 PM from December through April.

Sala dei Concerti, Conservatorio di Musica G. Verdi
Via del Conservatorio 12.   Tel.: 70 17 55; 70 18 54
Concerts of the RAI Orchestra and the Societa del Quartetto are given here.

Summer concerts are given in the Galleria, in the esplanade of the Castello
Sforzesco, in the public gardens near the Porta Venezia, and in the plaza of the
Fiera Campionaria.

Libraries and Museums

Archivio e Biblioteca Capitolare di Sant'Ambrogio [Ben. 185]
Basilica di Sant'Ambrogio, Piazza Sant'Ambrogio 15. Tel.: 87 20 59; 87 37 48
Hours: weekdays from 10:00 AM to noon and from 3:00 PM to 5:30 PM.
Description of the Collection: not exclusively a music library. Contains some
    liturgical music from the Middle Ages to the present. Also some treatises
    and prints.

Archivio Storico di Casa Ricordi (Casa Editrice) [Ben. 194]
Via Salomone 77.   Tel.: 50 16 41
Hours: Monday, Wednesday, and Friday by appointment. Closed in August.
Credentials: Apply in writing to Direzione Generale, G. Ricordi, Via Berchet 2,
    20121 Milan.   Tel.: 43 41 54
Description of the Collection: musical manuscripts, mostly autographs, showing the
    editorial activity of the house of Ricordi over the last five hundred years.
    About 4,000 items. Also copies of its own prints, mainly opera scores of the
    eighteenth and nineteenth centuries. Mostly works of Italian composers. In
    addition to opera, there are orchestral, chamber, vocal works from the
    seventeenth century to the present. Good collection of correspondence with
    musicians, directors, composers, musicologists. Emphasis on Puccini and
    Verdi material. May be studied with special permission.

Archivio della Cappella Musicale del Duomo [Ben. 186]
Archivio Generale della Veneranda Fabbrico del Duomo
Museo del Duomo, Palazzo Reale, Piazza del Duomo.   Tel.: 87 09 07
Hours: Monday through Friday from 10:00 AM to noon and from 3:00 PM to 5:30
    PM. Closed Christmas, Easter, August.

Credentials: For admission, apply to director.

Description of the Collection: three kinds of material: works composed by chapel masters; works of other composers performed in the chapel; works composed by candidates for position of chapel master. Arranged by Gaetano Cesari. Total collection ca. 5,000 vols, plus miscellaneous printed and manuscript editions.

Biblioteca Ambrosiana [Ben. 187]

Palazzo dell'Ambrosiana, Piazza Pio XI 2.   Tel.: 80 01 46

Hours: daily except Sunday from 9:00 AM to noon and 2:30 PM to 4:30 PM. Closed in August and Saturday Zafternoons.

Facilities: microfilm reader; makes photocopies. Catalogs.

Description of the Collection: Latin, Greek, and Byzantine liturgical manuscripts and fragments; theoretical treatises; sixteenth-century and seventeenth-century Italian editions. Heavy accent on Milanese composers' works. Opera and oratorio libretti.

Library was founded by Cardinal Federico Borromeo and opened to the public in 1609. It suffered considerable damage in World War II.

Biblioteca del Conservatorio di Musica Giuseppe Verdi [Ben. 192]

Via Conservatorio 12.   Tel.: 70 90 97

Hours: Monday to Friday 8:00 AM to 2:00 PM; Saturday 8:00 AM to 1:00 PM. Closed in August.

Credentials: identification required from the institution with which the visitor is connected. No admission fee for foreigners.

Facilities: microfilm reader; makes copies; complete catalogs.

Description of the Instrument Collection (Museo di Strumenti Musicale): mainly stringed instruments. Hours as above.

Description of the Collection: provincial depository for all books on music printed in Lombardy. Historical and practical collection numbering about 330,000 volumes. Special concentration on eighteenth- and nineteenth-century materials. Has acquired several private, public, and church collections.

The library of the Conservatory was founded in 1807 with material given to it by the Paris Conservatory through the intervention of Eugene Napolean. In 1850, the University of Pavia and the Braidense Library gave their music collection to the Conservatory as well. Scores of operas performed in Milan from 1816 to 1850, from the theaters and from La Scala help create an opera collection of major proportions. War damages sustained during bombardments of World War II destroyed part of the holdings. The building has now been restored and modernized.

Biblioteca dell'Istituto Lombardo di Scienze e Lettere

Via Borgonuovo 25.   Tel.: 87 18 97

Hours: daily from 9:00 AM to noon and from 2:00 PM to 4:00 PM. Closed August, Saturdays, and holidays.

Description of Collection: academic works only. Reference. 190,000 volumes.

Biblioteca Comunale, Sezione Drammatica e Musicale [Ben. 188]

Palazzo Sormani, Corso di Porta Vittoria 6.   Tel.: 79 52 44

Hours: 9:0 AM to 12:30 PM and 2:30 PM to 8:00 PM, Monday through Friday; 9:00 AM to 12:30 PM and from 2:30 PM TO 6:00 PM, Saturdays. Closed in August.

Facilities: microfilm readers; makes copies; ten listening stations; complete catalogs.

Description of the Collection: Located in the central branch of the Milan Public Library, the collection in the music section consists of approximately 1,150,000 works. Established in 1946, this collection contains many private bequests (including that of Achille Bertarelli), institutional gifts (from publisher Ricordi and from the Museo Teatrale alla Scala (see p. 38), and national donations (including modern American music donated by the former USIS library in 1965). The Fonoteca contains more than 7,000 recordings. Literature on music criticism in the Spettacolo section of the reference room.

Biblioteca Nazionale Braidense [Ben. 189]

Via Brera 28.   Tel.: 80 83 45; 86 12 70; 87 23 76

Hours: weekdays from 9:00 AM to 5:00 PM during winter; 9:30 AM to 12:30 PM and 2:30 PM to 5:30 PM, Monday to Saturday. Sundays and holidays, 9:30 AM to 1:30 PM. Closed during Holy Week and for the first fifteen days of August.

Description of the Collection: The Braidense is the provincial depository, but much of its music collection has gone to the Conservatory. The music division does have, however, some 4,000 libretti, many theoretical works, printed liturgical books from Parma, lute tablatures, the Corniani-Algarotti drama collection with sixteenth- to nineteenth-century opera and oratorio libretti and scores (special catalog), autograph letters of musicians.

This library was founded by Maria Teresa and opened to the public in 1786. The Brera Palace was formerly occupied by the Jesuits, who were suppressed in 1773. It was from these suppressed orders that the library received its first collections.

Special Section of the Braidense: Ufficio Ricerca Fondi Musicali.

Palazzo Clerici, Via Clerici 5.   Tel.: 87 01 42

Since 1965, catalogs of all Italian music collections with manuscripts and printed works dating to 1900 and printed libretti to 1800 have been in preparation under the direction of Claudio Sartori and Mariangela Donà. URFM issues the series *Bibliotheca Musicae.* Available to visits by accredited scholars Monday to Friday, 10:00 AM to 1:00 PM and 3:00 PM to 6:00 PM; Saturday from 9:00 AM to noon.

Biblioteca Trivulziana e Archivio Storico Civico [Ben. 191]

Castello Sforzesco, Foro Buonaparte. Tel.: 80 86 23

Hours: Monday to Saturday, 9:00 AM to noon; 2:30 PM to 5:00 PM except Saturday afternoons.

Facilities: microfilm reader; copies available; separate catalogs for each collection.

Description of the Collection: There are three distinctly separate collections pertaining to music housed in this Castello:

(1) Music book collection contains fourteenth- and fifteenth-century hymnals and antiphonaries; fifteenth-century Florentius *Liber musicus* and Codex Trivulziana; eighteenth-century chamber works.

(2) Civico Raccolta della Stampe, the civic collection of prints, contains over 11,000 engraved portraits of musicians and other theatrical personalities in the Bertarelli collection.

(3) Museo degli Strumenti Musicali (Musical Instrument Museum). The museum emanated from an exhibition prepared in 1953 by Signor Natale Gollini from his own collection. Later that collection was donated to the city of Milan, which, in cooperation with the Milan Museum, housed it in the Palazzo Morando, Via San Andrea 6. But the continued acquisition of new holdings required a much vaster space, which was found in the restored Castello Sforzesco.

The museum collection has an educational as well as an esthetic goal: to present a clear idea of the formation, development, and perfecting of several families of musical instruments from around 1500 to the present. The following families are represented:

Bowed instruments (all the violin family). Includes instruments of Brescian, Cremonese, Milanese, Venetian, Neapolitan, and Turinese origins as well as French and German instruments.

Plucked instruments, wind instruments, non-Western instruments, and folk instruments.

Struck instruments (organ, clavichord, spinet, virginal, cembalo, piano).

Among the most rare instruments in this collection are a Guarnari violin that belonged to Tartini, a glass harmonica that belonged to Pietro Verri, a Milanese spinet made by Scotti in 1753, which was played by Mozart, and a double virginal made by Ruckers in the sixteenth century, one of the oldest fortepianos in existence.

British Council Library

Via Manzoni 38. Tel.: 78 17 49; 78 20 16; 78 20 18

Open September through June. General collection. Periodical runs.

Museo Nazionale della Scienza e della Tecnica "Leonardo da Vinci" (Leonardo da Vinci National Museum of Science and Technology);

Sezione Acustica Applicata (Applied Acoustics Section)
Via San Vittore 21.   Tel.: 48 70 34; 46 40 69
Hours: 10:00 AM to 12:30 PM and 2:30 PM to 7:00 PM from Tuesday to Sunday.
Facilities: guided tours and educational services; concerts, lectures, sale of
    photographs.
Description of the Collection: In the Applied Acoustics Section of this national
    museum, there is a collection of approximately 100 European art in-
    struments, 80 of which were donated to the museum by Emma Vecla in
    1961.

Museo Teatrale alla Scala
Via Filodrammatici 2, Piazza della Scala.   Tel.: 89 34 18; 89 95 35
Hours: weekdays from 9:00 AM to noon and 2:00 PM to 7:00 PM. Saturday
    morning only. Holidays from 9:30 AM to 12:30 PM and 2:30 PM to 6:00 PM.
    The Museum is open during intermission of performances. Closed on
    Christmas, New Year's Day, Easter, and the afternoons of holidays when
    there are performances in the theater.
Description of the Collection: relating to the history of the theater in general and to
    La Scala in particular. The collections range from the sixteenth to the
    twentieth centuries, including such items as replicas of Verdi's rooms
    complete with the usual memorabilia, etc. The nucleus of the collection
    was the property of Giulio Sambon, purchased in 1911 by the Friends of La
    Scala. The Museum was officially inaugurated in 1913. There are regular,
    rotating exhibitions as well as exhibitions arranged to coincide with the
    specific operas being presented, thereby giving good background history of
    the production and the composition.
The Library: In 1954, the theater critic Renato Simoni bequeathed a collection of
    volumes on the theater and related subjects to the Museum in honor of his
    mother, Livia Simoni. The Livia Simoni Library has been considerably
    enlarged since that time and has become an important source of informa-
    tion for scholars of theatrical and musical subjects. The library has a
    reading room available to visitors and complete catalogs.

Conservatories and Schools

Conservatorio di Musica G. Verdi
Via del Conservatorio 12.   Tel.: 70 17 55
A national conservatory, subject to the same rules, regulations, and require-
ments as the Santa Cecilia in Rome (see p. 19).

*Centro di Perfezionamento Artisti Lirici (Center of Artistic Singing
Perfection)*

Segreteria dell'Ente Autonomo del Teatro Alla Scala
Via Filodrammatici 2.
During the 1946–47 season, this *scuola di perfezionamento* was organized for the training of young opera singers. Later called the Centro, it acquired international renown and many students came from all over the world.
For admission to the school, the future student must pass an entrance examination. The course lasts two years and includes technique and interpretation of opera, acting, theater history, makeup, mime, etc.
The maximum age for admission is 30 years for men, 27 for women. Applications must be submitted no later than May 15th for study in the following year.

Civica Scuola di Musica Villa Simonetta
Via Stilicone 36.   Tel.: 31 33 34

Civica Scuola Serale di Musica G. Donizetti
Via Marconi 44.   Tel.: 247 08 91
Both city music schools listed above are on a level just below that of a national conservatory.

Istituto Pontificio Ambrosiano di Musica Sacra
Via Gorizia 5.   Tel.: 839 04 00
Specializing in religious music skills and studies.

Scuolo Internazionale di Canto Giacomo Puccini
Porta Vittoria 16c.   Tel.: 70 21 19
Students of both sexes and all nationalities (maximum age 40) are welcome, subject to audition. Summer courses are organized as well.

Scuola Popolare di Musica e di Canto Corale
Corso Porta Vigentina 15.   Tel.: 54 14 16
Founded in 1863 as a school for instruction in choral singing and wind instruments only, it now offers music academy courses on a level just below the national conservatory.

Music courses are given within two university faculties:

Università degli Studi, Facoltà di Lettere e Filosofia
Istituto di Storia della Musica
Via Festa del Perdono 7.   Tel.: 89 24 43

Università Cattolica del Sacro Cuore, Facoltà di Lettere e Filosofia
Istituto di Storia della Musica
Piazza Sant'Ambrogio 9, Largo A. Gemelli 1.   Tel.: 87 92 25

Musical Landmarks

Casa di Riposa di Musicisti, Fondazione Giuseppe Verdi
Piazza Michelangelo Buonarotti 29.
In a little chapel at the back of the courtyard of this rest home for aged musicians, **Giuseppe Verdi** is buried next to his second wife, Giuseppina. A tablet there commemorates his first wife and two children who died very young. Verdi donated all his royalties for the building of this *casa di riposo,* nicknamed Casa Verdi, and supervised its construction. He died in January 1901.

Musical Organizations

Associazione Lirica e Concertistica Italiana (AS.LI.CO)
Via Mazzini 7.
Founded in 1950, the organization offers courses from January until April to prepare and present young singers training for careers in the musical theater. Open to foreign as well as Italian singers. Apply for information to the secretariat at the address above.

Ente Concerti del Politecnico
Aula Magna del Politecnico, Piazza Leonardo Da Vinci 32.
Founded in 1948, the first concert sponsored by this organization was given by the Trio di Trieste. Since 1955, they have had a resident chamber group of their own: Gruppo da Camera dei Concerti del Politecnico, directed by Claudio Scimone. The Ente sponsors symphonic and chamber concerts with invited guest soloists of international renown who perform with their own ensembles.

Gioventù Musicale d'Italia (Italian Musical Youth)
Via Rossari 2.
The Italian Musical Youth Society was founded in Milan in 1952 for the purpose of disseminating musical and artistic culture to all people under 30, regardless of social or economic class. The association activity ranges from the presentation of concerts, conferences, debates, and theatrical productions to the publication of an informative periodical. The central office is at Milan, but regional branches exist throughout Italy. An affiliate of the Fédération Internationale des Jeunesses Musicales, the UNESCO-sponsored youth-music network.

Orchestra da Camera dell'Angelicum
Piazza San Angelo 2.   Tel.: 63 27 48

The Angelicum, an independent entity since 1944, is a concert organization founded by P. Enrico Zucca. The organization and the chamber orchestra that bears its name are housed in a Franciscan monastery in Milan. The concert series extends from October through May on successive Monday evenings. Because of the multiplicity of its activity and its wealth, the Angelicum exerts a strong influence on the musical life of Milan. It publishes a periodical called *Educazione Musicale* (see p. 200) and sponsors courses, contests, and conferences.

Orchestra da Camera dell'Ente I Pomeriggi Musicali
Corso Matteotti 20.
The Ente dei Pomeriggi Musicali is a concert organization on the level of an established theater. Among other things, it sponsors the Concorso Internazionale di Composizione Sinfonico F. Ballo (see p. 185) and supports a chamber orchestra, which gives concerts on Saturday afternoons at 4:00 PM in the Teatro Nuovo from December through April.

Orchestra del Teatro alla Scala
(See p. 32.)

Orchestra Sinfonica della Radiotelevisione Italiana
Corso Sempione 27.   Tel.: 27 38 88
One of the four RAI performing organizations (the others are in Rome, Turin, and Naples) this group performs regularly in the hall of the Verdi Conservatory. The series, Concerti Sinfonici Pubblici della RAI are held on Friday evenings from December through April and broadcast. Tickets may be had by request.

Società Italiana per l'Educazione Musicale (SIEM)
Presso Circolo Filologico, Via Clerici 10.
Founded in May 1969, the first congress of this organization was held in September of the same year. Their aims are to integrate music into the educative and extracurricular life of the Italian student; to establish standards of professional accomplishment on a par with those in other countries; to decentralize music education and offer attractive music programs on a national, provincial, and regional level; to research the scientific bases and problems of educating for individual initiative. SIEM is an active participating member of the International Society for Music Education (ISME).

Unione Nazionale Compositori Librettisti Autori di Musica Popolare (UNCLA)
Galleria del Corso.
Organized in Milan in 1946, this professional performing rights organization protects copyright privileges of its members and monitors public performances of their works. Comparable to ASCAP or BMI in the United States.

The Business of Music

Literally hundreds of music publishers, music shops, record shops, instrument sales and repair establishments, and music managers thrive in this cosmopolitan and musical city. The firms listed below are merely a sampling of those found in Milan today, but they are selected in the belief that they would more than adequately serve the traveler's musical needs.

Music Publishers

(The "Big Five" each have retail outlets at which all the usual musical materials are sold: sheet music, records, music paper, instruments, books on music, etc. Because of their size and prominence, they are given here as the best retail music shops in the city.)

Carisch, S.P.A.
  Via General Fara 39.   Tel.: 65 07 41
Retail establishment with usual Milanese business hours. Major Italian music publisher. In addition, the firm is the agent for Hinrichsen, Chester, Mills, and Boosey & Hawkes.

Casa Musicale Sonzogno di Ostali Pietro
  Via Bigli 11.   Tel.: 70 00 65
Agents for Ascherberg and AMP.

Edizioni Curci, S.R.L.
  Galleria del Corso 4.   Tel.: 79 47 46
Publishes the periodical *Rassegna Musicale Curci* (see p. 205). Agent for several American firms in addition to having own publishing activity.

G. Ricordi & Co.
  Via Berchet 2.   Tel.: 89 82 42; 86 09 89
Has retail branches in all major Italian cities as well as in London, New York, and Paris.

Suvini Zerboni Edizioni
  Via Quintilicano 40.   Tel.: Q 50 84 (answering service)
The headquarters for this major publishing house is located at Via Passarella 4 (Tel.: 70 03 04). The address above is for the retail shop. In addition to the publication of a great deal of Italian contemporary music, the firm represents several American publishers abroad.

Record Shops

Records are sold in all of the major music retail shops, including, of course, those listed above. However, here are a few record specialty stores where a larger selection, especially in the popular area, would be available:

Alfa Record
    Via Chiossetto 6.   Tel.: 78 13 60
Bigi Dischi
    Piazzale Medaglie d'Oro 4.   Tel.: 89 86 35
Caruso
    Via G. Rasori 2.   Tel.: 43 56 53
C.D.I. (Compagnia Discografica Italiana)
    Via Ripamonti 7.   Tel.: 58 13 81
C.G.D. (Compagnia Gen. del Disco)
    Galleria del Corso 4.   Tel.: 70 25 63
Discografica Italiana
    Via Planna 45.   Tel.: 39 15 36
Erregi Dischi
    Via Aselli 26.   Tel.: 74 83 85
Meazzi ed. Discografiche
    Via dei Piatti 4/6.   Tel.: 86 73 61

Instrument Manufacture and Distribution

Alziatti Fratelli (manufacture of brass instruments and accessories)
    Viale Certosa 302.   Tel.: 308 36 33
Balbiani Begezzi Bossi (manufacturers of church organs)
    Via Padova 13.   Tel.: 28 76 52
Caretta (distributor for all major flute companies)
    Piazza Velasca.   Tel.: 86 08 37
Costamogna Fratelli (church organs)
    Viale Monza 117.   Tel.: 285 01 36
Eco Casa Musicale (distributor of all keyboard instruments, including harmoniums)
    Via San Antonio 5.   Tel.: 80 23 01
F.I.S.A.P. (percussion instruments and all accessories)
    Via Paulucci de'Calboli 20.
Furcht & Co. (pianos)
    Via Brera 16.   Tel.: 79 64 18
Kalison di Angelo Benicchio (wind and brass instrument manufacture)
Via Pelligrino Rossi 98.   Tel.: 645 30 60
Kosmos (distributors of Hohner harmonicas)
    Via L. Papi 14.

Messaggerie Musicali (distributes all makes of keyboard and percussion instruments)
Galleria del Corso 4.   Tel.: 79 45 98; 70 23 13
Monzino (manufacture of classical and electric guitars called MOGAR)
Via Donatello 5.
Abele Naldi (manufacture of violins, concert guitars, mandolins)
Via Turati, Segrate.
Pianoimport Prof. Henschel (distributor of major piano manufacturers)
Via Lorentaggio 41.   Tel.: 423 60 78
G. & C. Ricordi (distributors for major piano manufacturers)
Via Salomone 77.   Tel.: 50 16 41
Semprini-LIARE [Laboratorio Impiano Apparecchiature Radio Ellettroniche]
(stereophonic equipment, amplification, all electronic accessories)
Via Bissolati 22.   Tel.: 67 19 88; 69 10 50
Strumenti Musicali Paris di A. Paris (manufacturer of flutes)
Via Roma 79, Garbagnate.
Superton (accessories for string instruments)
Via Inama 19.   Tel.: 71 48 15

Instrument Repair

Cav. Celestino Farotto
Via Privata Asti 15.   Tel.: 43 06 78
Gerdinando Garimberti
Corso Concordia 10.   Tel.: 79 99 69
Mario Janes
Via Carlo Farini 10.
Carlo Ravizza
Via Boiardo 12.

Concert Managers

ACOM (Organizzazione Concertistica Internazionale)
Via Conca del Naviglia 10.   Cable: ACOM; Tel.: 84 36 70
ALCI (Affari Lirici Concertistici Internazionale)
Via Paolo da Cannobio 2.   Cable: ALCOTEA; Tel.: 80 60 18
OIC (Organizzazione Internazionale Concerti)
Via San Pietro all'Orto 24.   Cable: CONCERTI; Tel.: 79 12 52

NAPLES (Campania)   (Tel. prefix: 081)

Naples stands between hills and sea on a semicircular bay facing Ischia and Capri. As if to remind mankind that the proximity of tragedy exalts life, Vesuvius looms over that bay, a thin wisp of smoke continually curling over its momentarily peaceful peak. In his Neapolitan notes, Melville wrote: "Monstrous cruelty of a remorseless nature, memories of cities burnt under the lava . . . [yet Naples] . . . is the gayest city in the world." Travelers through the ages have remarked on the sharp contradictions of Naples—the gaiety and the noise, the filth and the vulgarity, the aristocratic rubbing elbows with the plebian. Mozart at the age of 14 was impressed by the strange and tumultuous festivity, and Goethe, in a letter dated May 1787, described "the festival of pleasure which is celebrated in Naples every day."

The origins of the city, first called Parthenope and later Neopolis, can be traced in the ruins of Cumae, which legend says was in existence in 800 B.C. The Romans were the first to appreciate the sybaritic potential of this lovely area, and built many of their palatial country homes there. Nero made his stage debut in Naples in the year 64 A.D. after studying singing in Rome. Suetonius reports that Nero disregarded an earthquake which was in the process of destroying the theater while he sang. The province of Campania went into a period of decline during the Middle Ages, only to blossom forth once again in the thirteenth century under Angevin rule. In the fifteenth century, it was taken over by the Aragons of Spain when, despotism and tyranny notwithstanding, the province thrived. The more benevolent rule of the Bourbons, who established the Kingdom of the Two Sicilies at the beginning of the eighteenth century, helped create the necessary atmosphere for the great accomplishments in music, art, architecture, and literature which immediately followed.

In music, most assuredly, these accomplishments had more than local reverberations. It was almost inevitable, after the establishment of a formula for music drama by the aristocratic Florentine *camerata,* in which the music was subservient to the text and action, that on the slow journey from Florence to Naples, this art form should be transformed to meet quite another set of needs and standards. The evolvement of a new kind of opera, in which the human voice and its exaltation supersede all other artistic and philosophical considerations, occurred in Naples and rapidly spread throughout the Western world. Neapolitan audiences were insatiable—it has been calculated that during the eighteenth century, forty local composers wrote approximately two thousand operas for immediate consumption! With Alessandro Scarlatti leading the way, the traffic in opera composers going in and out of the city was incredible. Bononcini, Jommelli, Caldara, Vivaldi, Pergolesi, Paisiello, and Cimerosa are only a few of the names that appeared regularly on the programs of the Teatro Real di San Carlo. Naples also had a tradition of great singers, from the castrato

Coffarello to the tenor Caruso. Inevitably the very best music instruction was made available, and in the eighteenth century there were four conservatories of international renown functioning simultaneously in the city. Today the Conservatorio di Musica carries on as the sole standard bearer of the rich conservatory tradition.

Music life in Naples is still firmly focused on the vocal cord. The opera season at San Carlo is a long and active one, and the festivals that take place during the idyllic summer months feature spectacles and music theater indoors and outdoors, while international music competitions for which the area has become famous concern themselves primarily with singing and singers. The Hollywood concept of the Neapolitan singer has its technicolor counterpart on almost every street in Naples, and for once the fiction is perhaps paler and less improbable than the fact. Present-day Naples is completely restored after having received considerable bombardment from both sides in World War II, and the flow of visitors into the Campania region recalls yet another description from ancient times of this place—"most blest by the Gods, most beloved by man."

Guides and Services

Ente Provinciale per il Turismo
Via Partenope 10.   Tel.: 41 89 88; 40 62 89

Azienda Autonoma di Soggiorno Cura e Turismo
Palazzo Reale, Piazza Plebescito.   Tel.: 41 87 44

Carnet del Turista-Napoli (Italian and English)

Published by the information offices of the Ente Provinciale Turismo di Napoli and the Azienda Autonoma di Soggiorno, Cura e Turismo. Appears monthly. Available gratis at the two offices listed above and at hotels.

Contains travel information, schedules, housing information, services, and describes cultural activities taking place in Naples and environs for the period covered in the issue. Called the *Tourist's Handbook*, it is presented in a very attractive and useful format.

Opera Houses and Concert Halls

Teatro di San Carlo
Piazza Trieste e Trento, Via Vittorio Emmanuele III. Tel.: 41 57 45; 40 52 08

Season: from October to the beginning of June: opera from December to June; symphony, October and November. Theater closed from June to September. Ballet performances at irregular intervals. Performances generally begin at 8:45 PM or at 6:00 PM.

Box Office: Biglietteria del San Carlo, Via San Carlo.   Tel.: 41 50 29; 41 85 60

Hours: 10:30 AM to 1:30 PM and 4:00 PM to the start of the performance. Open daily, including holidays when there are performances. No standing room.

Seating Capacity: 3,500; one of the largest houses in Italy.

San Carlo is one of the principal theaters for the performance of opera in Italy today. It is an *istituzione nazionale* (see pp. 4–5) and the jurisdiction of its directorate extends over the summer season, when opera and concerts are presented in open air and exotic locations. The theater was constructed in 1737 from a design by Giovanni Medrano, who was entrusted by Charles III of Bourbon, king of Naples, with the task of replacing the old Sala del San Bartolomeo, deemed inadequate for musical productions. Located in the center of the city close to the royal palace, it was one of the first manifestations of French influence succeeding the Austrian influence heretofore overwhelming the Neapolitan culture. The first performance in the hall was *Achille in Sciro* by Metastasio, music by Domenico Sarro. The interior was renovated by G. A. Bibiena in 1762, and then by F. Fuga in 1768. It was destroyed by fire and rebuilt in 1816 by A. Niccolini, a neoclassic architect who gave it a new timbered roof under which stage sets were stored. The auditorium, to this day, has an imposing and grandiose appearance because of this. The white and gold interior is one of the most beautiful in the world and should be visited, even out of season. The auditorium and foyer are open to visitors daily from 9:00 AM to noon. The theater's repertory today is among the most adventurous in Italy, and new works are introduced very often. From the standard repertoire can be heard works of Scarlatti, Pergolesi, Paisiello, and Cimarosa, in addition to the usual favorites from the nineteenth century.

Teatro de la Corte (Court Theater of the Royal Palace)
Piazza del Plebescito.

Hall redesigned as a theater by F. Fuga in 1768 and restored after it was damaged in World War II.

Auditorium del Centro di Produzione RAI
Via G. Marconi.   Tel.: 61 01 22

Chamber and symphonic concerts, beginning at 9:00 PM, are presented from one to three times a week, all broadcast. International repertory performed by local and guest artists.

Sala Scarlatti del Conservatorio di Musica San Pietro a Maiella
Via San Pietro a Maiella 35.   Tel.: 34 38 80

Chamber hall used to give concerts and recitals during the regular season.

Libraries and Museums

Archivio di Stato [Ben. 211]
Piazza Grande Archivio 5.   Tel.: 51 07 56; 20 45 94
Hours: daily 9:00 AM to 1:00 PM and 4:00 PM to 7:00 PM.
Description of the Collection: printed and manuscript nineteenth-century music.

Biblioteca del Conservatorio di Musica San Pietro a Maiella [Ben. 216]
Via San Pietro a Maiella 35.   Tel.: 21 17 64; 34 38 80
Hours: daily from 9:00 AM to 1:00 PM. Annual closing in August and at
   Christmas.
Facilities: Copies may be made; catalogs including autograph, libretto, and aria
   incipits.
Description of the Collection: (1) The library, reserved for the use of scholars or
   students at the Conservatory, contains 21,000 volumes and over 47,000
   manuscripts, as well as a collection of autographs and related musicological material. (2) Sezione Strumenti Musicale della Biblioteca del Conservatorio (music instrument collection) (Tel.: 45 92 55). In addition to the
   170 musical instruments comprising the collection and ranging from rare
   antiques that originally belonged to illustrious musicians to popular and
   folk instruments of the region, there is a vast collection of musical
   iconography consisting of paintings, sculpture, medals and photographs.
   Also a notable collection of autographs.
Originally founded in 1791 with the donation made by Saverio Mattei of his
personal library of the Conservatorio della Pietà dei Turchini, the present
impressive collection represents the total archives of at least four defunct music
academies.

Biblioteca della Società Napoletana di Storia Patria [Ben. 218]
Castelbuovo, Piazza Municipio, Maschio Angioino.   Tel.: 31 03 53
Hours: daily from 2:00 PM to 6:00 PM. Restricted to members of the society for
   borrowing purposes, but nonmembers may visit.
Description of the Collection: only partially music, important in regional history of
   Mezzogiorno. Many Medieval manuscript codices, private family letters,
   etc.
The Society was founded in 1875 and is most important in regional history. The
building was heavily bombed in 1943 and has been totally restored.

Biblioteca Lucchesi-Palli [Ben. 212]
Biblioteca Nazionale, Palazzo Reale, Piazza del Plebescito.   Tel.: 39 12 12
Entrance: Via Vittorio Emanuele
Hours: 9:00 AM to 5:00 PM weekdays. Closed during Holy Week and from August
   16 to 31.

Description of the Collection: The special music and theater section of the National
Library, given to the city in 1888 by the Count Lucchesi-Palli, consists of
about 60,000 volumes on opera and theater history. Manuscripts include
Neapolitan music of the seventeenth to twentieth centuries; autographs of
nineteenth-century musicians; current periodicals; reference and source
works. Completely catalogued.

Biblioteca Nazionale Vittorio Emanuele III [Ben. 213]
Palazzo Reale, Piazza del Plebescito.   Tel.: 40 28 42
Entrance: Via Vittorio Emanuele.
Hours: 9:00 AM to 8:00 PM weekdays. Closed for one week in spring, two in
summer.
Description of the Collection: music only part of collection. Some liturgical
manuscripts. Depository for works printed in the province.

Biblioteca Oratoriana dei Gerolamini [Ben. 214]
Casa dei Padri dell'Oratorio, Archivio Musicale, Via del Duomo 142.
       Tel.: 34 72 95
Hours: Monday to Friday from 9:00 AM to 1:00 PM, but difficult to get in.
Description of the Collection: sixteenth- to eighteenth-century prints, especially of
sacred music. Also madrigals, cantatas, oratorios of the Naples School
(1500–1800, when this city was the center of Italian musical life). Oldest
public library in city, opened in 1585.

Biblioteca Universitaria [Ben. 215]
Città Universitaria, Via Giovanni Paladino 39.   Tel.: 32 49 72
Hours: daily from 9:00 AM to 5:00 PM.
Founded in 1777, it was enlarged by the addition in 1816 of the Biblioteca
Gioacchina and of the Biblioteca del Collegio Reale (founded 1907). Damaged
in the 1930 earthquake.

Museo Archeologico Nazionale
Piazza Cavour.   Tel.: 21 01 61; 21 02 61; 34 04 18; or 21 13 41
Hours: 9:00 AM to 2:00 PM daily.
Facilities: guided tours, photographs for sale.
Description of the Collection: Within the national museum there are about 30
musical instruments including flutes and trumpets, percussion instru-
ments, harpsichords and several citterns.

Conservatories and Schools

Accademia Musicale Napoletana
Via San Pasquale 62.   Tel.: 39 77 08

Sponsors a summer course: Corso Internazionale di Interpretazione per Pianisti di Jacques Fevrier.

Conservatorio di Musica San Pietro a Maiella
Via San Pietro a Maiella 35.   Tel.: 34 38 80

A national conservatory and therefore subject to the same entrance requirements, same course structure, and same system as the Santa Cecilia in Rome
(see p. 19).

As the collective heir of four older conservatories all originating in the
sixteenth century (Santa Maria di Loreta, Sant' Onofrio a Capuana, Poveri di
Gesu Christo, and Pietà de'Turchini), the present institution has been housed in
the austere buildings of San Pietro a Maiella on the Via del Tribunali, a few
blocks south of the Muzeo Nazionale, since 1826.

Liceo Musicale di Napoli
Via Santa Brigida 68.   Tel.: 41 84 65

Ranked just below the National Conservatory and officially recognized by the
Ministry of Education, this school has a wide course offering and about fifteen
faculty members. Many of its graduates go on to the Conservatory. The school
was founded in 1898.

Musical Landmarks

A Gesualdo Jaunt
For the avid reader of whodunits, we recommend a visit to a gloomy building at
number 9 Piazza San Domenico Maggiore, just behind the Conservatory.
Although no sign of the blood remains, it was here that the great composer, **Don
Carlo Gesualdo,** Prince of Venosa, killed his wife and her lover in 1590. We will
leave it to the visitor so inspired to imagine what the scene must have been like
at the end of the sixteenth century. Today, the building is an apartment house
for about fifty families and no longer the palace of the Sansevero family. No
plaque marks the evil deed, but a painting depicting the murder is on view in a
Capuchin monastery at Gesualdo, a small town about forty-five kilometers east
of Naples. Gesualdo was buried in 1613 at the Church of Gesu Nuovo, Piazza
del Gesu, but the tombstone was destroyed by an earthquake in 1688. After it
was reconstructed, a bomb damaged it seriously in 1943. Should the disap-
pointed visitor find no tombstone to view, the church's Baroque organ case is
well worth a glimpse.

Chiesa di Santa Maria Montesanto
Piazza Montesanto.   Tel.: 21 28 75

The tomb of **Alessandro Scarlatti** (1660–1725) may be seen in a small chapel on the left side of the church.

Musical Organizations

Accademia Musicale Napoletana
Via San Pasquale 62.   Tel.: 39 77 08
The Coro Polifonico dell'Accademia and the Orchestra da Camera, plus the Gruppo Strumentale, are all part of the Accademia Musicale Napoletana, which sponsors concert series throughout the year.
The organization was founded in 1934 by Alfred Casella. The Gruppo Strumentale is the youngest member of the family of ensembles gathered under this umbrella organization, having been established in 1949. The concerts of the various Accademia organizations take place in the Sala del Conservatorio.

Fondazione Alberto Curci
Via Nardones 8.
Established in 1966 to honor the name of the musician Alberto Curci, the foundation awards scholarships to young string students of the Conservatory, sponsors cultural and artistic events, including conferences for the study of string teaching, and runs a competition annually (see p. 188).

Orchestra Alessandro Scarlatti della Radiotelevisione Italiana
Via G. Marconi 1.   Tel.: 61 01 22
This is one of the four RAI orchestras (Rome, Turin, and Milan house the other three). Both the orchestra and chorus perform throughout the year, not only at broadcast concerts, but also as part of the *Autunno musicale Napoletano* series and the *Luglio musicale.*

The Business of Music

Music Shops

S. Agneti & V. Agneto
    Via C. Porzio 81/87.   Tel.: 35 69 81
Figli Cimmino
    Via Santa Brigida 13.   Tel.: 39 13 13
Emporio Musicale
    Corso Umberto 250.   Tel.: 33 77 88
Gennaro Gallo
    Via C. Carafa 54.   Tel.: 32 41 94

Alfredo Pucci, Casa Musicale	
Vico Il Casanova 5.	Tel.: 35 32 27
G. & C. Ricordi	
Galleria Umberto 1.	Tel.: 39 34 36

Record Shops

EMG	
Via San Sebastiano 16.	Tel.: 34 98 27
Gilbert Record	
Piazza Garibaldi 73.	Tel.: 52 14 56
Jughans Records	
Via A. Poerio 51.	Tel.: 35 58 50
Phonotype Record	
Via Enrico de Marinis 4.	Tel.: 32 29 64

Instrument Makers or Distributors

Carlo Ardone (pianos)	
Via San Sebastiano 46.	Tel.: 34 25 08
Alfredo Contino (instruments)	
Vico Sant'Arpino a Chiaia 1.	Tel.: 39 68 08
Salvatore de Falco (instruments)	
Via San Sebastiano 40.	Tel.: 32 14 34
G. Loveri (instruments)	
Via San Sebastiano 8.	Tel.: 21 81 20

FLORENCE (Tuscany)   (Tel. prefix: 055)

Florence, a city of half a million people, sits on the banks of the Arno River almost at the exact center of the Italian peninsula. A network of superhighways links it to the rest of the country and minimizes the distances between the cities: 87 kilometers to Bologna, 283 kilometers to Milan, 80 kilometers to Pisa, 468 kilometers to Naples, and 267 kilometers to Rome. Siena is only 70 kilometers away. Today Florence boasts over 350 hotels and *pensiones*, which can accommodate 20,000 visitors. Restaurants and *trattorias* dot the landscape, savory witness to Tuscan gastronomy. And yet, at every street corner and at every piazza we are reminded that this is the city of Cimabue, Giotto, Brunelleschi, and Donatello; that it was here that Ghiberti, and the Della Robbias lived; and that it was in this place where the genius of Filippo Lippi, of Leonardo, and of Michelangelo held sway. Despite the automobiles trapped and braying in

narrow streets, despite the pseudo-authenticity of many of the bridges reconstructed after the bombings of World War II, and even in spite of the electric
wiring that somewhat defiles a Romanesque baptistery, we have stepped into
the Renaissance when we enter Florence.

Florence was founded by the Romans in the first century B.C.; it grew
slowly, and reached the highest peak of its development in the fifteenth century.
Then, as a prospering mercantile center, it came under the rule of the Medici,
who later became the Grand Dukes of Tuscany. This was the most splendid and
productive period in Florentine history, a period characterized by an urbanity
and worldliness that stood in sharp contrast to self-conscious piety—the spiritual
qualities so carefully cultivated in Rome. In the eighteenth century the city
became part of the House of Lorraine until 1860, when Tuscany as a whole
joined the Kingdom of Italy.

Literary studies were first established in Florence with Petrarch and
Boccaccio, and it has been claimed that the Italian language was born there.
Although one rarely can locate precisely the birthplace of any art form, there
can be no doubt that opera as we know it today was indeed born in Florence.

At 5 Via de' Benci, stands the palace of the Bardi family. Today the
building is a complex of apartments and shops. But at the end of the sixteenth
century, a group that came to be known as the Camerata Fiorentina met there
under the intellectual guidance of Giovanni de' Bardi and created out of the
combined elements of Greek tragedy and music the modern musical phenome-
non known as opera. Yet Florence has not enjoyed a rich tradition of opera
creation or performance since that auspicious beginning. Its opera season today
is virtually indistinguishable from that of any other city of its size and, aside
from the commercially-oriented Festival of May (see p. 165), quite unremark-
able. It is entirely possible that the city's monolithic accomplishments in the
plastic and graphic arts have served to discourage the musical ones. Certainly
the Medici family, during their long and prosperous reign, supported the entire
spectrum of humanistic endeavors with their patronage. And it may be that the
secular flavor that characterized Florentine music during the Renaissance,
reflected the high values they placed on entertainment and social graces.

The concert life of present-day Florence follows a straight line from those
conditions that prevailed in the time of the Medicis. The operative word is
spectacle (spettacolo). The productions of the "Musical May" are often genuinely
innovative; the inspiring surroundings of Florentine art are used to advantage
as the sites for concerts, recitals, musical melodramas. There are "Musical
Afternoons" in the Palazzo Pitti and organ recitals in the monumental
churches, as well as the more traditional orchestral and solo recitals at the
Teatro Comunale and the Teatro della Pergola. The pageants and parades, the
musical entertainments in the Boboli Gardens, all conspire with the theatrical
beauty of the setting to enhance, to entice, and to enjoy.

Guides and Services

Ente Provinciale per il Turismo
Via A. Manzoni 16.   Tel.: 67 88 41

Azienda Autonoma di Turismo
Via Tornabuoni 15.   Tel.: 21 65 44 or 21 65 45
Piazza Rucellai.   Tel.: 29 89 06 or 21 74 59
Publishes a variety of tourist aids, such as *Firenze: Informazioni Turistiche,* a
small-format booklet of 54 pages, into which are crammed hundreds of useful
names, addresses, and telephone numbers; or *Manifestazioni a Firenze,* a flyer
printed annually in which the major events of the year are listed.

Movimento Forestieri
Via Veccheitti 22.   Tel.: 27 06 27
This is the central clearinghouse for tickets and information concerning all
musical activities in Florence. All foreign languages are spoken here and tickets
may be purchased for all concert and opera events. It is advisable, however, to
buy tickets as early as possible, but often they do not go on sale until two or three
days before a performance.

Ufficio Guide Turistiche
Viale Gramsci 9/a.   Tel.: 67 91 88

Centro di Cultura per Stranieri
Via Bolognese 52.   Tel.: 49 62 72

Agenzia Universalturismo
Via Speciali 7r.   Tel.: 21 72 41
This agency services visitors by obtaining tickets for them, informing them
about current events in Florence, and taking care of their travel plans.

Opera Houses and Concert Halls

Teatro Comunale
Corso Italia 12.   Tel.: 26 30 41
Mailing address: Via Solferino 15, 50100 Florence.
Season: December to February for opera. October to November and February to
    April for the symphony season. Summer: Maggio Musicale season, early
    May to end of June (see p. 165). Ballet season in July. Closed in August.

Evening performances usually begin at 9:00 PM; opera matinees at 4:00 PM; Sunday afternoon orchestral concerts at 5:00 PM.

Box Office: Biglietteria del Teatro Comunale, Corso Italia 16.   Tel.: 21 62 53
Hours: 9:00 AM to 12:30 PM and 3:00 PM to 6:30 PM daily except Monday.
300 standing-room places are sold one hour before a performance.

Seating Capacity: 1,806.

One of the best and most modern lyric theaters in Italy, the Comunale, formerly called the Politeama Fiorentino Vittorio Emanuele, was originally built in 1862. It was radically transformed between 1935 and 1937 and finally completed in 1961 by Alessandro Giuntoli and Corinna Bartolini. The Teatro has a permanent orchestra, a ballet school, and preparatory school for young singers. It is an *istituzione nazionale.*

During the winter opera season, approximately six works (opera, ballets, and spectacles) are presented in the three-month period. The autumn and spring concert seasons feature the orchestra and chorus of the Maggio Musicale Fiorentino with guest soloists and conductors. A total of approximately twenty-five concerts (many presented twice) are given in the two-part season. The ticket prices tend to be much lower than for the operas.

Sala Bianca (The White Hall)

Palazzo Pitti, Piazza Pitti.   Tel.: 23 440

Season: March to May, concerts sponsored by AIDEM (see p. 61). Other performances all through the year. In the courtyard, open-air concerts called the Serate Musicale Fiorentine (FME) are held from July to September.

Box Office: Palazzo Pitti. Hours: Daily from 9:00 AM to noon and 3:00 PM to 6:30 PM. No standing room.

Teatro della Pergola (La Pergola)

Via della Pergola 12–32.   Tel.: 27 09 97

Public entrance: Via della Pergola 18.

Season: October 1 to June 30. Annual closing July 1 to September 30. Chamber music, chamber operas during the Maggio Musicale. Used extensively for spoken drama.

Box Office: All tickets are available after 7:00 PM at the box office. 100 standing-room places go on sale one hour before the performance.

Seating Capacity: 1000.

The Teatro della Pergola was commissioned in 1652 by the Accademia degli Immobili, an organization made up of the Florentine aristocrats and protected by Cardinal Gian Carlo de Medici. Ferdinando Tacco constructed the theater on a spot formerly occupied by a wool factory. Originally built of wood, the theater was reconstructed of masonry in 1755. An elegant opera house, it retains an air of past refinement, although there is very little visible today that has not been renovated. The Pergola has an important record of first performances of operas by Mozart, Meyerbeer, Verdi, Gluck, Salieri, Paisiello, and Mascagni. Today, the Amici della Musica have a concert season there, and occasional opera performances are given during the Maggio. But the major portion of its use is for *prosa*—spoken drama. For a small gratuity, the superintendant, who lives at number 20, will take you on a conducted tour of the hall when it is not in use.

Sala del Conservatorio di Musica
Piazza Belle Arti 2.   Tel.: 27 21 80

Teatro del Palazzo dei Congressi
Pratello Orsini 1, Via Valfonda.   Tel.: 26 22 41; 21 75 42

Teatro Verdi
Via Ghibellina 99.   Tel.: 29 62 42
Used primarily for spoken drama and musicals.

Environs of Florence

Teatro Comunale Metastasio
Via Cairoli, Prato (12 kilometers outside Florence).   Tel.: 2 61 37
                                                         Box Office   Tel.: 2 62 02
Designed by Cambray-Digny and opened in 1838, it is the site of concerts and opera performances held throughout the year.

Summer concerts are given in places of historical and artistic interest all over Florence. For example, large-scale events have been presented in the courtyard of the Palazzo Vecchio, concerts of the Maggio are given in the Basilica di San Lorenzo, and chamber music recitals *en plein air* are given in the Boboli Gardens.

Libraries and Museums

Acquinas Library, Pius XII Institute [Ben. 122]
Graduate School of Fine Arts, Villa Schifanoia, Via Boccaccio 123.
                                                         Tel.: 57 61 95
Hours: weekdays in summer, 9:00 AM to noon. Weekdays in winter, 9:00 AM to noon and also on Monday, Wednesday, and Friday from 3:00 PM to 6:00 PM. Closed August.
Credentials: a bona fide affiliation with any university in Florence, or membership in the German, French, British, or Dutch Institute.

Description of the Collection: musical monuments and historical sets. Research and reference tools for the musicological research that forms part of the school's graduate program. Works on contemporary, electronic, and computer music.

American Library
American Cultural Center, Lungarno Vespucci 46.   Tel.: 21 65 31
Hours: daily from 9:00 AM to 12:30 PM and 2:30 PM to 5:00 PM. Closed on Saturday.
Description of the Collection: reference library primarily for Italians interested in the United States.

Archivio di Stato [Ben. 123]
Loggiato degli Uffizi.   Tel.: 21 16 29; 29 20 58
Hours: Monday to Friday, 9:00 AM to 2:00 PM and 3:30 PM to 7:00 PM. Saturday from 9:00 AM to 1:00 PM.
Description of the Collection: Much of the music collection was transferred to the Conservatory library in 1892. A few nineteenth-century prints and some eighteenth-century manuscripts remain. Local composers.

Archivio Musicale dell'Opera di Santa Maria del Fiore [Ben. 130]
Piazza del Duomo.   Tel.: 23 229
Hours: summer, 9:30 AM to 1:00 PM and 2:30 PM to 6:00 PM; winter, 9:30 AM to 4:30 PM. Holidays, 10:00 AM to 1:00 PM. Closed for part of July through September.
Description of the Collection: sixteenth- to eighteenth-century polyphony, manuscripts, prints, scores and parts, sacred music, madrigals. The Archivio Musicale is separate from the Archivio Storico dell'Opera.

Biblioteca Domenicana [Ben. 124]
Chiesa Santa Maria Novella, Piazza della Stazione 4a.
Hours: summer, 9:00 AM to 5:00 PM; winter, 9:00 AM to 4:00 PM. Holidays 9:00 AM to noon. Closed July to September.
Description of the Collection: sixteenth- to nineteenth-century printed liturgical music (missals, antiphonaries, invitatories, offices, psalteries, etc.). Library belongs to Dominican order of Friars Preachers (Frati Predicatori) and specializes in history.

Biblioteca del Conservatorio di Musica Luigi Cherubini [Ben. 129]
Via degli Alfano 80.   Tel.: 27 21 80
Public Entrance: Piazza Belle Arti 2.
Facilities: exclusively musical; copies possible, catalogs.

Description of the Collection: more than 71,000 volumes, 4,500 letters, and other documents. Rare theoretical and practical works. Autographs of Monteverdi, Scarlatti, Rossini, Wagner, Cherubini, Donizetti, Verdi.

The library was founded in 1862 with collections of the ducal court of Toscana and of the music school of the Accademia di Belle Arti, formerly the Casa Rinuccini. Gifts were added from the Basevi, Corsini, Picchi, and other families. There was some flood damage to four rooms in November 1966, involving approximately 10,000 pieces of material.

Biblioteca dell'Istituto Francese
Piazza Orgnissanti 2.   Tel.: 28 75 21
Hours: 10:00 AM to 12:30 PM and 3:30 PM to 6:00 PM daily.
Description of the Collection: 75,000 volumes, predominantly in French, including music and music periodicals.

Biblioteca del British Institute of Florence
Palazzo Lanfredi, Lungarno Guicciardini 9.   Tel.: 28 40 31
Hours: 10:00 AM to 12:30 PM and 4:00 PM to 6:30 PM daily. Closed Saturday and the first Monday of every month.
Description of the Collection: 30,000 volumes, mostly in English, including music section and current periodicals.

Biblioteca della Facoltà di Lettere e Filosofia dell'Università degli Studi
[Ben 134]
Via degli Alfani 31.   Tel.: 26 18 31
Hours: winter, weekdays 8:00 AM to 7:45 PM; Saturdays 8:30 AM to 12:45 PM.; summer, opens at 8:00 AM; closes at 8:00 PM in June, at 5:00 PM from July 10th to 31st, and from September 1st to 10th. Open six days a week. Closed all of August.
Credentials: student identification card.
Description of the Collection: reference materials for classes on the history of music. Sixteenth- to nineteenth-century literature on music, theoretical treatises, prints.

Biblioteca Marucelliana [Ben. 125]
Via Cavour 43.   Tel.: 27 06 02
Hours: weekdays from 9:00 AM to 1:00 PM and from 3:00 PM to 8:00 PM. Saturdays from 9:00 AM to 1:00 PM. Rare materials available only in the morning.
Description of the Collection: 10,000 libretti of operas and oratorios from Bonamici di Livorno. A great deal of music for the dance. Provincial depository. Musical works from convents, literature on music, prints.

Biblioteca Medicea-Laurenziana [Ben. 126]
Piazza San Lorenzo 9.   Tel.: 27 07 60

Hours: 8:00 AM to 2:00 PM. Saturdays from 8:00 AM to 1:00 PM. Closed Easter week and September 1–15.

Credentials: documents of identity and letter of recommendation.

Description of Collection: Squarcialupi codex; twelfth- to fourteenth-century Greek hymnologia; treatises, manuscripts, Medici codex. Library is primarily devoted to manuscripts, incunabula, and other rare materials. Library opened in its present location in 1571, later received the collections of suppressed convents.

Biblioteca Nazionale Centrale (incorporating Magliabechiana and Palatina) [Ben. 127]

Piazza Cavalleggeri 1. Tel.: 28 70 48

Hours: Monday to Saturday, 9:00 AM to 1:00 PM and 2:00 PM to 7:00 PM, except Saturday afternoon. Closed August 15–31.

Description of Collection: old music in department of *Manoscritti e Rari*. Printed works, manuscript volumes, theoretical works, fourteenth-century Laudi. Horace Landau memorial collection. Since 1886, library is depository for all music published and books printed in Italy.

All items in *Catalogo di Musica Antica* escaped damage in the 1966 flood. Italy's largest and richest library.

Biblioteca Riccardiana e Moreniana [Ben. 128]

Via dei Ginori 10. Tel.: 27 25 86

Hours: 8:00 AM to 2:00 PM. Saturdays 8:00 AM to 1:00 PM. Closed August 15–31.

Credentials: identification papers or passport.

Description of Collection: manuscripts including theoretical works, libretti, fifteenth- through eighteenth-century editions.

Library was established at the end of the sixteenth century by Riccardo Romolo Riccardi and passed to the state in 1815. It is now run by the Ministry of Public Instruction. Shares functions and services with the Biblioteca Moreniana.

Museo di Strumenti Musicale del Conservatorio Luigi Cherubini

Piazza Belle Arti 2. Tel.: 27 05 02; 27 21 80

The collection, which is found within the Conservatory itself, was begun by Ferdinando de' Medici and includes three Stradivari, two Amati, the first vertical piano (1739), a marble psaltery built for the Medici family, and a Roman bugle-horn.

Museo di Antropologia ed Etnologia

Via del Proconsolo 12. Tel.: 24 049

Hours: Monday and Thursday, 9:30 AM to 12:30 PM.

Guided visits to collection of ethnic instruments.

Conservatories and Schools

Accademia Nazionale Luigi Cherubini di Musica, Lettere e Arti
Via Alfani 80.   Tel.: 27 05 02
This is a national conservatory, subject to the same general course of study, prerequisites, examinations, and diploma awards as all the others. The Conservatory not only serves an educative function, but also promotes musical, literary, and artistic events, scholarly meetings, competitions for musical and artistic compositions, historical, critical, and aesthetic works, and the construction of musical instruments.

Università degli Studi, Facoltà di Lettere e Filosofia
Istituto di Storia della Musica, Piazza Brunelleschi 1.   Tel.: 26 07 05
The Institute has a Center of Culture for Foreigners. Its program of academic study for foreigners includes the history of music.
Dates: four sessions annually of two and a half months each.
Information: Secretary, Center of Culture for Foreigners, Via Bolognese 52.

Villa I Tatti
The Harvard University Center for Italian Renaissance Studies
Via Vincigliata 26, 50014 Fiesole (Florence).   Tel.: 60 32 51; 60 89 09
Advanced research in art, music, literature, history of the Italian Renaissance. No faculty. Twelve to fourteen students, usually between 25 and 40 years of age with doctorates. No tuition. Grants no degree; normally nominated by the Dean of the Graduate School at Harvard or senior scholars.
Library hours: Monday to Friday, 9:00 AM to 1:00 PM and 2:30 PM to 6:00 PM. Saturday, 9:00 AM to 1:00 PM. Closed last two weeks in August.

Villa Schifanoia Graduate School of Fine Arts.
Via Boccaccio 123.   Tel.: 57 62 97; 57 61 95
Winter Program: two semesters (October to June). Intensive Italian language study program precedes all courses. Application deadline September 28 and February 1.
Summer Workshop: six weeks in June and July.
For further information: Villa Schifanoia Admissions Committee, Rosary College, 7900 W. Division, River Forest, Illinois 60305.
A branch of Rosary College, the school is housed in a sumptuous sixteenth-century Tuscan villa, surrounded by pools and gardens. The Master of Music diploma is offered with courses in literature, applied music, and voice.

Musical Landmarks

The Birthplace of Opera: Palazzo de Bardi
Via dei Benci 5.

On the wall of this fifteenth-century palazzo, designed by the great Filippo Brunelleschi, there is a plaque marking it as the place where the group of intellectuals and musicians now known as the Camerata Fiorentina regularly met toward the end of the sixteenth century. The palace was owned by the group's benefactor, a Florentine aristocrat, Count Giovanni de' Bardi, mathematician, poet, and musician. The Camerata concerned itself with ideas and with esthetics. It numbered among its members some of the leading minds of Florence, fired by the spirit of the Renaissance and eager to revive the glories of Greek drama in a contemporary setting. The social circle or club included **Vincenzo Galilei,** a lute player and theoretician better known today as the father of the astronomer, Galileo; **Giulio Caccini** and **Jacopo Peri,** singers and composers; **Emilio de' Cavalieri,** nobleman and composer; **Girolamo Mei,** scholar; and **Ottavio Rinuccini,** poet and librettist. Out of the Camerata's announced intention to support a more direct, more human kind of music, arose a declamatory style which became known as *recitativo* and which remains, to this day, an essential aspect of Italian opera. The first opera, *Euridice,* was based on a libretto by Rinuccini, music by Peri; the first performance took place on the evening of October 6, 1600, in the Pitti Palace apartment of Don Antonio dei Medici.

Musical Organizations

Associazione Amici della Musica
Via Rondinelli 10.   Tel.: 29 62 33; 27 28 66

Sponsors important concert series at La Pergola from October to May. Approximately twenty-five concerts, featuring soloists and ensembles of international reknown.

Associazione Italiana per la Diffusione dell'Educazione Musicale (AIDEM)
Via Maggio 39.   Tel.: 29 63 19; 29 67 18

This organization, the Italian Association for Musical Development and Education, sponsors annual competitions, concert series, and other musical activities calculated to increase musical education and appreciation throughout Italy. In Florence, it supports an orchestra, the Orchestra di Palazzo Pitti, which performs regularly under its auspices. The concert series presented by this group is called Incontri con la Musica (Encounters with Music).

The Business of Music

Here is a short list of reliable professional establishments:

Music Shops

G. and C. Ceccherini
    Piazza Antinori 21.   Tel.: 21 87 23; 27 00 31
Saporetti & Cappelli
    Via dei Conti 12/r.   Tel.: 2 42 23
Messaggerie Musicali
    Via Il Prato 13r.   Tel.: 26 06 01
Brizzi & Niccolai
    Via Pecori 10/r.   Tel.: 29 66 77

Record Shops

Alberti s/p.a.
    Via dei Pucci 16.   Tel.: 28 43 36
    Via dei Pecori 9.   Tel.: 29 42 71
Discoteca Fiorentina
    Via Oriuolo 1/3.   Tel.: 2 38 54
Disclub
    Piazza San Marco 11.   Tel.: 28 28 69
Minimarket del Disco
    Via Verdi 47.   Tel.: 26 38 61

Instrument Manufacture and Distribution

Gastone Bargelli (violin making and repair)
    Via Saponai 12.
Carlo Bisiach (violin making and repair)
    Via Puccinnoti 94.
F. Maestrini & Figli (pianos)
    Via Anguillara 10.   Tel.: 29 66 22

Music Publisher

Edizioni Musicali
    Via Nazionale 23.   Tel.: 28 77 02

Music Antiquarian

Libreria Antiquaria Leo S. Olschki
    Piazzo del Pozzetto.   Tel.: 68 74 44

PALERMO (Sicily)   (Tel. prefix: 091)

Palermo, a city of some 730,000 permanent residents, records on its face the traces of many transient civilizations. It is a city of many aspects: Phoenician in origin, Roman in the mosaics of the Villa Bonnano, Arab in the mosques that serve as churches today, French, German, Spanish in its monuments, architecture, and street names. It is a city that is outranked only by Rome, Milan, Naples, and Florence in the number of concert and opera performances presented yearly and in the variety and imagination of its musical activity. Its Teatro Massimo not only has the third largest opera stage in the entire world (exceeded in dimension only by Paris and Vienna), but an artistic policy that is decidedly unprovincial in outlook. Experimental works and new operas are frequently given premieres in Palermo. Music that is influenced by Sicilian folklore is guaranteed a hearing. The support received from the government is put to good use in deemphasizing pure box-office considerations and in mounting a movement to vitalize the Italian audience. Finally, the fact that Palermo enjoys one of the most idyllic climates in the world attracts a constant flow of visitors throughout the winter season, serving to augment the excitement of performances and maintain the high professional level of performance.

Guides and Services

Ente Provinciale per il Turismo
Piazza Castelnuovo 35.   Tel.: 58 61 22; 24 50 80

Azienda Autonoma di Turismo di Palermo e Monreale
Villa Igiea.   Tel.: 24 23 43
Stazione Ferrovie State (Central Railway Station).
                              Tel.: 54 01 41; 54 01 43; 54 01 98
Hours: 9:00 AM to 1:00 PM, Monday through Saturday. Tickets for most musical
    events can be obtained at the villa Igiea branch.

Opera Houses and Concert Halls

Teatro Massimo
Piazza Giuseppe Verdi.   Tel.: 33 19 88; 33 44 54; 58 46 72
Season: The season as whole runs from mid-September to the end of May,
    divided as follows: symphony, mid-September to mid-November; opera,
    beginning of December to end of May. The summer opera season, under

the auspices of the Teatro Massimo, is held at the Teatro del Parco di Villa Castelnuovo (see p. 169). Ballets, concerts, and opera are presented.
Seating Capacity: 2,500.
Box Office: in lobby of theater.   Tel.: 21 45 12
Hours: daily from 10:00 AM to 1:00 PM and 4:00 PM to 7:30 PM.
Customary Dress: a dark suit is required for first nights.
The Teatro Massimo, an *istituzione nazionale* (previously known as *ente autonomo*), was designed by Giovanbattista Basile, who won a public competition for this project in 1864. It was completed by his son Ernesto, and thirty-three years later it opened with a performance of Verdi's *Falstaff,* to which the composer was not invited. Because things are done in Sicily in ways that do not appear immediately obvious to the mainlander, it took another fifty years before a Mozart opera was performed on the stage of the Massimo (1947, *Le Nozze di Figaro*). That stage measures 3,600 square feet, making possible the most elaborate presentations. The schedules nowadays invariably include interesting works, both old and new, reflecting a very enlightened artistic policy and adventurous audience. There is a Center of Opera Studies attached to the opera house (see p. 66) as well as a museum. The theater has its own symphony orchestra, one of the two performing all year long in Palermo.

Teatro Biondo
Via Roma.   Tel.: 58 93 61; 24 53 61
Primarily a dramatic theater, the Biondo is used for solo recitals, especially by visiting international artists.

Teatro del Parco di Villa Castelnuovo
Viale del Fante 78b.   Tel.: 51 65 61
The summer season of the Teatro Massimo takes place here with opera, ballet, and concerts throughout August. Known as the Festival di Palermo (see p. 169).

Teatro Politeama Garibaldi
Piazza Settimo Ruggero.   Tel.: 21 23 34
Constructed according to a design by Giuseppe Damiana Almeyda and inaugurated in 1875, this theater is Pompeian in style and has a circular structure lightened by a double portico. The principal access consists of a grandiose entrance reminiscent of the Arc de Triomphe.

Church concerts are held in the Duomo di Monreale, the Palermo Cathedral, and the churches of San Domenico, Santo Spirito, and Santa Maria di Gesù, to name but a few.

Libraries and Museums

Biblioteca Comunale [Ben. 242]
Piazzetta Lucrezia Brunaccini.   Tel.: 28 06 09
Hours: Monday to Saturday from 9:00 AM to 5:00 PM. Closed for fifteen days in
September.
Description of the Collection: only partly musical. The collection contains printed
and manuscript works, including liturgical works, autographs of Bellini
and Fiamengo.
Founded by Ferdinand IV and opened in 1760, the Library received the
collections of suppressed religious orders. Strong in literary and historical
studies.

Biblioteca del Conservatorio di Musica Vicenzo Bellini [Ben. 244]
Via Squarcialupo 45.   Tel.: 21 18 03
Hours: Monday through Saturday, from 9:00 AM to 1:00 PM. Closed August.
Credentials: apply to conservatory director or librarian for admission.
Description of the Collection: exclusively musical. The collection consists of musical
editions up to the present as well as some theoretical treatises and
manuscripts from the collection of the Baron Pietro Pisani, received in the
mid-nineteenth century.

Biblioteca dell'Archivio di Stato [Ben. 240]
Corso Vittorio Emanuele 31.   Tel.: 24 06 93; 24 34 26
Open primarily to scholars, the small music collection includes first edition of
Corelli Opus 5 and documents concerning E. d'Astorga. Founded in the
eighteenth century.

Biblioteca dell'Istituto di Storia della Musica [Ben. 245]
Facoltà di Lettere, Università degli Studi, Viale delle Scienze.   Tel.: 23 56 51
Hours: Monday to Friday, 9:00 AM to 1:00 PM; Tuesday to Friday also 4:00 PM to
7:00 PM. Closed July 15 to September 15.
Description of the Collection: Part of the university library, this exclusively musical
section was developed for basic research and instruction in Renaissance
Sicilian music, of which a microfilm collection is being made.

Biblioteca Nazionale [Ben. 243]
Corso Vittorio Emanuele 429-431.   Tel.: 21 17 62; 21 46 02
Hours: weekdays from 9:00 AM to 7:00 PM. Closed August 15-31.
Description of the Collection: Founded in 1778, the entire collection has 485,000
volumes including *siciliana rara*. Music items are scattered but cataloged.
Depository for works printed in the province.

Museo Etnografico Siciliano G. Pitre
Parco della Favorita. Tel.: 51 61 41
Hours: 9:00 AM to 3:00 PM, Monday to Saturday; 9:00 AM to 1:00 PM, Sunday.
Facilities: library and sale of photographs.
Description of the Collection: There is, within this provincial museum, a collection
of 67 Italian folk music instruments.

United States Information Service Library
Via Vaccarini 1. Tel.: 29 66 36
General collection with current periodicals and large library of recordings.

Conservatories and Schools

Conservatorio di Musica Vincenzo Bellini
Via Squarcialupo 45. Tel.: 21 18 03; 24 02 41
This is a national conservatory, subject to the same organization, programs, and
diploma schedule as the Santa Cecilia in Rome (see p. 19).

Università degli Studi, Facoltà di Lettere e Filosofia
Istituto di Storia della Musica, Via Maqueda 172. Tel.: 22 37 14
One of the few universities in Italy with a musicological institute that gives
courses and offers degrees in music.

Summer Schools

Centro di Avviamento al Teatro Lirico (Center for Opera Studies)
Mailing Address: Teatro Massimo, Via Volturno. Tel.: 58 99 36
School Address: Teatro del Parco di Villa Castelnuovo, Viale del Fante 78b.
Tel.: 51 65 51
Age Limit: women: 17 to 27; men: 18 to 28.
Deadline for Application: beginning of February.
Admission Requirements: competitive examination only, which can be taken in the
spring in Palermo or in Rome. Applications must be forwarded to Palermo
through Italian diplomatic representatives and include curriculum and
documentation of studies by the applicant in an accredited institution.
Course of Study: In addition to all the aspects of music theater performance,
students may take part in the opera season at the Teatro del Parco for
first-hand experience in performance.

Musical Organizations

Associazione Siciliana Amici della Musica
Via Bari 8.   Tel.: 21 06 65
Organizes concerts throughout the year. Member of the AIAC (Italian Association for Concert Activity).

Ente Autonomo Orchestra Sinfonica Siciliana
Via Giuseppe La Farina 29.   Tel.: 26 65 99; 29 64 47
Independent entity on the same level as the established theaters. Performs at the auditorium of Santo Salvatore.

The Business of Music

Music and Record Shops

Salvatore D'Alfonso
    Via Dante 55.   Tel.: 23 18 25
Disco Service
    Via Cavour 98.   Tel.: 20 10 42
G. & E. Ricordi
    Via R. Settimo 24/a.   Tel.: 21 85 81
Giacinto Sacco (also sells musical instruments)
    Via Maqueda 132.   Tel.: 23 32 13
Cinevox
    Via A. Paternostro 48.   Tel.: 21 31 49

Instrument Repair

Prof. Sebastiano Imbesi
    Via La Mantia 146.   Tel.: 20 35 51.

VENICE (Veneto)   (Tel. prefix: 041)

Venice is a physical improbability which lies on a lagoon in the Adriatic Sea about two and a half miles from the mainland. It is a compromise between land and water, about 37 miles long and 5 miles wide. The city is spread over 118 islands linked by 177 canals over which there are 400 bridges. The Grand Canal divides the city into two unequal parts, and the houses, about 15,000 in all, are for the most part, built on pilings, with their facades on a main canal and their doors on a side or back canal.

Venice is the Queen of the Adriatic—a city that captures the imagination of all who visit—a place with a mysterious aura of high drama—a tired courtesan who hints at past glories. More books have been written about the physical qualities of Venice than of any other place in Italy. For the architect, there is the widest possible collection of styles: Byzantine, pointed Gothic heavily laced with Arab influence, Lombardian, and Renaissance. For the painter, there is something rewarding at every turn—from the Greek mosaics in San Marco to the works of Giovanni Bellini and his most famous pupils Giorgione and Titian; from Tintoretto to Veronese; and from the two Canaletti to the incomparable Guardi. For the city planner and the urban economist, Venice is a triumph of man against the sea, a challenge to nature that has been going on since the Venetians began building the "Palatium Ducis"—the Doge's Palace—by reinforcing the insecure subsoil with close and deeply driven wooden pilings.

For the musician, Venice starts with San Marco. As surely as we must look to the Vatican for the dominant force in Roman music, to the university for the prime influence in Bologna, to the opera house in Milan and to the Renaissance court in Florence, so do we turn to San Marco for some of the early answers about Venetian music. We can begin with a fact: high above the altar and on each side of it are two choir lofts. In each loft, there has been an organ since 1316, reflecting the Byzantine practice of antiphonal singing, which was traditional in St. Mark's. The *maestro di cappella* played the first organ and his most gifted student, the second. The continuity thus guaranteed did, indeed, carry through from the fifteenth to the seventeenth century, when the music of Venice knew no equal. Jean Mouton, Adrien Willaert, Cypriano de Rore, the two Gabrielis, Heinrich Schütz, Giacomo Carissimi, and Claudio Monteverdi are some of the names that come to mind. All of them contributed to the brilliance of the Venetian style during that long period.

The first printed music originated in Venice. In 1501, Ottaviani Petrucci published a collection of the best music he could find and called it *Harmonice Musices Odhecaton A*. Fine examples of this and subsequent works of Petrucci's are preserved in the Biblioteca Nazionale Marciana and can be seen today— superb specimens of clarity, design, and workmanship.

The transition from church to theater, which took place all over musical Italy in the seventeenth century, was personified in the life and works of Monteverdi. He was *maestro di cappella* of San Marco for the last thirty years of his life. Nevertheless, he combined his churchly duties and functions with the writing of operas—the last of which, *L'Incoronazione di Poppea*, was the first to deal with an historical rather than Biblical subject. It was performed at the Teatro San Giovanni e Paolo in 1642, one year before his death.

Opera did more than flourish in Venice in the late seventeenth century; it was rampant. The houses were large and well-equipped, the audiences enthusiastic, and the productions nothing short of stupendous.

It was not until the beginning of the eighteenth century, however, that a violinist in the orchestra of St. Mark's began to make his presence felt, and we have our next figure of major international importance appearing on the horizon. Antonio Vivaldi, called the *prete rosso* (the red priest), was not actually of a very reverent disposition, although he most assuredly had red hair. His works number over fifty operas and more than five hundred concertos, and his influence on the music of his time was profound. The nineteenth century in Venice slipped by on the gilded skirts of La Fenice. Opera composers made their royal round of opera houses, and La Fenice was surely one of the most illustrious stopping points. Wagner made the supreme gesture and died in Venice in 1883.

And today? Surely, there is the solid season at the opera house and a slightly incestuous Biennale; there are the moderately inane band concerts in the Piazza San Marco and the worthy efforts of the Fondazione Cini. And what of the musical glories that were Venice's? Gone, perhaps, and almost forgotten, for the traditions that stubbornly persisted, like the excellent singing of the choir of San Marco, is seldom heard by Venetians today. Yet the words of Nietzsche haunt us like the city and we recall that he said: "When I search for a word to replace that of music, I can think only of Venice."

Guides and Services

Ente Provinciale per il Turismo
Castello, Calle del Remedio 4421.   Tel.: 2 23 73; 2 86 93

Azienda Autonoma Soggiorna e Turismo
Palazzo Martinengo, Rialto 4089.   Tel.: 2 61 10

Information offices of the EPT and AAST are at:
    San Marco, Ascensione 71C.   Tel.: 2 63 56
    Santa Lucia Railway Station.   Tel.: 2 13 37
    Piazzale Roma.   Tel.: 2 74 02
    Marghera, Autostrada.   Tel.: 97 46 38
The EPT and the AAST publish *Venice Events* annually in English. The publication includes a brief outline of the major events of the year, listed by month. Available gratis at the offices listed above.

Opera Houses and Concert Halls

Teatro La Fenice
Campo San Fantin 2519.   Tel.: 2 51 91; 2 44 73; 2 82 26; 2 44 73

Season: The grand opera season runs from December through May, with an
opera festival in the summer (see p. 176). The symphony season (Orchestra
La Fenice) takes place before and after the opera season: spring, May to
June; autumn, October and November; plus a summer season of concerts
in the Ducal Palace courtyard. Monday evening lecture series in the winter.
Box Office: open daily from 10:00 AM to 12:30 PM and from 4:00 PM to 7:00 PM.
Tel.: 2 39 54
Seating Capacity: 1,500.
The Teatro La Fenice, an *istituzione nazionale* and one of the primary locations
for opera in Italy today, was designed by Antonio Selva and opened in 1792
with a performance of a Paisiello opera. The principal entrance to the house is
on San Fantin, the back one on a canal. When the theater was gravely damaged
by fire in 1836, it was reconstructed by the brothers Meduna, after the original
plans, substituting only the interior decor. La Fenice has seen premieres of
Ernani, Rigoletto, La Traviata; Wagner conducted his C-major Symphony here,
and Toscanini saw service in the orchestra pit in his time. There are interesting
programs at La Fenice; rare operas as well as important first performances such
as *The Rake's Progress* (1951), but the season is not really designed for the
convenience of the tourist. One work is performed several times consecutively,
then another one is presented for a period, instead of a system of rotation which
would allow the opera lover passing through the city for a short time to see
different productions.

Of all the Venetian houses in which opera has been presented, La Fenice is
the only one currently being used for this purpose. The Teatro San Cassiano,
which was the first public opera house in the city, opened in 1637, no longer
stands. The Teatro San Moisè, which opened in 1638 with Monteverdi's *Arianna*
is also only a memory. The Teatro San Salvatore, opened in 1661, was renamed
the Teatro Goldoni in 1875 and refurbished in 1962 as a dramatic theater. The
Teatro Malibran, originally opened in 1687, is a most magnificent hall. It can be
seen, along with a dubbed double feature, for the price of admission, as it is now
a cinema.

The interior of La Fenice is gilt and pink plush, complete with pink cherubs
swooping down from the ceiling. At a gala performance, the theater attendants
wear wigs and embroidered costumes, and the ambience is of a glamorous
consistency that often outdoes the performance itself.

Under the sponsorship of the Fondazione Cini, the Circolo Artistico, the
Amici della Musica and other organizations, concert series in the winter as well
as the summer take place in various palaces, courtyards, and churches through-
out Venice. To mention but a few places used in this way, one could cite the
Palazzo delle Prigioni, the Palazzo Vendramin Calergi (where Wagner died),
Chiostro dei Cipressi, Salone degli Arazzo, Scuola de San Rocco, Chiesa della
Pietà, Ca'Pesaro, and the Museo Correr.

In order to find out what concerts are being given precisely where, and perhaps even what the program will be (although this last-mentioned is even more uncertain than the uncertainties that precede it), the visitor may consult the arts page of the local newspaper and hope for the best. A better probability is to search out the ubiquitous posters that are plastered over many walls in the city to advertise the musical events of the two weeks immediately ahead. The posters announce not only the above information, but the price of tickets as well.

Libraries and Museums

Archivio del Teatro la Fenice [Ben. 414]
Campo San Fantin 2519. Tel.: 2 51 91; 2 44 73
Hours: open daily Monday through Saturday. Closed in August.
Description of the Collection: The working archive of the opera house contains manuscripts and prints of nineteenth century music, including an autograph score of Rossini's *Semiramide*. For the most part, opera materials for use by the orchestra.

Biblioteca d'Arte e Storia Veneziana del Museo Civico Correr [Ben. 410]
Piazza San Marco 52. Tel.: 2 56 25
Description of the Collection: In this general collection on Venetian art and history, there are a few eighteenth-century manuscripts, as well as prints from the sixteenth to the nineteenth centuries. Most of the music holdings were deposited in 1961 in the Conservatory library (see next entry). Part of the Correr collection of musical instruments is still housed in this museum.

Biblioteca del Conservatorio di Musica Benedetto Marcello [Ben. 405]
Palazzo Pisani, Campo Pisani 2809. Tel.: 2 56 04
Hours: open weekdays. Closed August.
Description of the Collection: Wiel and Pascoluto bequests of eighteenth-century Venetian manuscripts. Collections of the Ospedaletto, Museo Correr e Giustinian. Manuscripts of the later Venetian school of sacred music and opera. Prints of Corelli, Geminiani, Boccherini, Albinoni, and Haydn. Conservatory music materials of a practical nature.

Biblioteca del Seminario Patriarcale [Ben. 413]
Campa della Salute-Dorsoduro 1. Tel.: 2 55 58
Hours: open daily upon request to the seminary director. Closed August.
Description of the Collection: private library originally formed from the collections of suppressed convents. Many sixteenth- through eighteenth-century prints and manuscripts, including works by Anfossi, Asioli, Bertoni, Cimarosa, etc. Over 80,000 volumes in all.

Biblioteca dell'Archivio di Stato [Ben. 402]
Campo dei Frari 3002.   Tel.: 2 22 81
Public Entrance: Rio Terra San Tomà.
Hours: Monday through Saturday, 8:30 AM to 1:30 PM. Closed for fifteen days in
   August.
Facilities: microfilm reader; makes copies. Catalogs.
Credentials: for use of archive personnel, but scholars may consult with director's
   permission.
Description of the Collection: psalters, hymn books, and some codices from San
   Marco. Occupies site of former Convento dei Frari, called the Ca'Grande.

Biblioteca della Casa di Goldoni [Ben. 404]
Istituto di Studi Teatrali, Palazzo Centrani,
Calle Terrà dei Nomboli 2798, San Tomà.   Tel.: 3 63 53
Hours: open weekdays from 9:00 AM to noon and from 2:00 PM to 6:00 PM. except
   Saturday afternoon. Closed in August.
Facilities: catalogs; study space for the visitor in the library.
Description of the Collection: A library of theatrical material, it contains an
   exceptional collection of libretti, with emphasis on Venetian operas from
   1637 on. Texts of operas by Monteverdi and Cavalli, some with lost music.
The library was established in 1954 with materials from the Civico Museo
Correr and other museums. The Istituto Veneziano di Studi Teatrali, a section
of the Civici Musei Veneziani was formed at the same time in the Casa di
Goldoni. The collection numbers over 20,000 volumes, 300 manuscripts, and
3,000 documents in all.

Biblioteca dell'Archivio Storico d'Arte Contemporanea
San Marco 1364a, Cà Giustinian.   Tel.: 70 03 11
Contemporary arts, including theater, music, film. Has slides, photos, clippings,
exhibition catalogs, current periodicals. Very current collection.

Biblioteca della Fondazione Giorgio Cini, Centro di Cultura e Civiltà
[Ben. 408]
Scuola di San Giorgio per lo Studio della Civiltà Veneziana,
Isola di San Giorgio Maggiore.   Tel.: 8 99 00
Hours: Monday to Saturday from 9:15 AM to 12:30 PM and 3:15 PM to 7:00 PM.
   Closed in May.
Credentials: references required.
Description of the Collection: mainly a microfilm collection of musical treatises in
   manuscript. Also 35,000 libretti from the library of Ulderico Rolandi.
   Sixteenth- to eighteenth-century works from Aron to Zacconi, listed in
   URFM. Film and photocopies of sixteenth- to eighteenth-century Vene-
   tian music. Monographs, bibliographic studies, scores, periodicals, etc.

Malipiero collection. Sponsors compositions, performances, festivals, publications.

Biblioteca della Fondazione Querini-Stampalia [Ben. 406]
Palazzo Querini-Stampalia, Calle Querini-Stampalia 4778.   Tel.: 2 52 35

Hours: Monday to Saturday, 2:00 PM to 11:00 PM; Sunday from 3:00 PM to 7:00 PM. Closed New Year, Easter, May 1, June 2, November 4, Christmas, July 16–31.

Facilities: photocopies; catalogs. For access apply to librarian.

Description of the Collection: seventeenth- and eighteenth-century musical codices of vocal music by Legrenzi, Sartorio, etc. Manuscripts of Clementi, Galuppi, Marcello, etc. Printed works by Gossec, Haydn, Hoffmeister, etc.

Biblioteca della Fondazione Ugo Levi, Centro di Cultura Musicale Superiore [Ben. 407]
Palazzo Giustinian Lolin, Rio di San Vidal 2893.

Although the library is difficult to enter, it contains a rich collection of sixteenth- and seventeenth-century madrigals and sacred music in Italian editions. Works from San Marco.

Biblioteca Nazionale Marciana [Ben. 403]
Piazzetta San Marco 7.   Tel.: 2 00 19; 2 50 01

Hours: Monday to Friday from 9:00 AM to 5:00 PM; Saturday from 9:00 AM to 3:00 PM.

Facilities: separate music section has microfilm reader; make films, slides. Catalogs.

Description of the Collection: permanent exhibition in the great Sala Sansonniana dei Filosofi and Anticola. Collection includes illuminated manuscripts, illustrated ancient books, historical bindings, *gradulai, antifonarii,* etc. Repository for music from city churches. Includes some Petrucci prints of Josquin and Moutin. Provincial depository as well.

The library was founded in 1468 in Sansovino's old palace of the Zecca (mint), across from the Doge's Palace on the Piazzetta San Marco.

Conservatories and Schools

Conservatorio di Musica Benedetto Marcello
Palazzo Pisani, San Marco 2809.   Tel.: 2 56 04

This is a national conservatory and subject to the same entrance requirements and internal organization as the Santa Cecilia in Rome (see p. 19). Sponsors a concert season.

Istituto di Musica, Lettere e Teatro della Fondazione Giorgio Cini
Isola di San Giorgio Maggiore.   Tel.: 8 99 00
Founded in 1958 and set up in the monastic buildings of San Giorgio Maggiore, the work of the great Palladio. Since 1951, when Count Vittorio Cini rescued these buildings, which had been used for years as Austrian barracks, and completely restored them, they have been the home of a group of institutes named in memory of Count Cini's son and devoted to the study of various aspects of Venetian civilization. An open-air theater with marble seats, guarded from the elements by a screen of cypresses, is used for opera and concert performances in the summer.

Venezia Isola degli Studi, Fondazione Querini-Stampalia.
Campo Santa Maria Formos, Castello.   Tel.: 2 52 35
For information contact: Venice Island of Studies, Liberty Trust Building, Philadelphia, Pennsylvania 19107.
Dates: last week of September through second week of June.
Entrance Requirements: adequate background and motivation; permission of parents; financial solvency and good health.
Areas of Specialization: The faculty is drawn from the University of Venice, the Institute of Architecture, the Conservatory of Music, and the Institute of Industrial Design for concentration in these subject areas.

Corsi Superiori di Studi Musicali per Stranieri (Advanced Courses of Musical Studies for Foreigners)
Corsi di Alta Cultura sulla Musica Italiana.
Segretaria dei Corsi, Via Vittoria 6, Rome.
The sessions of the Advanced Courses of Musical Studies for Foreigners, which take place in Venice, coincide with the sessions of the Vacanze Musicali (see below) but are of a higher order. The entire program, which is sponsored by the International Center of Studies for the Dissemination of Italian Music, extends from midsummer to midwinter. The first part of it takes place in Venice, the balance in Rome. The courses covered include musicology, conducting, organ, voice, opera. These are given in the form of seminars and are supplemented by lessons and concerts.
Admission Requirements: Foreigners in possession of a degree or diploma from an accredited conservatory or academy in their own country may apply. Age limit: 35 years old.
Deadline for Applications: June 16th.
Study prizes and scholarships are available upon application to the Centro.
     The Ottorino Respighi Fund is offered annually by the G. Cini Foundation to the prize-winning student of the course.

Summer Schools

Vacanze Musicale (Musical Vacations in Venice)
Ca'Vendramin, Calergi, Venice.
Applications should be made to the Conservatorio di Musica di Santa Cecilia, Via dei Greci 18, Rome.
Dates: six weeks in the summer (August–September).
Program: The program of the Musical Vacations follows the lines of the Advanced Course of Musical Studies outlined above. However, the entrance requirements are a bit more relaxed, and there are provisions for auditors who observe the courses but do not actively take part in them. There are sessions in composition, orchestration, conducting, singing, and instrumental instruction given by prominent Italian musicians. There are study prizes and scholarships available for the Vacations as well as for the Advanced courses and the examinations and credit program are very similar.

Corso Estivo di Canto Gregoriano e Musica Sacra
PP. Benedetini di San Giorgio Maggiore, Fondazione Cini.
For information concerning these special courses in Gregorian chant and sacred music, contact the Fondazione Cini.

Musical Landmarks

Among the musical landmarks of this illustrious city, one may visit the Ospedale della Pietà on the Campo Santi Giovanni e Paolo where **Antonio Vivaldi** (ca. 1678–1741) was choirmaster from 1703 to 1740. **Claudio Monteverdi** (1567–1643) is buried in the large church of Santa Maria dei Frari on the Campo dei Frari. **Igor Stravinsky** and **Serge Diaghilev** are both at rest in the island cemetery of San Michele.

Musical Organizations

Istituto Internazionale di Musica Comparata
Fondazione Cini, Isola di San Giorgio Maggiore.   Tel.: 8 99 00
This is the Italian bureau of the Berlin-based, UNESCO-sponsored organization that concerns itself primarily with East-West exchange and ethnomusicological problems. Has an interesting publications program of books and recordings.

The Business of Music

Music and Record Shops

Carlo Berrera
    San Marco 4948.
Antonio Bracaleon
    San Marco 5476.
Ulderico Frison
    Cannaregio 5575.   Tel.: 3 46 89
Mario Gasparini
    San Marco 4943.
Casare Wolf
    San Marco 2765b.   Tel.: 3 09 64
Robinson Records
    Via Comuffo 22.   Tel.: 97 06 04
Dicobolo
    Via Mestina 25.   Tel.: 5 19 17

Instrument Manufacture and Repair

Giuseppe Garatti
    Sottoportico del Fornes.
Nicolo Ulcigrai
    Cannaregio 1432a.   Tel.: 8 10 10
Luigi Vistoli
    Cannaregio 3047.

BOLOGNA (Emilia-Romagna)   (Tel. prefix: 051)

Bologna today has a population of almost half a million and is one of the most active and important trading centers of the Po Valley. By virtue of its function as the gateway from southern and central Italy to the rest of Europe, it also serves as a natural meeting place for all currents of culture and thought.

Originally an Etruscan village called Felsina, then a Roman colony, then a municipality called Bononia, the city became celebrated in the early Middle Ages as a center for the study of law—its university being the oldest in Europe.

The University of Bologna was founded in the eleventh century and very early on established itself as a mecca for students from all lands. The first chair in music was decreed by papal order in the middle of the Quattrocento. The tradition of musical scholarship which has since that time characterized Bolognese life, was firmly established by the eighteenth century, when the great

theoretician and musicologist Giovanni Battista Martini (known as Padre
Martini, 1706–84), lived and worked in the city. Young musicians from all over
Europe sought his counsel as well as confirmation of their own gifts. To cite a
few, one might mention Dr. Charles Burney of England, the "little German,
Mozart" (to quote the former), Johann Christian Bach (1735–82), and Niccolo
Jommelli (1714–74). Martini amassed during his lifetime a formidable and
unique musical library, which reposes, after a complicated journey, in the
Civico Museo Bibliografico Musicale (see p. 80).

Today Bologna is a center of wealth as well as learning—a thriving
metropolis and a gourmets' paradise. (Few will challenge the supremacy of
Italian cuisine "alla Bolognese.") The city is a marvelous pastiche of porticos
and portfolios—modern businessmen and students from all countries. The
concert life is restrained but dependable, the relatively short season being
supplemented by interesting concerts of an experimental nature, musical
collegia, and special festivals to delight the local resident as well as the foreign
visitor.

Guides and Services

Ente Provinciale per il Turismo

Via Marconi 45.	Tel.: 23 74 13/14
Branches of the EPT may be found at Via Leopardi 1.	Tel.: 23 66 02
Stazione Centrale Ferrovie Stato, Piazza Medaglie d'Oro 5.	
	Tel.: 37 22 20
Autostrada del Sole-Cantagallo, Casalecchio di Reno.	Tel.: 57 22 63
Autostazione, Piazza XX Settembre.	Tel.: 27 32 69

Bologna Incontri (Meet Bologna)

Published monthly by the EPT and available, in Italian, gratis at ETP offices
and major hotels. Feature articles concerning events and activities in and
around the city. Map and brief digest of the month's calendar.

Opera Houses and Concert Halls

Teatro Comunale

Piazza del Teatro.   Tel.: 23 71 89; 26 75 25; 27 67 89; 27 96 24
Public Entrance: Via Zamboni 28–30.
Season: The opera season runs from November (or December) to March (or
    April). The concert season takes place both before and afterward, begin-

ning in September and running until the end of May or the beginning of June. The house is closed in August.

Box Office (Biglietteria): Large Respighi 1.   Tel.: 22 29 99

Hours: 10:00 AM to 1:00 PM and 4:00 PM to 6:30 PM daily except Monday, when there are no performances. There is no standing room.

Seating Capacity: 1,500.

The Teatro Comunale was designed by Antonio Galli Bibiena, third generation of that esteemed family, and opened its doors on May 14, 1763, with a performance of Gluck's *Il Trionfo di Clelia* (libretto by Metastasio). The building is splendid, having one of the most magnificent interiors in the world. The house does not have a spectacular record of first performances, although Wagner's *Lohengrin* was given there, the first performance of a Wagner opera in Italy. A bronze relief of the German composer joins one of Verdi to dominate the lobby of the hall. The Comunale is an *istituzione nazionale* and receives both city and state support. If its repertory has not been venturesome, it has made up for this deficiency somewhat in the imagination of its scenic design and the novelty of its productions.

Sala Mozart, Accademia Filarmonica

Via Guerrazzi 13.   Tel.: 22 29 97

Chamber and symphonic music concerts are given here in the spring. Occasionally concerts by the student association (ORUB) of the University are programmed.

Sala Bossi, Conservatorio G. B. Martini

Piazza Rossini 2.   Tel.: 22 14 83

Extraordinary hall, the walls of which are hung with one hundred and thirty-two paintings of musicians, collected by Padre Martini. Chamber music concerts are held here, especially those of the Amici della Musica.

Organ music and church concerts may be heard in the following, among others: Santa Maria dei Servi, Strada Maggiore; Basilica di San Petronio, Piazza Galvani; and Chiesa di San Vittore, Porta San Mamolo.

In the summer, concerts are given in the squares and palace courtyards throughout the city, as well as in the basilicas, cloisters, and gardens.

Libraries and Museums

Archivio della Cappella di San Petronio, Basilica di San Petronio [Ben. 46]

Piazza Galvani 5.   Tel.: 22 93 30; 22 92 30

Hours: open daily in the afternoon. Apply to the archivist for entrance. Closed in August.

Description of the Collection: many examples of the Bolognese school of instrumental music, including trumpet sonatas and *concerti grossi* of Vitali, Torelli, etc. Sixteenth- and seventeenth-century brass and string music.

Archivio di Stato [Ben. 36]

Piazza Celestini 4.   Tel.: 22 38 91

Hours: daily from 8:30 AM to 11:30 AM. Closed for fifteen days in July or August.

Description of the Collection: The small music collection includes fragments of liturgical books from various epochs; tenth- to eleventh-century psalters; manuscripts from suppressed religious orders. Primarily for personnel working in archive.

Biblioteca Americana

Via Belmeloro 11.   Tel.: 22 37 77; 22 38 57; 22 38 93

The Johns Hopkins University Center at Bologna was founded in 1955. Contains Americana and general collection, as well as periodicals. Closed in August.

Biblioteca Braille dell' Istituto dei Ciechi Francesco Cavazza

Via Castliglione 71.   Tel.: 23 36 68

Restricted to faculty, students, and blind persons, this library contains over 3,500 music scores.

Biblioteca Comunale dell'Archiginnasio [Ben. 38]

Palazzo dell'Archiginnasio, Portici dei Pavaglione, Piazza Galvani 1.

Tel.: 22 55 09

Hours: weekdays from 10:00 AM to 5:00 PM. Closed legal holidays and from August 15 to August 31.

Facilities: reference and circulating library; photocopying equipment. Separate music catalogs.

Description of the Collection: illuminated choirbooks, antiphonaries, vocal music. Rossini sketches; musical literature; libretti, especially Bolognese editions. Liturgical manuscripts formerly here are now deposited at the Civico Museo.

Biblioteca del Conservatorio di Musica G. B. Martini [Ben. 42]

Piazza Rossini 2.   Tel.: 23 39 75

Hours: open daily. Closed in August.

Facilities: microfilm and microfiche readers. Listening facilities. Catalogs.

Description of the Collection: exclusively musical, with over 17,000 titles and 1,000 discs. Recipients of Lino Livabelli and Filippo Ivaldi bequests. When the Liceo Musicale became a state institution, the library stayed with the community as a separate institution (see Civico Museo, below). Reference collection, collected editions, periodicals, etc.

Biblioteca del Convento di San Francesco [Ben. 45]

Piazza Malpighi 9.   Tel.: 22 17 62

The collection contains 1,300 manuscripts, volumes of choral music and liturgical works from other convents in the area, nineteenth-century music, as well as twentieth-century music from the libraries of Martini, Mattei, Capanna, Pozzi, etc.

Biblioteca dell'Accademia di Belle Arti e Liceo Artistico

Via Belle Arti 54.   Tel.: 23 79 61

Hours: 10:00 AM to noon and 3:30 PM to 5:30 PM on weekdays during the academic year.

Description of the Collection: stage drawings, designs; special collections of musical theater.

Biblioteca dell'Accademia Filarmonica [Ben. 35]

Via Guerrazzi 13.   Tel.: 22 29 97

This exclusively musical collection exists for the convenience of the Academy's associates, but others may request access from the archivist. The library was established in 1666, the same year the Academy was founded by Count Vincenzo Maria Carrati. Contains the Lonati collection of libretti.

Biblioteca Universitaria [Ben. 39]

Palazzo Universitario, Via Zamboni 35.   Tel.: 23 11 83

Hours: open Monday through Saturday, 8:00 AM to 2:00 PM and 3:00 PM to 6:00 PM, except Saturday afternoon; July–September 8:00 AM to 2:00 PM only.

Description of the Collection: Music is included with other materials. Music collection includes liturgical codices, rare printed editions of works by Casini, Merulo, Perti, etc. Important opera and oratorio libretti collection.

British Library

British Institute, Via Santo Stefano 11.   Tel.: 23 38 82

Collections of the British Consulate in Rome. General, with periodicals and standard reference books in English. Closed August.

Biblioteca del Civico Museo Bibliografico Musicale [Ben. 40]

Piazza Rossini 2.   Tel.: 27 09 17

Formerly called Biblioteca del Liceo Musicale and erroneously called the Biblioteca del Conservatorio di Musica Giovanni Battista Martini.

Hours: Monday through Saturday, 9:00 AM to 1:00 PM. Closed Easter, Christmas, and August.

Facilities: A large, beautiful fifteenth-century room, the Sala Vecchia del Museo Bibliografico, has recently been completely restored and refurbished for use as a working room for visitors.

Description of the Collection: one of Italy's most important collections of early music with medieval manuscripts, autographs, rare editions, and over 10,000 opera libretti. The nucleus of the library belonged to Padre Martini, and additional bequests have greatly enriched the collection.

Biblioteca Ambrosini, Cassa di Risparmio [Ben. 37]
Via Farini 22.   Tel.: 22 05 74; 23 06 68; 23 11 97
The main purpose of the library is to produce scores, transcriptions, and performance materials for use in the Schola Cantorum of some churches and secular schools of Bologna.

Biblioteca della Capella Musicale Santa Maria dei Servi [Ben. 47]
Via Bersaglieri 1.   Tel.: 22 68 07
Hours: weekdays from 8:00 AM to noon and from 2:00 PM to 9:00 PM. Closed July to August 19.

Description of the Collection: completely musical collection belonging to the Order of the Servants of Mary. Contains illuminated manuscripts, music history, theory, biography, and reference works.

Museo Civico (Sezione Medioevale)
Via Musei 8.   Tel.: 22 18 96
Hours: 9:00 AM to 2:00 PM daily; 9:00 AM to 12:30 PM holidays.
Facilities: library and photographic archive.
Description of the Collection: There are approximately 190 musical instruments in this municipal museum: 109 are European; 17 African; 58 Asian. Among the European art instruments, there are 76 wind instruments originally made in Bologna.

Conservatories and Schools

Conservatorio di Musica Giovanni Battista Martini
Piazza Rossini 2.   Tel.: 22 14 83; 23 21 88
Entrance at Via Zamboni 33.
This is a national conservatory and subject to the same entrance requirements, course structure, and diploma awards as the Santa Cecilia in Rome (see p. 19). Its illustrious forebear, the Liceo Filarmonico, was organized in 1804 with the

purpose of channeling all the Bolognese musical currents into one stream. Renamed the Liceo Musicale G. B. Martini, it became a state-supported school in 1963 with the status of national conservatory.

Istituto di Studi Musicale dell'Università
Palazzo Aldini-Sanguinetti, Strada Maggiore 34.
Tel.: 26 98 20; 27 29 33; 22 58 20

Musical Organizations

Accademia Filarmonica
Via Guerrazzi 13.   Tel.: 22 29 97
Founded in 1666 by Count Vincenzo Maria Carrati, this illustrious organization sponsors concerts, primarily in the Mozart Hall (see p. 78), throughout the year. It also owns a library of considerable value (see p. 80) and generally functions as one of the prime musical movers of Bologna.

The Business of Music

Publishers

Arnaldo Forni Editore
    Via Triumvirato 7.   Tel.: 38 58 02
The Istituto di Studi Musicale of the University of Bologna sponsors a large list of publications on music, including the *Biblioteca Musica Bononiensis,* which are brought out by this house.

Music Publishers

BDM S.p.A. Casa Musicale
    San Petronio Vecchio 17/19.   Tel.: 23 38 90; 22 39 08
Francesco Bongiovanni Stab. Musicale
    Via Rizzoli 28/e.   Tel.: 22 57 22

Music and Record Shops

Alfredo Bergonzoni
    Via San Felice 20.   Tel.: 23 39 13
Faril
    Piazza San Francesco 11.   Tel.: 23 23 83

Borsari e Sarti (musical instruments)
    Piazza Cavour 9.   Tel.: 27 95 12
Casa del Disco
    Via Indipendenza 30.   Tel.: 23 42 24
Il Disco d'Oro
    Via Marconi 41.   Tel.: 26 09 07

Instrument Repair, Manufacture, and Distribution

Casale Bauer
    Via Zanardi 41.   Tel.: 36 88 66; 36 88 67
    Major distributor of all instruments from Besson and Conn to Wittner.
Bruno Fanello
    Via San Mamalo 17.   Tel.: 23 04 66
Enrico Piretti (guitars)
    Via Solferino 16/18.   Tel.: 26 47 49

GENOA (Liguria)   (Tel: prefix: 010)

Guides and Services

Ente Provinciale per il Turismo
Via Roma 11-14.   Tel.: 58 14 07; 58 14 08

Opera Houses and Concert Halls

Teatro Comunale dell'Opera
Via XXV Aprile 1.   Tel.: 54 27 92; 53 992
Formerly the Teatro Carlo Felice, the Teatro Comunale, an *istituzione nazionale,* was designed by C. Barabino and opened in 1828 with a performance of Bellini's *Bianca e Fernando.* It bore its original name during the nineteenth century and early years of the twentieth. The theater was badly damaged by bombs during World War II and only superficially repaired in 1948. It was recently declared too unstable for occupancy by large groups, and both opera and concert seasons are being held elsewhere while renovations are completed.

Teatro Margherita

Via XX Settembre 20.   Tel.: 59 16 99
Mailing Address: Via XX Settembre 33.
Season: September to July. Opera season: March to June. Presents opera, ballet, and concerts. Symphony season includes guest artists, orchestra, conductors, as well as Genoa's own groups. Summer open-air concerts of popular music. Theater closed in August.
Box Office: Tel.: 58 93 29
    Hours: 10:00 AM to 1:00 PM; 3:00 PM to 8:00 PM, daily including holidays.

Sala di Politeama Genovese

Via Martin Piaggio.   Tel.: 89 26 58
Symphony orchestra season moved here in 1971, pending reconstruction of the Teatro Comunale. Ordinarily concerts include symphonic works, ballet programs, and recitals by visiting soloists from various countries.

Falcone Theater

Palazzo Reale, Via Balbi 10.   Tel.: 20 68 51
The Superintendent of Galleries and Works of Art, Monuments, and Antiquities of Liguria has his office in the Royal Palace, also known as the Palazzo Balbi-Durazzo. The small theater within the palace is used for chamber and solo recitals.

Other halls and chambers used for concerts in Genoa include the Little Auditorium at Via Del Campo 10; the Oratorio di San Filippo Neri (Via Lomellini 12); the Palazzo Rosso (Via Garibaldi 18), popular during the summer months; and a very special hall known affectionately as Paganini's Parlor (Via Caffaro 10).

Libraries and Museums

Biblioteca Civica Carlo Berio [Ben. 144]

Palazzo Accademia, Piazza De Ferrari 5.   Tel.: 56 52 74
Hours: daily from 9:00 AM to noon; 2:00 PM to 7:30 PM. Manuscript section open Monday to Friday, 4:00 PM to 7:00 PM.
The library was opened to the public in 1775 by the Abbot Berio and presented to the community in 1824. Most of the holdings were destroyed during World War II. A small collection of music manuscripts remains in a predominantly nonmusical library.

Biblioteca del Conservatorio di Musica Niccolò Paganini [Ben. 147]

Villa Bombrini, Via Albara.   Tel.: 36 07 47

Hours: open weekdays from 9:00 AM to noon. Closed July to September.
Description of the Collection: exclusively musical collection containing many
manuscripts and mementos of Paganini. Standard reference collection.

Biblioteca Franzoniana [Ben. 145]
Piazza Corvetto 3.   Tel.: 55 341
Mailing Address: Piazzetta Santa Maria 3, I-16122 Genova.
Hours: Monday to Saturday from 10:00 AM to noon and 2:30 PM to 7:00 PM,
     except Saturday afternoon.
Collection originally belonged to the Abbot Franzone (who died in 1927) and
now belongs to the Sacerdoti Secolari (detti Franzoniani). Since 1965 it has
occupied quarters in the Chiesa Santa Maria. Small number of music holdings.

Biblioteca Universitaria [Ben. 146]
Via Balbi 3.   Tel.: 28 144
Hours: Monday to Saturday from 9:00 AM to 1:00 PM and from 3:00 PM to 8:00
     PM, except for Saturday afternoon.
Facilities: microfilm reader, quick photocopies, catalogs (for music, author
     catalog only).
Description of the Collection: acquisitions from several different sources: the Jesuit
     College, Gaslini, Calonghi, and De Gaudenzi collections. Music reference
     works in separate department. Early manuscripts, lute and choir books.
     Opera libretti in Miscellany Department.

Istituto Mazziniano, Museo del Risorgimento e Museo delle Guerre
[Ben. 149]
Casa di Giuseppe Mazzini, Via Lomellini 11.   Tel.: 20 75 53
Hours: Monday to Friday from 9:00 AM to noon, 3:00 PM to 6:30 PM except
     Wednesday afternoon. Closed in August.
There are a small number of music manuscripts and prints of a patriotic nature
in this predominantly historical collection founded in 1915. There is also a
special collection of Mazzini autographs.

Conservatories and Schools

Conservatorio di Musica Niccolò Paganini
Villa Bombrini, Via Albaro.   Tel.: 36 07 47
This is a national conservatory and subject to the same requirements and
internal organization as the Santa Cecilia in Rome (see p. 19). Founded in
1829 as a free school of song, the Conservatory has only recently moved to its
new quarters in the Villa Bombrini.
     There is a bronze statue of Paganini by the sculptor Guido Galleti in the

main hall of the Conservatory. Paganini's violin is kept in a glass case at the Palazzo Tursi, right next to the mayor's office. Once a year a distinguished violinist is invited to take it out and play it.

Among the schools in Genoa where one may find musical instruction, the level of which is maintained and scrutinized by the Ministry for Public Instruction, there are: the Istituto Musicale G. Rossini (Via Verdi); Liceo Musicale A. Gasparini; Istituto Musicale G. Martucci; Accademia Musicale Genovese; Liceo Musicale Zanella; and the Scuola Musicale G. B. Pergolesi.

Musical Landmarks

The birthplace of **Niccolò Paganini** (1782–1840) may be found at 30 Passo di Gatta Mora, in one of the oldest sections of Genoa. There is a plaque identifying the building with the words: "Great destiny from a humble place. In this house, on 27 October 1782, Niccolò Paganini, unsurpassed master of the heavenly art of music, was born for the glory of Genoa and delight of the world."

Musical Organizations

Enti Manifestazioni Genovesi
Via Garibaldi 14.   Tel.: 28 15 48; 29 24 93
Promotes concert series, musical performances of all kinds.

Giovane Orchestra Genovese
Via G. D'Annunzio 2.
Gives about fifteen performances a year with soloists. Founded in 1912.

Teatro dell'Opera Giocosa della Città di Genova (Centro Culturale Sperimentale Lirico Sinfonico)
Corso Torino 12.
Founded in 1956 for the purpose of producing early Italian operas not found in currently existing editions. Private, nonprofit organization. Composers whose works have been resurrected by this group include Paisiello, Galuppi, Salieri, etc.

The Business of Music

Music Publishers

Azalea
    Via San Martino 65/3.   Tel.: 30 39 56
Euterpe
    Via Santa Zita.   Tel.: 58 17 77

Instrument Makers and Distributors

Andrea Albertelli (violinmaker)
    Via Carlo Orgiero 3/5, Sampierdarena, Genoa.
Lorenzo Bellafontana (violinmaker and repairer)
    Corso Torino 10/2.
Renato Bucchi (clarinets and saxaphones)
    Via Montevideo 6.   Tel.: 36 05 63
Antonio Celestino (lutier)
    Piazza Pellicceria 2/r.
Luigi Gaggero (new and used pianos)
    Vico Scuole Pie 1.   Tel.: 29 48 24
Ditta Paganini (new and used pianos)
    Via XX Settembre 87 a/r.   Tel.: 54 30 46
Vittorio Salvi (harps)
    Via Cesarea 11.   Tel.: 54 19 38; 54 25 42
Sisme Strumenti Musicali (pianos, guitars, drums, organs, amplification, hi-fi)
    60028 Osimo Scalo.   Tel.: (071) 7 90 12

Music Shops

Casa Musicale F.lli Gaggero (guitars, electric organs, wind instruments, music, repairs)
    Via di Fossatello 13.   Tel.: 20 49 88
Ernani Paganetto
    Piazza San Matteo 17.   Tel.: 29 38 23
S. Pittalugo (pianos, organs, music, repairs, tuning)
    Via A. Cantore 127.   Tel.: 45 90 17
G. & C. Riccordi (music, instruments, repairs)
    Via Fieschi 20/r.   Tel.: 54 33 31; 54 33 33
Storti (instruments, music, accessories)
    Via D. Fiasella 25/r.   Tel.: 54 35 69

Record Shops

Al Juke Box (records and musical instruments)
Corso A. De Stefanis 129/r.   Tel.: 89 19 93
Alta Fedelta'
Lg. XII Ottobre 41.   Tel.: 58 77 93
Disco Club
Via San Vincenzo 20.   Tel.: 54 24 22
Juke Box Records
Via Diaz 35.   Tel.: 58 55 12
Music Corner
Corso Buenos Aires 26.   Tel.: 59 54 02
No-El Distribuzioni (records, hi-fi)
Via Casaregis 38/1.   Tel.: 58 55 32
Orlandini Dischi
Piazza Soziglia 110.   Tel.: 29 68 66

Concert Managers

Musical Bureau
Via San Martino 160/17.   Tel.: 20 77 31

CREMONA (Lombardy)   (Tel. prefix: 0372)

Guides and Services

Ente Provinciale del Turismo
Galleria del Corso 3.   Tel.: 2 17 22

Opera Houses and Concert Halls

Teatro Amilcare Ponchielli
Corso Vittorio Emanuele 52.   Tel.: 2 03 70
Season: February through March for opera. There is a symphony season both
    before and after the opera season.
Box Office: Corso Vittorio Emanuele 54.   Tel.: 2 17 66
Seating Capacity: 900.

This is one of the seventeen "traditional" theaters in Italy—that is, a theater that is not nationally owned but has considerable artistic and historical merit and which serves to extend musical activities beyond the provincial capitals and urban centers of the country. For reasons of practicality and economy, some of the traditional theaters join forces and engage in cooperative regional activities, such as exchanging performances and sharing expenses of new productions.

Originally named the Teatro Concordia when it was opened in 1808, the Ponchielli was renamed after the Cremonese composer of *La Gioconda*. It was rebuilt in 1821, and the interior of the house is still very attractive. When the theater is not in use, it may be visited by applying to the custodian who lives in the building just to the left of the opera house.

Libraries and Museums

Biblioteca Governativa e Civica, Sala di Musicologia Gaetano Cesari
[Ben. 103]
Palazzo Affaitati, Via Ugolini Dati 4.   Tel.: 2 92 79
Hours: summer: daily except Sunday from 9:00 AM to 12:30 PM and from 3:00 PM to 7:00 PM; winter: Monday to Saturday, same as above. Sunday from 10:00 AM to noon. Closed the week before Easter and from August 1 through August 15.
Facilities: microfilm reader, makes copies, catalogs.
Description of the Collection: musicological and paleographic collections. In addition to standard reference works and theoretical texts, there is a small special library of slides and discs. Other collections added to the Cesari collection upon which the library is based include those from the Pia Istituzione Musicale (chiefly operatic eighteenth- and nineteenth-century prints), Banda Musicale (nineteenth-century sacred and operatic works), and Della Corna Mainardi (piano-vocal reductions of operatic works). Depository for the province.

Museo Civico di Organologia (also called the *Museo di Liuteria* or the *Stradivarius Museum*)
Palazzo dell'Arte, Piazza Marconi.   Tel.: 2 23 58
Hours: summer: 9:00 AM to noon and 3:00 PM to 6:00 PM; winter: 9:00 AM to noon and 2:00 PM to 5:00 PM. Closed all day Monday, Sunday afternoon, and holidays.
Description of the Collection: The museum, which is attached to the Scuola Internazionale di Liuteria (see p. 90), may be reached from the Stradivari House via a succession of musical streets (see p. 90). On display is a complete array of tools, forms, patterns, materials, models, drawings, and paper cuts used by Stradivari and belonging to him. There are also a handful of Amati drawings and many stringed instruments.

Saletta dei Violini, Palazzo Comunale
Piazza del Comune (opposite the cathedral and the city hall).
Hours: weekdays: 8:30 AM to 12:30 PM and 2:30 PM to 5:30 PM. Saturdays and
    Sundays and holidays: 9:00 AM to 11:00 AM.
Description of the Collection: The Stradivarius, once owned by Joseph Joachim,
    was purchased from an American dealer after a sum of thirty million lire
    (approximately $50,000) was raised for the purpose by the people of
    Cremona. It rests, together with an Andrea Amati of 1566 and a Niccolò
    Amati of 1658, in a glass cabinet next to the mayor's office. Any of these
    rare violins may be played by a qualified person upon request.

Conservatories and Schools

*Istituto Professionale Artigianato Liutario e del Legno (Scuola
Internazionale di Liuteria)*
Palazzo dell'Arte, Via Bell'Aspa 3.   Tel.: 2 71 29
This school, called the Stradivari School of String Instrumentmaking as well as
the more elaborate titles given above, represents the official attempt to keep the
violinmaking tradition alive by training and issuing diplomas to masters in
violin-building. The Institute is government sponsored and supported.

*Università degli Studi di Parma: Scuola di Paleografia e Filogia
Musicale*
Corso Garibaldi 178c.   Tel.: 2 55 75
A branch of the University of Parma, two-year courses are offered in basic
musical formation, and the transcription of ancient texts is taught to an
international student body.

Musical Landmarks

Aside from the Museo Civico di Organologia and the violins in the Saletta dei
Violini, mentioned above, Cremona abounds in musical references, reflecting
its rich musical heritage. Streets called Amati, Guarneri, and Stradivari are a
commonplace; the great organ in the Duomo was the cause of a famous
contretemps in the mid-sixteenth century which involved **Monteverdi**'s teacher
Ingegneri; a statue of the Cremonese **Amilcare Ponchielli** stands in a park close
to the Stradivari tomb. That tomb is in the center of Cremona's finest park, only
steps away from the house in which **Antonio Stradivari** (1644–1737) lived most
of his life (Piazza Roma 1, now a modern shop with no marker indicating its
illustrious origins).

Musical Organizations

Società dei Concerti
Via Verdi 14.   Tel.: 3 08 13
A private organization founded in 1908 which has sponsored public concerts
since 1948. The season runs from October to April. Concerts are held in the
Teatro A. Ponchielli.

The Business of Music

Music and Record Shops

Aurelio Cappelletti
    Via de Calboli 13.   Tel.: 2 75 16
Leonardo Desidera
    Corso Garibaldi 13.   Tel.: 2 03 12
La Cartomusica di Carenzi Giuliano
    Via C. Monteverdi 4.   Tel.: 2 92 19
Noe' Ettore
    Corso Campi 64.   Tel.: 2 89 87

Music Publishers

Astra
    Via Bissolati 81.

Instrument Making and Repair (violins)

Secondo Biachini
    Via Genola 42.
Cavaollotti
    Via Teatro.
Pietro Conti
    Via XI Febbraio 25.   Tel.: 2 11 60
Lorenzo Marconi
    Via Giordano 104.   Tel.: 2 06 34
Giobatta Morassi
    Via Cadore 27.   Tel.: 2 79 33
Dante Tolomini
    Via Palestro 40.   Tel.: 2 81 11

LUCCA (Tuscany)   (Tel. prefix: 0583)

Guides and Services

Ente Provinciale per il Turismo
Via Veneto 13.   Tel.: 4 69 15

Opera Houses and Concert Halls

Teatro Comunale del Giglio
Piazza Puccini.   Tel.: 4 61 47; 4 72 17
The first theater on this site was called the Teatro San Gerolamo, inaugurated
in 1692. When it collapsed in 1817, the architect Giovanni Lazzarini was
commissioned to reconstruct and remodel the building. It reopened in 1819
with a performance of Rossini's *L'Aureliano in Palmira*. The present name Giglio
(fleur de lys) was taken from the coat of arms of the Bourbon family when the
house was rededicated in the nineteenth century. The elegant neoclassic facade
is decorated with bas reliefs and musical symbols. An exhibit hall, the Ridotto,
is the location of special displays and collections during the season.

Summer Concerts

During the summer, concerts are held at the Anfiteatro Romano; the Baluardo
San Regolo; the Museo Nazionale di Villa Guinigi, Via del Bastardo; the
Giardino Botanico; the Palazzo Mansi, Via Galli Tassi; and the gardens of the
Palazzo Pfanner and the Villa Oliva.

Church Concerts

Organ recitals and concerts of sacred music are held throughout the year in the
Cattedrale di San Martino (Duomo), Piazza San Martino; Basilica di San
Frediano, Piazza del Collegio; Chiesa Monumentale dei Servi, Via dell'Arcive-
scovato; and San Romano, Piazza San Romano.

Libraries and Museums

Biblioteca dell'Istituto Musicale Luigi Boccherini [Ben. 169]
Piazza San Ponziano.   Tel.: 4 51 61

Hours: summer: 9:00 AM to noon, weekdays; winter: 9:00 AM to noon, weekdays except Monday and Thursday. Closed Easter, Christmas, the month of August, and other legal holidays.

Credentials: For admission, apply to the librarian.

Description of the Collection: manuscripts of the youthful works of Puccini and other Lucca composers. Collection from the Istituto Giovanni Pacini foundation and from the Fondo Bottini. Rossini, Boccherini manuscripts; sacred and secular music from the seventeenth century to the present. Record collection.

Biblioteca Manoscritti, Archivio di Stato [Ben. 166]

Via San Andrea and Piazza Guidiccioni 5.   Tel.: 4 14 65

Hours: daily from 8:30 AM to 12:30 PM; Monday, Wednesday, Friday also 3:00 PM to 6:00 PM. Closed August 6 to 31.

Description of the Collection: leaves of the famous Lucca codex; early Italian-French vocal works; music in the Mancini and Strohm codices.

Biblioteca del Seminario Arcivescovile [Ben. 170]

Sezione Musicale, Via Monte San Quirico, Borgo Giannotti.   Tel.: 4 52 79

Hours: open by appointment only. Apply to seminary director or librarian. Closed July and August.

Description of the Collection: manuscripts of Lucchese composers. Theoretical works. Collection is based on the joint collections of the Seminario di San Martino and the Seminario di San Michele, plus the Guerra and Bernini collections.

Biblioteca Statale e Governativa di Lucca [Ben. 168]

Via Santa Maria Corte Orlandini 12.   Tel.: 4 50 70

Hours: Monday to Saturday from 9:00 AM to 1:00 PM, 3:00 PM to 5:00 PM except Saturday afternoon; summer from 8:00 AM to 2:00 PM. Closed week before Easter and from August 16 to 30.

Facilities: microreader. Copies available through Archivio di Stato. Catalogs.

Description of Collection: eleventh- to eighteenth-century manuscripts and printed works. Printed books, treatises from the sixteenth century to the present. Liturgical manuscripts and books, autograph letters of Verdi, Rossini, etc. Libraries of the Società Orchestrale L. Boccherini, convent of Santa Maria Corte Orlandini and Baralli. Provincial depository.

Conservatories and Schools

Istituto Musicale Luigi Boccherini

Piazza San Ponziano 6.   Tel.: 4 51 61

Formerly called the Istituto Musicale G. Pacini after its first director, the school was founded in 1842. In 1943 it was renamed in honor of the two-hundredth anniversary of the birth of the renowned native musician. Although it does not normally admit foreigners, special dispensation may be obtained through the Ministero della Pubblica Istruzione. This is an "equalized" institute of music, much like that at Genoa. There are faculty members who instruct in instruments, history, theory, chamber music, choral music, etc.

Musical Landmarks

Museo Puccini
Villa Giacomo Puccini, Viale Puccini 266, Torre del Lago (Lucca)
Tel.: 4 14 45

Hours: daily, winter and summer from 9:00 AM to noon; summer, also from 3:00 PM to 7:00 PM; winter from 2:00 PM to 5:00 PM. No annual closing.
Condition of Admission: a maximum of twenty-five visitors at any one time. No photographs.

Torre del Lago is twenty-five kilometers from Lucca. **Puccini** lived there from 1891 until 1921. When he died, he was buried in a wall behind the Förster upright piano upon which he worked on his operas, from *La Bohème* to *Turandot*. The director of the museum will guide visitors around the villa and explain all the details of the collection housed there. Torre del Lago may be reached easily by public or private transit from Viareggio or Lucca.

The house in which Puccini was born in Lucca was donated by his descendants to the town. It is located at Via di Poggio 30, and plans are in progress to turn the building into a national monument.

Boccheriniana
Another native of Lucca who was a great composer was **Luigi Boccherini** (1743–1805), born at Via Fillungo 71. A bronze plaque on the building attests to this fact. A virtuoso violoncellist, Boccherini spent his entire life travelling throughout Europe, finally ending his days in Madrid. In 1927, one hundred and twenty-two years after his death, his remains were returned to Lucca, where they are entombed in the left wall between the second and third altars at the church of San Francesco. Next to Boccherini's tomb, a tablet serves as a memorial to **Francesco Geminiani** (1679–1762), a Lucchese who spent most of his life in England and Ireland.

Musical Organizations

Associazione Musicale Lucchese
Via C. Battisti 17.
Sponsors both summer and winter concerts. Member of the AIAC (Associazione Italiana fra le Attività Concertistiche—Italian Society for Concert Activity). Gives concerts of music by Lucchese composers at the Provincial Palace. Founded in 1964.

The Business of Music

Music and Record Shops

Casa Della Musica	
Via Fillungo 4.	Tel.: 4 79 53
Italradio	
Via Sarzanese 197.	
G. Pietrasanta	
Via dei Gallo 1.	Tel.: 4 72 70
Annibale Simonetti	
Via Santa Croce 13.	Tel.: 4 22 29

PARMA (Emilia Romagna)   (Tel. prefix: 0521)

Guides and Services

Ente Provinciale per il Turismo	
Piazza Duomo 5.	Tel.: 3 39 59
Information office	Tel.: 3 47 35

Opera Houses and Concert Halls

Teatro Regio di Parma	
Via Garibaldi.	Tel.: 2 20 03

Season: a "traditional" opera house in which opera, concerts, and some drama are presented. Annual closing in the summer. Concert season before and after the opera season, which runs from December through February.

Box Office: open daily from 10:00 AM to 1:00 PM and 3:00 PM to 7:00 PM. Open on all days when there are performances. No standing room.

Seating Capacity: 1,300.

The Teatro Regio was commissioned by Marie Louise, wife of Napoleon and benefactress of Parma, from the architect Niccolò Bettoli. It was inaugurated in 1829 with a performance of Bellini's *Zaira,* specially written for the occasion. (Fragments of this disastrously unsuccessful score may be heard in *I Capuletti e I Montecchi.*) The theater was somewhat renovated in 1853 under the supervision of Girolamo Magnani. A house with an illustrious record in the performance of operas (it is said to have produced twenty-three of Verdi's total output of twenty-six operas—an admirable record indeed!), the Regio represents the musical heart of the city of Verdi and Toscanini. It has one of the most beautiful interiors of all the opera houses in Italy and a very elegant Green Room, which is worth a visit in itself.

Environs of Parma: Busseto

Teatro Verdi

Built into the right wing of the Rocca dei Marchesi Pallavicino, this intimate theater, inaugurated in 1869, seats 600. Verdi was not in favor of its construction. Nevertheless, Toscanini conducted *Falstaff* here in 1913 to celebrate the centennial of Verdi's birth.

Environs of Parma: Fidenza

Teatro Municipale Girolamo Magnani

Via Bacchini 2.   Tel.: 2 0 44

Designed by the same Bettoli of the Teatro Regio, this theater was opened in 1861. The opera season takes place in October.

Libraries and Museums

Archivio Storico del Teatro Regio [Ben. 253]

Via della Repubblica 41.   Tel.: 3 40 88

Hours: open daily. For admission, apply to board of cultural activities.

Description of the Collection: libretti and music of works performed at the Regio since 1829. Iconography of composers, performers, and other artists; also autographs.

Biblioteca dell'Archivio di Stato [Ben. 252]
Strada Massimo d'Azeglio 43/45.   Tel.: 3 31 85
Hours: 8:30 AM to 1:30 PM daily. Closed August 1–15.
Facilities: microfilm reader. Makes copies. Author catalog.
Description of the Collection: parchment manuscripts with fragments of thirteenth-through fifteenth-century works. Also works by Caserta, Cicogna, Feraguti, etc.

Biblioteca della Deputazione di Storia Patria per le Province Parmensi
Vicolo San Marcellino 1 and Via Cavestro 14.   Tel.: 3 86 05
Special collections on the theater in Parma.

Biblioteca dell'Istituto di Studi Verdiani [Ben. 255]
Strada della Repubblica 57.   Tel.: 2 60 44
Hours: daily, except Saturday afternoons and all day Sunday, from 9:00 AM to 1:00 PM and from 3:00 PM to 7:30 PM. Annual closing August 10–16.
Description of the Collection; printed works of Verdi and his contemporaries. Literature concerning Verdi and theater documentation. Collection of Verdi letters and archival documents concerning him.

Biblioteca Palatina, Conservatorio di Musica Arrigo Boito
Via del Conservatorio 27.   Tel.: 2 22 17
Hours: 8:30 AM to 12:30 PM and 2:00 PM to 4:00 PM weekdays. Closed in August.
Description of the Collection: This library is made up of the music collection of the original Biblioteca Palatina, which held the collections of the Bourbons and of the Empress Marie Louise. Important holdings, as well, in fourteenth-century parchment manuscripts; treatises; 7,000 libretti. The library has its origins in the singing school founded in 1818 at the Ospizio delle Arti. It was given to the state in 1889.

Conservatories and Schools

Conservatorio di Music Arrigo Boito
Via del Conservatorio 27.   Tel.: 2 33 20
This is a national conservatory and is subject to the same organization, requirements, course structure, and diploma rules as the Santa Cecilia in Rome (see p. 19). It is housed in an old Carmelite convent and contains a well-preserved four-foot positive organ built toward the end of the sixteenth century. Arturo Toscanini received his formal training in this establishment.

Musical Landmarks

Teatro Farnese

Palazzo della Pilotta, Via della Pilotta 4.   Tel.: 3 37 18

Hours: summer, daily from 9:30 AM to 1:00 PM and from 3:00 PM to 6:00 PM;
   winter, daily from 9:00 AM to 1:00 PM and from 2:00 PM to 4:30 PM. Sunday
   and holidays from 9:30 AM to 1:00 PM.

The hours outlined above are the hours that the National Gallery, which is
housed in the Palazzo della Pilotta is open. The visitor entering the courtyard
should turn right before going up to the picture gallery. By the time these words
are printed, the Teatro Farnese, which has been undergoing extensive restoration since it was virtually destroyed by a bomb in 1944, should be open to the
public. Designed by the architect Giovanni Battista Aleotti, who was much
influenced by the Teatro Olimpico of Palladio in Vicenza (see p. 148), the
Teatro Farnese was opened in 1628 with a wedding show for the Duke Farnese
and his bride, Margherita de Medici. The composer of the festival music was
none other than Monteverdi, and the machinery, performers, and the audience
of 4,000 were far more elaborate than anything that had been done before.
There have been no performances in the Teatro Farnese since 1732.

Casa natale di Arturo Toscanini

Borgo Rodolfo Tanzi 13.

One of Italy's most famous conductors was born in this poor section of Parma in
1867. A plaque marks the house. **Toscanini** returned to his native town many
times before his death in 1957, to conduct in its various theaters and concert
halls.

Busseto

Le Roncole and Giuseppe Verdi

Verdi was born at Le Roncole, a hamlet within the township of Busseto. The
house in which his parents lived is now a national monument. The upstairs
room where he first saw light of day is open to the public. In 1813 it was a village
inn and general store run by Giuseppe's father, Carlo Verdi. In 1823, the family
moved to the larger town of Busseto, three miles away.

   The church in Le Roncole, where Verdi played the organ as a child, still
stands. In 1900 the organ was restored at Verdi's expense.

   In Busseto, the central piazza is named after Verdi and dominated by a
statue of him. On that piazza, the Teatro Verdi is housed within the castle (see
p. 96). Across the way is the house of Antonio Barezzi, a wealthy merchant who
was Verdi's patron and the father of his first wife.

Villa Sant'Agata

Open to the public in the summertime.
The Villa Sant'Agata was Verdi's home from the mid-nineteenth century until his death in 1901. It is still inhabited on its upper floors by the descendants of his adopted daughter, and the entire villa is kept much as it was when Verdi was alive. The villa is in a tiny village about three miles outside Busseto, actually in the province of Piacenza. Verdi spent much time and energy remodeling the house and planning the gardens. Inside the house one finds memorabilia, piano, large library of music and literature, billiard room, photos, statues and souvenirs, plus a large collection of paintings. The villa is set in its own fifty-acre park by a lake.

Musical Organizations

Istituto di Studi Verdiani

Strada della Repubblica 57. Tel.: 2 60 44
Institute established in 1959 for the purpose of studying the works of Verdi, supervising scholarly editions of his operas, gathering a complete archive of documents relating to his life and work. Publishes a bulletin and holds international congresses.

Società dei Concerti di Parma

Via del Conservatorio 2. Tel.: 3 78 90
Private organization that sponsors concerts and musical conferences. Gives regular season with guest artists and ensembles from Italy and abroad. Heirs to the tradition of concert activities established in the nineteenth century by Count Sanvitale.

Società Italiana di Musicologia

Via del Conservatorio 2.
National musicological society of Italy. Official publication, *Rivista Italiana di Musicologia,* see p. 206.

The Business of Music

Music Shops

Guido Belletti
  Via XXI Luglio 25. Tel.: 2 12 67

Lisetta Bolzoni
    Via d'Azeglio 45.   Tel.: 2 90 94
Casa Musicale
    Via Garibaldi 22 and Via Cavour 39.
Ermete De Simoni
    Via Repubblica 80.   Tel.: 3 56 08
Gold Music
    Viale Duca Alessandro 9.   Tel.: 3 74 18
Musica per Tutti
    Via M. Melloni 5.   Tel.: 2 13 18
Soncini & Garimberti
    Borgo del Correggio 32.   Tel.: 3 02 87
L. Varese
    Corso Garibaldi 39.   Tel.: 2 95 15

Record Shops

Mario Aleotti (radio, TV)
    Via Farini 92.   Tel.: 2 57 34
Davoli Records
    Via F. Lombardi 6/8.   Tel.: 4 08 83/85
Il Discobolo di Schmidt
    Via XX Marzo 1.   Tel.: 6 62 30
Discoteca 33 di R. Schmidt
    Via Goldoni 1.   Tel.: 2 95 67

Instrument Manufacture, Distribution, and Repair

Davoli
    Via F. Lombardi 6/8.   Tel.: 4 08 83/85
Renato Scrollavezza
    Via Gramsci 11.   Tel.: 2 48 69
Pietro Sgarabotto
    Via Gorizia 11.   Tel.: 3 50 95

Antiquarian Book and Music Dealer

Carboni
    Via XXII Luglio

Music Publishers

Aquila
    Via Parmigianino 10.

Crispoli
    Via Farini 5.   Tel.: 2 95 08
Giuseppe Gambarini
    Viale Rimembranze 6, Salsomaggiore (Parma).
Ugo Guanda, Editore (magazzino)
    Strada San Niccolò 8.   Tel.: 3 02 29

SIENA (Tuscany)   (Tel. prefix: 0577)

Guides and Services

Ente Provinciale per il Turismo
Direzione e Uffizi: Via di Citta 5.   Tel.: 4 70 51

Azienda Autonoma di Turismo
Banchi di Sotto 20.   Tel.: 4 22 09
Information: Piazza del Campo 55.   Tel.: 28 05 51
Office at the Railway station open from April 1 to October 31.   Tel.: 4 45 25
The Azienda Autonoma puts out a tourist information bulletin in English called *Siena 1978* (1979, 1980, etc.), which contains useful data on the highlights of festivals, parades, celebrations, etc. It also contains useful hotel information and addresses and telephone numbers of restaurants and museums. The Calendar of Events tends to be rather general.

Opera Houses and Concert Halls

Teatro dei Rinnovati
Piazza il Campo 1.   Tel.: 28 92 92
Box Office: same location.   Tel.: 28 93 17
Originally the council hall in the Palazzo Pubblico, it was converted into a theater in the sixteenth century. Built entirely of wood, the theater burned down twice. Its present incarnation, refurbished in 1950, follows the eighteenth-century design of one of the Galli-Bibienas. Both orchestral and operatic performances sponsored by the Settimana Musicale Senese (see p. 174) and the conducting classes of the Accademia Musicale Chigiana (see p. 104) are held here. To see the inside of the theater when there is nothing scheduled, the visitor is advised to go through the door at the right rear of the left courtyard.

Sala dei Concerti, Palazzo Chigi Saracini
Via di Città 89.   Tel.: 4 04 51
Season: In addition to the concerts of the Settimana Musicale Senese, which
follows the conclusion of the Accademia summer season, there are concerts
held in this Baroque hall from January to April. Recent plans are to begin
the season earlier, in November. Italian and foreign guest artists and
orchestras.
Seating capacity: 500.
The courtyard (*cortile*) of the Palazzo Chigi Saracini is also used in the summer
months for public concerts along with the Galleria d'Arte.

Teatro dei Rozzi
Accademia dei Rozzi, Via di Città 34–36.   Tel.: 28 01 22
Public Entrance: Piazza Indipendenza.
The theater opened its doors in 1690 and represents the finest eighteenth-century theater architecture, valid and attractive to this day. It is actually a private
concert hall, belonging to the Accademia dei Rozzi and used for chamber events
and solo recitals.

Sala del Mappamondo, Palazzo Comunale
Piazza il Campo.   Tel.: 28 08 13
This large "Map of the World" Room in the Town Hall is used for occasional
large-scale events. The town hall itself is open to the public daily.

Music in Churches

Organ recitals and other concerts of sacred music may be heard from time to
time in the Siena Cathedral and in Santa Maria della Scala, where the organ
dates from 1518.

Libraries and Museums

Biblioteca dell'Accademia Musicale Chigiana [Ben. 346]
Palazzo Chigi Saracini, Via di Città 89.   Tel.: 4 61 52
Hours: Monday to Friday and Saturday mornings. Closed May.
Credentials: apply to Academy office.
Facilities: microfilm reader; makes copies; catalogs.
Description of the Collection: sixteenth- and eighteenth-century editions of works
   by Agazzari, Anerio, Haydn, Spontini, Vecchi, etc. Rich in Italian opera
   and chamber music. English music from British Council in Rome. Gig-
   liucci bequest of Novello editions.

Biblioteca dell'Archivio di Stato [Ben. 347]
Palazzo Piccolomini, Via Banchi di Sotto 52.   Tel.: 4 12 71
Hours: Monday to Saturday 9:00 AM to 1:00 PM. Closed Sunday and from August
    15 to 31.
Facilities: microfilm reader; makes copies; author catalog.
Description of the Collection: small music collection in large library. Fifteenth-cen-
    tury music manuscripts.

Biblioteca Comunale degli Intronati [Ben. 348]
Via della Sapienza 5.   Tel.: 28 07 04
Hours: Monday to Friday from 9:30 AM to noon and from 4:30 PM to 8:00 PM.
    9:00 AM to 1:00 PM Saturdays. Closed on Sundays and from October 1 to 15.
Description of the Collection: troubadour songs, fifteenth-century treatises. Six-
    teenth- to eighteenth-century printed works. Depository of works printed
    in province.
The library began in 1758 with a gift by Sallustio Bandini of his own collection
to the university. Transferred to the city in 1810. The Accademia degli Intronati
(Academy of the Stunned) was one of the oldest and most elegant clubs of the
city, active in the sixteenth century and of a highly intellectual character.

Biblioteca Piccolomini e Opera Metropolitana, Archivio Musicale [Ben.
349]
Piazza del Duomo.   Tel.: 2 30 48
Hours: Monday, Wednesday, Friday, 9:00 AM to 12:30 PM. Occasionally closed.
Description of the Collection: illuminated choirbooks exhibited in the Biblioteca
    Piccolomini and first floor of the Museo dell'Opera Metropolitana. The
    Archivio Musicali has fifteenth- to eighteenth-century editions of works by
    composers ranging from Agazzari to Wert. Sacred music from nineteenth
    and twentieth century in manuscript.

Conservatories and Schools

Istituto Comunale di Musica Rinaldo Franci
Via Garibaldi 42.   Tel.: 28 07 66
One of the oldest schools in Tuscany, the Franci was founded in 1834 as a school
of *solfeggio*. In 1840 a school for string players was added, and in 1923, it became
a full-fledged music school with a complete faculty at a level just below that of
national conservatory. Courses include instruction in all instruments, *solfeggio*,
theory. Foreigners are admitted.

Summer Schools

Fondazione Accademia Musicale Chigiana
Palazzo Chigi Saraceni, Via di Città 89.   Tel.: 4 61 52
Dates: two months, between July and September. Deadline for application,
   June 20.
Courses: for professional and advanced musicians. Master classes in instruments,
   voice, composition, chamber music, conducting, musicology, opera production, etc.
About five hundred students are admitted annually to the program. Public
concerts by students and student groups are part of the extracurricular activity
during the summer. Master classes are taught by artists of international
reputation. The Academy was founded in 1932. Information and application
forms may be obtained from the Segreteria at the address above.

Siena Session, North Carolina School of the Arts
Dates: two two-month sessions running from mid-June to mid-August and from
   mid-July to mid-September.
Courses: All courses are held at the Accademia Musicale Chigiana and include
   performance in a symphony orchestra, chamber ensemble, or opera group
   as well as instruction in theory and instrument.
For information, apply to the Director, Siena Session, North Carolina School of
the Arts, P.O. Box 4657, Winston-Salem, North Carolina 27107.

*Scuola di Lingua e Cultura Italiana per Stranieri (School of Italian
Language and Culture for Foreigners)*
Scuola di Lingua e Cultura, Università degli Studi, Via Banchi di Sotto 55.
                                                                          Tel.: 2 37 65
Dates: mid-July to mid-September.
Courses: elementary, intermediate and advanced courses in Italian. Also classes
   in Italian literature, history, philosophy, art, cinema, and history of music.

The Business of Music

Music and Record Shops

Guglielmo Aldrovandi
      Via di Città 121.   Tel.: 2 11 15
Renato Brogi
      Piazza Gramsci 1.   Tel.: 2 09 56

Lorenzo Corsini
    Piazza Matteotti.   Tel.: 2 05 45
Vittorio Fornacelli
    Via Garibaldi.   Tel.: 2 38 29
Alberto Olmi (instrument sale and repair; music; records)
    Via Banchi di Sotto 49.   Tel.: 4 71 90
Mario Raveggi & Fratello
    Via Pellegrini.   Tel.: 2 00 95

TRIESTE (Friuli-Venezia Giulia)   (Tel. prefix: 040)

Guides and Services

Ente Provinciale per il Turismo
Via Rossini 6.   Tel.: 3 55 52

Azienda Autonoma di Turismo
Piazza dell'Unità d'Italia 4.   Tel.: 3 87 51

Movimento Forestieri
Information offices: Radice Molo Audace.   Tel.: 6 07 52
                 Viale Miramare 2.   Tel.: 42 08 69
These offices are open from June to September only.

Opera Houses and Concert Halls

Teatro Comunale Giuseppe Verdi
Piazza Verdi 1.   Tel.: 6 29 31
Season: The opera season runs from November to April (approximately twelve
    operas in forty-eight performances); the symphony season from October
    through June (about twenty concerts).
Seating Capacity: 1,400.
An *istituzione nazionale*, the Giuseppe Verdi presents opera, concert, and ballet
programs for a rather longer season than most houses. Its architecture and
tradition contribute also to making it one of the most important opera houses in
the country. Designed by Matteo Pertsch on a plan by Antonio Selva, it was

opened as the Teatro Nuovo in 1801 with a work by Simone Mayr. From 1861, when it was acquired by the city of Trieste, it was called the Teatro Comunale, and on the 27th of January, 1901, when Verdi died, it was given its present name.

Many Verdi works have been performed here. In about 1900, however, Trieste became the most Wagnerian city in all of Italy because of its appetite and appreciation for the works of that composer. The twentieth century has seen a broadening of repertory to include works by Britten, Strauss, and Menotti.

Il Politeama Rossetti

Viale XX Settembre 45.   Tel.: 76 35 83

Designed in 1878 by Niccolò Bruno and dedicated to the eminent Triestino, Domenico Rossetti, this theater was recently reopened and is primarily a showcase for spoken drama. However, the Società dei Concerti holds its concert events in this hall.

Summer Concerts

Castello San Giusto Portineria

Piazza del Castello 3.   Tel.: 79 38 56

Built between 1470 and 1630, this *castello* contains a courtyard (called the Milizie Courtyard) in which opera and ballet performances are given during the summer season.

Libraries and Museums

Biblioteca Civica Attilio Hortis [Ben. 386]

Piazza Attilio Hortis 4.   Tel.: 6 89 21

Hours: Monday to Friday, 8:30 AM to 1:30 PM and 5:00 PM to 7:30 PM. Saturday from 8:30 AM to 1:30 PM. Closed from August 1 to 20.

Facilities: microfilm reader; makes copies; special music catalogs.

Description of the Collection: Predominantly humanistic, with one of Europe's richest collections of Petrarch, this is a provincial depository with a small musical collection.

Biblioteca dei Civici Musei di Storia ed Arte [Ben. 387]

Via della Cattedrale 15.   Tel.: 74 17 08

Open to scholars only, the musical part of the collection focuses on seventeenth- and eighteenth-century editions from the Chapel of San Giusto.

Biblioteca del Conservatorio di Musica G. Tartini [Ben. 389]
Via Carlo Ghega 12. Tel.: 3 00 87
Hours: weekdays. For access, apply to the librarian. Closed for one month during the summer.
Description of the Collection: about 20,000 exclusively musical volumes. Sixteenth- to eighteenth-century editions; *opera omnia* of several composers. Tartiniana. A special section is reserved for works by Trieste composers and others from the Friuli-Venezia Giulia area. Complete musicological and reference section.

Biblioteca della Fondazione Giovanni Scaramangà di Altamonte [Ben. 390]
Via Fabio Filzi 1. Tel.: 3 15 85
Hours: Tuesday and Friday from 10:00 AM to 12:30 PM upon written request. Closed August.
Description of the Collection: lute tablature editions of the sixteenth century. Collection mostly related to the history of Trieste.

Library of the RAI [Italian Radio and Television]
Via Fabio Severo 7. Tel.: 73 51
Collection of folksongs of the Friuli-Venezia Giulia region, in addition to performance materials and reference books.

Civico Museo Teatrale di Fondazione Carlo Schmidl [Ben. 388]
Piazza G. Verdi 1. Tel.: 3 72 16
Hours: 10:00 AM to 1:00 PM daily and during the first two intermissions of performances at the Teatro Verdi, next door. Closed during May.
Facilities: special catalog of performers and composers of ballet, opera, drama, and symphonies. Guided Tours. Sound archives.
Description of the Collection: A music and theater collection with 2,500 libretti, 840 opera scores, 1,500 photographs and mementos, 3,700 books on music, and 4,100 manuscripts, the library also holds documents from the archives of the Teatro Verdi and from the Cappella Civica.
The Museum of the Carlo Schmidl foundation is, after the one at La Scala (see p. 38) considered the best theater museum in Italy. In addition to the library collection described above, the Museum contains collections of scenic designs, programs of the Theater, a collection of posters; rare instruments are displayed in the mezzanine of the Theater during the season. The Museum also arranges special displays pertinent to the works being performed.

Conservatories and Schools

Conservatorio di Musica G. Tartini e Scuola Media Statale Annessa
Via Ghega 12.   Tel.: 3 00 87
A national conservatory, arranged along the same lines as the Santa Cecilia in
Rome (see p. 19), but with a lower school annexed to it. The Conservatory has
about 53 faculty members and 135 students; the lower school about 10 faculty
and 124 students. There are free courses for foreigners. The director has the
option of accepting a few students without previous records at a recognized
school of music who show sufficient talent to warrant such action.

Three schools at a slightly lower level than the Conservatorio, but under the
supervision of the Ministry of Public Instruction are the Scuola Provinciale di
Fisarmonica, the Ateneo Musicale Triestina, and the Liceo Musicale Triestino.

Musical Organizations

Società dei Concerti
Via San Spiridione 1.   Tel.: 3 80 15
Founded in 1932, the Society does not have its own hall, but sponsors concerts in
the Politeama Rossetti and the Teatro Comunale. Usually organizes evenings of
chamber music, but has on occasion featured opera groups, orchestras, etc.

The Business of Music

Music and Record Shops

A.B.C. Dischi e Musica de Steno Permuda
    Corso Italia 26.   Tel.: 74 40 02
Casa del Disco
    Via Mazzini 37.   Tel.: 3 50 16
Antonietta Bacchelli
    Via Pascoli 24.   Tel.: 9 05 52
G. Bardelli (also musical instruments)
    Via Imbriani 10/a.   Tel.: 6 17 36
Micol & Pascucci Stabilimento Musicale
    Via Madonnina 15.   Tel.: 9 00 84
Radio Serbo (records)
    Via Mazzini 7/a.   Tel.: 3 87 43

Sergio Rossoni (also sells instruments)
    Via Carducci 15.   Tel.: 2 49 57
Stabilimento Musicale G. Verdi
    Via Reti 12.   Tel.: 3 02 88

Publishers

Casa Musicale Giuliana, Eddizione Fabbri
    Via F. Venezian 24.   Tel.: 3 65 66

Instrument Manufacture and Repair

Luigi Paoli
    Via Romenico Rossetti 76/1.   Tel.: 74 17 59
Francesco Zappelli
    Via San Giacomo in Monte 10.

Concert Managers

Giovanni Kurlaender
    Via N. de Rin 7.   Tel.: 9 03 82

TURIN (Piedmont)   (Tel. prefix: 011)

Guides and Services

Ente Provinciale per il Turismo
Via Roma 222.   Tel.: 53 51 81
Information centers of the EPIT may also be found at:
    Porta Nuova Central Station entrance hall.   Tel.: 53 13 27; 53 83 76
    Turin Exhibition Building, Valentino Park.   Tel.: 6 00 56

Opera Houses and Concert Halls

Teatro Regio
Piazza Castello 215.   Tel.: 54 91 26
Season: September to July. Closed during August. Symphony season before and
    after opera repertory.

The original Teatro Regio di Torino was finished in 1738–39 from a design by Benedetto Alfieri, first architect to His Majesty, Carlo Emmanuele III and decorated by Bernardino Galliari, who even painted the curtain. This house, modelled after the great San Carlo of Naples and containing room for 2500 spectators, was destroyed by fire in 1936. The new Teatro Regio was a long time in reconstruction. It was opened in 1973 with a production of Verdi's *I Vespri Siciliani,* staged by Maria Callas. The most recent among the great Italian theaters, it has a horseshoe shaped hall with seats for 1800. In addition, there is a second hall, the Piccolo Regio, with a seating capacity of 400, where special concerts (such as the series Lunedi Musicali [Musical Mondays]), vocal recitals, and contemporary music events are given, often free of charge.

Teatro Nuovo
Corso Massimo d'Azeglio 17 (Turin Exhibition Building).   Tel.: 68 29 90
Season: September to July. Closed during August.
Box Office: Via Petrarca 37.
      Hours: 9:30 AM to 12:30 PM and 3:30 PM to 7:30 PM, daily except Sunday.
Seating Capacity: 1,240.
Formerly known as the Teatro della Moda, it was damaged by bombing in 1942. When it reopened in 1949 with a performance of Handel's *Messiah,* it had been completely rebuilt and decorated by prominent Italian artists. A regular opera and operetta season runs from January to May, with two periods of symphonic music intervening. It is contemplated that, with the reopening of the Regio, the Nuovo will be used more and more for dramatic performances.

Auditorium i Concerti di Torino della RAI
Via Rossini 15.   Tel.: 57 57
The *Stagione Sinfonica d'Autunno* concerts, given and broadcast weekly on Friday evenings at 9:15, are held here.

Summer Concerts

In the summer, concerts are given in the open-air theater gardens of the Royal Palace in the Piazza Castello.

Libraries and Museums

Biblioteca di Storia dell'Arte, Museo Civico [Ben. 372]
Via Magenta 31.   Tel.: 54 36 21
Hours: Monday to Friday, 3:00 PM to 5:45 PM all year except August.
Description of the Collection: This library specializes in art history, and there are
      only a few items of musical interest. However, the museum to which this
      library is attached, has a general instrument collection of note.

Biblioteca del Conservatorio Statale di Musica G. Verdi [Ben. 370]
Via Giuseppe Mazzini 11.   Tel.: 54 52 27; 53 07 87
Hours: 9:00 AM to 1:00 PM daily except holidays (national and religious). Closed
in August.
Description of the Collection: primarily reference and practical performance
materials, with some autographs of operas performed in Turin and works
by Turinese composers. Recordings and listening facilities.

Biblioteca dell'Archivio di Stato [Ben. 366]
Viale Alessandro Luzio 4.   Tel.: 54 03 82
Hours: weekdays from 9:00 AM to 2:00 PM. Closed June 1 to 15.
Description of the Collection: sixteenth-century madrigals. The depository for
music is now the Biblioteca Nazionale Universitaria (see below).

Biblioteca Musicale Andrea Della Corte [Ben. 367]
Via Roma 53 (3rd floor, above the Teatro Carignano).   Tel.: 53 85 44
Hours: Monday to Friday, 3:00 PM to 6:30 PM. Closed in August.
Description of the Collection: This is the music section of the Biblioteche Civiche e
Raccolte Storiche. Contains musicological reference works and the con-
tents of several important collections, including: Società di Concerti del
Teatro Regio (manuscript and printed orchestral scores and parts); Banda
Civica (formerly the National Guard, with manuscript and printed scores
and parts); Scuola di Canto Corale Municipale; Valentino Carrera (sev-
enteenth- to twentieth-century opera and ballet libretti); and over one
thousand American recordings from the USIS center closed in 1964.

Biblioteca Nazionale Universitaria [Ben. 368]
Via Po 19.   Tel.: 55 50 64
Hours: summer: weekdays 8:00 AM to 2:00 PM, Saturday, 8:00 AM to noon;
winter: 8:00 AM to 5:30 PM, Saturday as in the summer. Closed from August
1 to 15, Sundays, and holidays.
Description of the Collection: Vivaldi manuscripts; Foa and Giordano collections.
University library. German tablatures, medieval manuscripts. Rich in
Baroque music.

Biblioteca Reale [Ben. 369]
Piazza Castello 191.   Tel.: 54 38 55
Hours: Monday to Saturday, 9:00 AM to 1:00 PM to qualified specialists. Closed
August.
Description of the Collection: music collection of 1,800 manuscripts and 1,000
prints, scores, libretti, and musicological items. Recently acquired the
Pallavicino-Mossi collection.

Archivio Musicale, Radiotelevisione Italiana (RAI) [Ben. 373]
Via Rossini 15.   Tel.: 5 71 01

Hours: open Monday to Friday to personnel of RAI.
Description of the Collection: practical musical materials.

Conservatories and Schools

Conservatorio Statale di Music G. Verdi e Scuola Media Annessa
Via Mazzini 11. Piazza Bodoni.   Tel.: 53 07 87
This is a national conservatory, founded in 1867 and subject to the same course
structure, entrance requirements, and diploma as the Santa Cecilia in Rome
(see p. 19). The lower school attached to the conservatory offers a degree that is
prerequisite for entrance into the Conservatory.
     Concerts are given in the concert hall, sponsored either by the Conserva-
tory or by the Unione Musicale (see below).

Istituto di Storia della Musica
Università degli Studi, Facoltà di Lettere e Filosofia,
Via Carlo Alberto 10.   Tel.: 54 05 05
Institute for musical study within the university context.

Among the pre-conservatory music schools in Turin supervised by the Ministry
of Public Instruction, there is a Civico Istituto Musicale and an Accademia di
Musica (Via Lagrange 7).

Musical Organizations

RAI Orchestra (Italian Radio and Television Symphony Orchestra)
Via Rossini 15.
One of the four RAI performing organizations in Italy and, along with the
Rome RAI, one of the best. Gives public concerts as well as transmitted ones at
the RAI auditorium year-round.

Unione Musicale
Piazza Castello 29.   Tel.: 54 45 23
Originally founded in 1946 as a student organization, it sponsors an annual
series of chamber concerts. In 1966–67, the Unione Musicale was responsible for
no less than forty-four concerts during the year. Since 1964, it has been the only
concert society in Turin with a major concert series.

The Business of Music

Music Shops

Silvio Bertotto (also musical instruments)
Via Cherubini 49.   Tel.: 27 33 31
Casa Musicale Zaccagnini
Via Bertola 23.   Tel.: 51 94 83
Paolo Maschio (also musical instruments)
Piazza Castello 51.   Tel.: 54 27 22
Ricordi
Via Lagrange 35.   Tel.: 54 01 56; 51 08 30
Ruggero Visconti
Via A. Gramsci 3.   Tel.: 54 43 37

Record Shops

Artis
Piazza L. Facta 3, Pinerolo (Turin).   Tel.: 26 23
Folklore, S.r.l.
Via Pietro Micca 17.   Tel.: 51 86 68
Fonit-Cetra
Via Bertola 34.   Tel.: 57 53
Golden Record
Corso Svizzera 147.   Tel.: 21 59 26; 54 76 09
S.I.L.
Via G. Ferrari 3.   Tel.: 87 17 26

Instrument Manufacture, Distribution, and Repair

A.M.A.T. (percussion instruments)
Via Gaudenzio Ferrari 4.   Tel.: 8 13 09
Egidio Cipriani, Strumenti Musicali
Via Lagrange 47.   Tel.: 54 48 03
F.A.C.A.T. (guitars)
Via Thures 10/A.   Tel.: 79 37 85
Morutto (accessories)
Via XX Settembre 77.   Tel.: 54 64 81
Royal (instrument market)
Via dei Mille 32.   Tel.: 87 20 24
Samina dei F.lli Neirotti (pianos)
Via Basse di Dora 42.   Tel.: 79 08 64
Domenico Zoppo (pianos)
Via Tancredi Canonico 34.   Tel.: 24 04 87

Antonio Lajolo (keyboards and percussion)
Via Gaudenzio Ferrari 2.   Tel.: 87 64 45
Arnaldo Morano (repair)
Corso San Maurizio 20 bis.   Tel.: 88 51 64
Società Steinbach (pianos, harmoniums)
Corso San Maurizio 75.   Tel.: 87 63 78

Cities Briefly Noted

BARI (Puglia)

Guides and Services

Ente Provinciale per il Turismo
Piazza Roma 33-A.   Tel.: 36 92 28

Opera Houses and Concert Halls

Teatro Petruzzelli
Corso Cavour.   Tel.: 21 81 32
Seating Capacity: 4,000.
One of Italy's largest theaters, the Petruzzelli was designed by A. Masseni and
opened in 1903. A "traditional" theater, it houses an opera season in the spring
and a concert season in the winter.

Libraries and Museums

Biblioteca Nazionale Sagarriga Visconti-Volpi [Ben. 22]
Piazza Umberto 1.   Tel.: 21 66 67
Hours: weekdays from 8:30 AM to 1:00 PM and 3:30 PM to 6:00 PM; summer, closed
    in the afternoon.
Description of the Collection: includes works by Bari composers Nicola De Giosa
    and Giovanni Cammarota. Depository for works printed in the province.

Conservatories and Schools

Conservatorio de Musica Niccolò Piccini
Via Brigata Bari 26.   Tel.: 34 79 62
A national conservatory founded in 1925 by Giovanni Capaldi. Also has working library for use by students and faculty.

Musical Organizations

Accademia Polifonica Barese
Via Gironda 22.   Tel.: 21 35 00
Organization founded in 1926 which sponsors concerts by local and foreign composers. The chorus of the Accademia has participated in international competitions.

Fondazione Concerti Niccolò Piccini
Via Nicolai 77.   Tel.: 23 53 32
Founded in 1949 as a private organization, the Foundation puts on concerts in which major works of international character are featured.

The Business of Music

Music and Record Shops
Cangiano
    Via Principe Amadeo 145.   Tel.: 1 93 54
Discorama
    Corso Cavour 99.   Tel.: 21 60 24
Morquin Record
    Via Nicola de Gemmis 16.   Tel.: 25 87 08
G. & C. Ricordi
    Via Sparano 18.   Tel.: 21 80 28

BERGAMO (Lombardy)   (Tel. prefix: 035)

Guides and Services

Ente Provinciale per il Turismo
Viale Vittorio Emanuele 11/4.   Tel.: 24 22 26

Opera Houses and Concert Halls

Sala Piatti
Via San Salvatore.
Concert season, solo recitals, chamber music.

Teatro Donizetti
Piazza Matteotti 13.   Tel.: 24 96 31
Season: A fall opera season takes place in October and November. In addition,
there is a series called Teatro della Novità, which features little-known
works from the classical as well as the contemporary reportoires.
The theater was designed by G. Lucchini and opened in 1791. It was rebuilt in
1797 after a fire and given its present name in 1897 in honor of Bergamo's most
famous composer, who died at Via di Gaetano Donizetti 1 at the age of fifty.

Libraries and Museums

Biblioteca del Civico Istituto Musicale Gaetano Donizetti [Ben. 33]
Via Arena 9.   Tel.: 23 73 74
Hours: open daily. Closed in August.
Description of the Collection: In addition to reference works and performance
materials, the library holds several special collections: the Piatti-Lochis
library of 2,000 volumes from cellist Alfredo Piatti; Archivio della Basilica
di Santa Maria Maggiore (sacred music manuscripts and prints); Museo
Donizetti (see below).
An active center for Donizetti research, a concert season is presented here by the
Friends of the Institute.

Biblioteca Civica Angelo Mai [Ben. 32]
Piazza Vecchia 15.   Tel.: 24 49 20

Hours: weekdays from 9:00 AM to noon and 2:30 PM to 6:00 PM; summer, from 8:30 AM to noon and 3:00 PM to 6:30 PM.

Description of the Collection: contains the *Fondo Musicale Mayr* as well as sixteenth- to nineteenth-century prints, choirbooks from Santa Maria Maggiore and other Bergamo churches.

Museo Donizettiano
Via Arena 9.   Tel.: 23 73 74

Hours: 9:00 AM to noon, 2:00 PM to 6:00 PM, daily and by appointment.

This intimate Donizetti museum contains memorabilia and music manuscripts, editions, letters, musical instruments, and documents, all cataloged by the curator. This catalog was published in 1970 by the Centro di Studi Donizettiani.

Conservatories and Schools

Civico Istituto Musicale Gaetano Donizetti
Via Arena 9.   Tel.: 23 73 74

Founded by Simone Mayr in 1805, this "officially recognized" institute offers instruction in all instruments, theory, and history of music. There are approximately twenty faculty members.

Musical Landmarks

The church of Santa Maria Maggiore has been the musical center of the town since 1450, when music lessons in voice and instruments began to be given as a regular part of the clerical education. In 1566, two Antegnati organs were installed there, of which only the empty cases may be seen today. The church had a double choir of at least forty voices during its heyday, plus wind and string instruments supplying accompaniment. Both **Simone Mayr** (1763-1845)—who founded the Istituto Musicale as well as two charitable institutions for aging musicians and was a guiding force of the opera house—and his pupil **Gaetano Donizetti** (1797-1848), who was born in the old section of Bergamo on the Borgo Canal, are buried in the church of Santa Maria Maggiore, where their tombs may be seen. There is also a plaque in the church commemorating **Amilcare Ponchielli**'s tenure as choirmaster from 1882 until his death in 1886.

The Business of Music

Music and Record Shops

Bottego della Musica
    Via T. Tasso 31.
Bottega del Disco
    Piazzale Autolinee 10.
Rinaldi S.p.A.
    Via Stoppani 5.   Tel.: 24 68 46

Instrument Makers

Fratelli Piccinelli
    Via Maggiore 41.   Tel.: 57 10 95
The first factory specializing in the construction of the mechanical organ and
the restoration of old organs.

Music Publishers

Casa Musicale Carrara
    Via Calepio 4.

BRESCIA (Lombardy)   (Tel. prefix: 030)

Guides and Services

Ente Provinciale per il Turismo
Corso Zanardelli 38.   Tel.: 4 50 52

Opera Houses and Concert Halls

Teatro Grande
Via Paganora 19a.   Tel.: 4 24 00
Season: September and October, January and February, as well as festival
    seasons.
Box Office: Tel: 5 94 48

Seating Capacity: 1,070.

The Teatro Grande, a "traditional" theater, is located in the center of town. The visitor wishing to view only the lavish stucco and gilt interior, which was added to the wooden hall in the 1860s, may search out the custodian at the back of the building. The house was built in the late seventeenth or early eighteenth century and has been altered and enlarged over three centuries by a wide variety of architects, including one of the Bibienas. It was given its present name in 1810. The hall has excellent proportions and acoustics. It was in this theater that *Madama Butterfly* was rehabilitated after its initial failure in Milan in 1904.

Libraries and Museums

Archivio Musicale del Duomo [Ben. 56]

Via Mazzini 2, Piazza del Duomo.   Tel.: 4 01 26

Hours: open by appointment only. Apply to the priest.

Collection especially rich in sixteenth- and seventeenth-century manuscripts of local composers.

Biblioteca Civica Queriniana [Ben. 55]

Palazzo Querini, Via Mazzini 1.   Tel.: 4 40 13

Hours: Monday to Saturday, 8:30 AM to noon and 2:30 PM to 8:00 PM (Monday, Wednesday and Friday only to 6:00 PM). Closed July 15 to August 15.

Description of the Collection: choirbooks from San Francesco monastery and works from other suppressed convents. Sixteenth- and seventeenth-century editions and prints.

Biblioteca del Seminario Vescovile

Via Bollani 20.   Tel.: 30 00 41

A private library containing a small collection of eighteenth- and nineteenth-century music prints. Open to teachers and students.

Biblioteca dell'Ateneo di Scienze, Lettere e Arti [Ben. 54]

Via Tosio 12.   Tel.: 4 10 06

Has Giovanni Tebaldini bequest, mainly tenth-century prints and manuscripts.

Biblioteca dell'Istituto Musicale A. Venturi [Ben. 57]

Corso Magenta.

Manuscripts and printed music of the nineteenth century. School is in former Augustinian convent of San Barnaba. Entrance through garden of Palazzo Liceo Ginnasio Arnaldo (formerly called the Palazzo Poncareli).

Musical Landmarks

In the church of San Giuseppe, approached from the Piazza della Loggia via the street Gasparo da Salò, is what many experts call the best organ in Italy, built by **Antegnatus** of Brescia in 1581. A plaque outside the church commemorates the fact that **Gasparo da Salò**, "the inventor of the modern violin," was buried there in 1609. (His tombstone can no longer be found.) The tombstone of **Benedetto Marcello** (1686–1739) can be seen toward the front of the middle aisle.

CAGLIARI (Sardinia)   (Tel. prefix: 070)

Guides and Services

Ente Provinciale per il Turismo
Piazza Deffenu 9.   Tel.: 65 19 46

Opera Houses and Concert Halls

Teatro Massimo
Viale Trento.   Tel.: 65 89 43
Season: opera in winter and spring, with concert season before and after.
Seating Capacity: 2,500.
The Teatro Massimo was destroyed during the war and rebuilt in 1947.

Libraries and Museums

Biblioteca del Conservatorio di Musica G. Pierluigi da Palestrina
[Ben. 69]
Via Bacaredda.   Tel.: 6 26 88
Hours: weekdays from 8:00 AM to 2:00 PM and from 5:00 PM to 6:00 PM. Closed
     August.
Facilities: listening and recording equipment; makes copies. Catalogs.
Description of the Collection: Founded in 1926 from the libraries of disbanded
     musical institutions in the town (band, orchestra, city chapel, Istituto

Civico Musicale, etc.), the present collection consists of 20,230 volumes, 2,814 manuscripts (including some autographs of contemporary composers), and over 17,000 scores.

Biblioteca e Archivio Comunale di Studi Sardi [Ben. 66]
Galleria Comunale d'Arte, Giardino Pubblico.   Tel.: 48 78 57
Hours: weekdays from 9:00 AM to noon and from 4:30 PM to 6:30 PM. Closes for two weeks sometime between July 15 and September 15.
Description of the Collection: Of the total collection of 500,000 volumes, the music holdings constitute a very small part, consisting mainly of music and prints of nineteenth- and twentieth-century origin once belonging to a city band.

Biblioteca Universitaria [Ben. 67]
Via Università 32/A.   Tel.: 6 46 95
Hours: weekdays from 9:00 AM to 2:00 PM and from 4:00 PM to 6:00 PM.
This is the most important library in Sardinia; the small music collection consists chiefly of opera scores and a few manuscripts. It is the depository for all works printed in the province.

Conservatories and Schools

Conservatorio di Musica G. Pierluigi da Palestrina
Via Bacaredda.   Tel.: 49 40 48
A national conservatory founded in 1921, it is subject to the same standards of organization, course offerings, and diploma as the Santa Cecilia in Rome (see p. 19). An Istituzione dei Concerti del Conservatorio is quartered within the school for the purpose of organizing and sponsoring concerts throughout the year. Some of these concerts feature the chamber orchestra of the Conservatory.

Musical Organizations

Istituzione dei Concerti e del Teatro Lirico
Via Regina Margherita 6.   Tel.: 65 92 14
This organization is considered, along with the Accademia Nazionale Santa Cecilia, to be the quivalent of an *istituzione nazionale*. It unites under one management opera and concert activity. Since the Istituzione does not have its own house, as yet, it leases the Teatro Massimo for the operas it sponsors. Besides an opera season, it organizes a symphony season and one of chamber music that lasts throughout the year. This musical activity is carried on by the Istituzione in all the cities of Sardinia.

Istituzione Concertistica Giovanni Pierluigi da Palestrina
Conservatorio di Musica, Via Bacaredda.   Tel.: 49 40 48
A concert management, arranging events mostly at the Conservatory.

CATANIA (Sicily)   (Tel. prefix: 095)

Guides and Services

Ente Provinciale per il Turismo
Largo Paisiello 5.   Tel.: 27 87 20

Opera Houses and Concert Halls

Teatro Massimo Vincenzo Bellini
Piazza Bellini.   Tel.: 31 20 20
Season: Concert and symphony seasons take place before and after the opera
    season, which runs from October to May.
Seating Capacity: 1,470.
The Teatro Massimo Bellini was begun in 1873 to replace the old and
inadequate Arena Pacini. The architect Carlo Sada completed the work in 1890
from the original design of Andrea Scala. The first opera performed in this hall
was Bellini's *Norma*. The house is famous for its acoustics and the lush
fin-de-siecle interior decoration.

Concerts of a religious nature are often held at the Chiesa di San Niccolò
l'Arena, an eighteenth-century structure and the largest church in Sicily. Its
enormous, five-manual organ with three consoles and almost three thousand
pipes is one of the major tourist attractions of the area.

Libraries and Museums

Biblioteca Americana J. F. Kennedy
Via Manzoni 90.
Formerly the library of the USIS and now a gift to the city of Catania, this
collection specializes in North American culture, including music. Recordings
as well as standard English musical reference works.

Biblioteca Comunale Vincenzo Bellini
Giardino Bellini, Via Manzoni 90.   Tel.: 31 12 61
Collection includes music manuscripts from the eighteenth and nineteenth centuries.

Biblioteca dell'Archivio di Stato [Ben. 79]
Via Vittorio Emanuele 156.   Tel.: 22 38 60
Collection includes liturgical codex from the thirteenth century.

Biblioteca della Società di Storia Patria per la Sicilia Orientale [Ben. 82]
Piazza Stesicoro 29.   Tel.: 27 59 20
Among the many special collections concerning Sicilian history, there is a small collection of manuscripts by Catanese composers of the eighteenth century.

Biblioteche Riunite Civica e Antonio Ursino Recupero [Ben. 80]
Via Biblioteca 13.   Tel.: 27 58 83
Specializes in Sicilian culture and contains fifteenth-century theoretical manuscript of Jacobus Borbo, as well as some eighteenth- and nineteenth-century manuscripts.

Museo Belliniano
Piazza Francesco d'Assisi 3.   Tel.: 22 82 60
Hours: open daily from 8:30 AM to 11:30 AM and from 4:30 PM to 7:00 PM.
Small museum housed in the building where Bellini was born in 1801. It was made into a national monument in 1923 and opened to the public in 1930. The collection includes Bellini manuscripts, some of the early works, and the second version of *I Puritani*. There are also mementos of nineteenth-century Catania and the manuscript of an oratorio by Bellini's father.

Conservatories and Schools

Istituto Musicale Vincenzo Bellini
Via Vittorio Emanuele 282.   Tel.: 22 51 51
An "equalized" institute, on a level immediately below that of the National Conservatory. Offers full range of instrumental and theoretical instruction.

Musical Landmarks

In addition to the Bellini Museum described briefly above, there are other evidences that Catania is proud to claim the composer as their own, although

Bellini returned to the city only once during his lifetime after leaving it at the age of eighteen. The Bellini Gardens is the name given to the huge public park in the northern part of the city. In addition, a square in front of the nineteenth-century opera house (as well as the house itself) is named for him. A statue portrait is located in the centrally located Piazza Stesicoro; around him are statues of the characters in his most famous operas: *Norma, I Puritani, Il Pirata,* and *La Sonnambula.* His tomb, where his remains were placed forty-one years after his death, may be seen in the Duomo.

The Business of Music

Music and Record Shops

Attilio Cappellani & Co.
  Via Etnea 247.
Edizione Musicale Galatea
  Via Lorenza Bolano 2.
Estudiantina
  Via Nino Martoglio 3.
Prospero Sanfilippo
  Via Gemellaro 48.   Tel.: 27 46 72; 21 45 29

FERRARA (Emilia-Romagna)   (Tel. prefix: 0532)

Guides and Services

Ente Provinciale per il Turismo
Largo Castello 28.   Tel.: 2 12 67

Opera Houses and Concert Halls

Teatro Comunale
Corso Mostri della Libertà 5.   Tel.: 3 42 00
Season: December to March. Symphony season before and after the opera season. The Teatro Comunale is a member of the Associazione Teatri Emiliani Riuniti (ATER), a cooperative venture between six cities of the province of Emilia-

Romagna for the staging and production of operas that tour all the towns in the group. The Teatro Comunale was designed by Roschini and opened in 1792. It has recently been refurbished and restored.

Libraries and Museums

Biblioteca Comunale Ariostea [Ben. 118]
Palazzo Paradiso, Via Scienze 17.   Tel.: 3 40 29
Hours: Monday to Friday, 9:00 AM to 12:30 PM and 2:30 PM to 7:00 PM. Closed August 1–15.
Description of the Collection: This is a provincial depository and the holdings exceed 150,000 volumes. Among the special collections are a group of sixteenth- to eighteenth-century manuscripts and rare prints, especially from the Este court.
The Library was named for the poet Lodovico Ariosto, whose tomb rests there since the beginning of the nineteenth century. Since 1862, the Library has been separated from the University.

Biblioteca dell'Archivio del Capitolo Metropolitano [Ben. 117]
Piazza della Cattedrale.   Tel.: 2 53 41
Collection includes liturgical and sacred polyphonic manuscripts.

Civico Museo di Schifanoia
Via Scandiana 21.   Tel.: 3 73 26
Hours: daily except Tuesday. Summer: weekdays 9:00 AM to noon and 3:00 PM to 6:00 PM. Winter: weekdays from 10:00 AM to noon and from 2:00 PM to 5:00 PM. Holidays from 9:00 AM to noon.
Description of the Collection: archeological collection mainly from the Renaissance, including illuminated manuscript choirbooks from churches.

Conservatories and Schools

Conservatorio di Musica G. Frescobaldi
Via Previati 22.   Tel.: 2 17 28
Recently made a national conservatory and therefore subject to the same organization and diploma facilities as the Santa Cecilia in Rome (see p. 19). It has a *liceo musicale pareggiato* attached to it, which serves at the level immediately below the Conservatory.

MANTUA (Lombardy)   (Tel. prefix: 0376)

Guides and Services

Ente Provinciale per il Turismo
Piazza Andrea Mantegna 6.   Tel.: 2 16 01

Opera Houses and Concert Halls

Teatro Sociale
Piazza T. Folengo 4.   Tel.: 36 27 39
Season: February to April.
Seating Capacity: 1,400.
A "traditional" theater designed by L. Canonica and opened in 1822.

Libraries and Museums

Biblioteca Comunale [Ben. 177]
Palazzo degli Studi, Via Roberto Ardigò 13.   Tel.: 2 15 15
Hours: Tuesday to Saturday, 9:00 AM to noon and 3:00 PM to 6:00 PM. Closed
      August 1–15.
Description of the Collection: sixteenth-century madrigals and canzonettes, as well
      as nineteenth-century works by Giuseppe Acerbi.
The collection was founded in 1780 by Maria Theresa of Austria.

Biblioteca dell'Archivio di Stato [Ben. 175]
Via Roberto Ardigò 11.   Tel.: 2 44 41
Some liturgical and chant manuscripts of the fourteenth and fifteenth centuries.
Also inventory from Capitolo di Santa Barbara di Mantova's music collection,
most of which is in Milan. Monteverdi autographs.

Biblioteca dell'Archivio Storico Diocesano [Ben. 176]
Curia Vescovile, Piazza Sordello.   Tel.: 2 20 51
Of the Archive's five sections, three have music: Basilica ex Palatina di Santa
Barbara; Basilica di Sant'Andrea (fifteenth- to seventeenth-century graduals
and antiphonaries) and Capitolo della Cattedrale (early polyphonic manu-
scripts). Open by appointment.

Biblioteca dell'Accademia Virgiliana di Scienze Lettere ed Arti [Ben. 174]
Archivio Musicale, Via dell'Accademia 47.   Tel.: 2 03 14
Hours: weekdays from 10:00 AM to noon and 3:00 PM to 6:00 PM.
The Library, which was established in 1768, is strong in science, art, and
literature. The music archive contains, for the most part, manuscripts of vocal
and instrumental works of the eighteenth and nineteenth centuries.

Biblioteca dell'Istituto Musicale Lucio Campiani [Ben. 179]
Largo XXIV Maggio 12.   Tel.: 2 46 36
Primarily autograph manuscripts of Lucio Campiani's works make this practi-
cal conservatory collection distinctive.

Conservatories and Schools

Istituto Musicale Lucio Campiani
Largo XXIV Maggio 12.   Tel.: 2 46 36
Founded in 1761 by the Accademia Filarmonica, this music school is under the
supervision of the Ministry of Public Instruction and is authorized to give
diplomas at a level just below that of national conservatory.

Musical Landmarks

Sala degli Specchi (Gallery of Mirrors)
Palazzo Ducale, Piazza Sordello.   Tel.: 2 02 83
Hours: summer from 9:00 AM to 12:30 PM and from 2:30 PM to 6:00 PM; winter
    from 9:00 AM to 4:00 PM. Sundays and holidays from 9:00 AM to 1:00 PM.
    Guided tours are available.
To the left of the entrance to the Gallery of Mirrors is a sign which reads:
" 'Ogni Venere Di Sera Si Fa Musica Nella Sala Degli Specchi' Cl. Monteverdi
al Card. Ferdin. Gonzaga Da Mantova Il 22 Giugno 1611." (" 'Every Friday
evening there is music in the Gallery of Mirrors' Claudio Monteverdi to
Cardinal Ferdinand Gonzaga of Mantua, 22 June 1611.") **Claudio Monteverdi**
(1567–1643) was employed as court musician to the Duke of Mantua from 1590
to 1612. His opera *La Favola d'Orfeo* was performed in Mantua in 1607 and was
such a great success that Monteverdi wrote two additional operas for the
wedding celebrations of Francesco Gonzaga and Margarita of Savoy in 1608.
They were *L'Arianna* and *Ballo dell'Ingrate*. All these operas were performed in
the Sala degli Specchi, as well as in other theaters of the period.
    Salomone Rossi shared the labors at the Gonzaga court with Monteverdi.

Although he was a Jew, he was so esteemed by the Gonzagas that he was allowed to move around the city without the yellow headdress that customarily identified people of his faith at this time.

Teatro Scientifico (now called *Teatro Accademio del Bibiena*)
Via dell'Accademia 47, near the Piazza Dante Alighieri.   Tel.: 2 76 53
The Teatro Scientifico first opened its doors in 1769 as a private club called the Accademia Vigiliana. The hall was designed by the famed Antonio Galli-Bibiena, who was also responsible for the Teatro Comunale of Bologna. In 1770, the fourteen-year old Mozart gave a concert there, a fact commemorated by a plaque on the wall of the building to this day. In total ruins for many years, the Scientifico was completely restored to its original magnificence, renamed, and reopened in April 1972. It is one of the most perfect examples of eighteenth-century architecture in use today.

The Business of Music

Music and Record Shops

Franco Bonfà
    Via Fratello Cairoli 18.   Tel.: 2 25 08
Continental
    Piazza Cavallotti 11.   Tel.: 59 88
Eredi Mojetta
    Corso Umberto 1/33.
Recordmusic
    Viale Mondello 8.

MODENA (Emilia-Romagna)   (Tel. prefix: 059)

Guides and Services

Ente Provinciale per il Turismo
Corso Canalgrande 3.   Tel.: 23 74 79

Opera Houses and Concert Halls

Teatro Comunale

Corso Canalgrande 31.   Tel.: 22 51 83

Season: December through March. Member of ATER in the province of Emilia-Romagna (see p. 125 for further details). The concert season precedes and follows this.

Seating Capacity: 1,400.

Originally called the Teatro Regio di Modena, the theater was inaugurated on 2 October 1841 with a performance of *Adelaide di Borgogna al Castello di Canossa,* composed for the occasion by the court composer of the Duke Francesco IV d'Este, Alessandro Gandini (1807–71). The building was designed by Francesco Vandelli and has *bas reliefs* by Luigi Righi. This is one of the "traditional" theaters, along with the Petruzzelli of Bari, the Bellini of Catania, and the Sociale of Mantua.

Teatro Ducale

Palazzo dei Musei, Piazzale Porta Sant'Agostino.

A very small theater used for chamber music and solo recitals of an intimate nature.

Libraries and Museums

Archivio Capitolare del Duomo [Ben. 201]

Via Lanfranco 6.   Tel.: 05 31

Open weekdays by appointment, this collection includes manuscripts and printed works of the sixteenth and seventeenth centuries.

Biblioteca del Liceo Musicale Orazio Vecchi [Ben. 202]

Corso Canalgrande 60.

Working library with a good collection of printed music.

Biblioteca dell'Accademia Nazionale di Scienze, Lettere ed Arti [Ben. 197]

Corso Vittorio Emanuele II 59.   Tel.: 22 55 66

Hours: weekdays from 5:30 PM to 7:00 PM. Closed August.

Printed and manuscript works, chiefly related to opera; libretti of eighteenth to twentieth centuries. Contains the collection of musicologist Vincenzo Tardini, who died in 1903.

Biblioteca dell'Archivio di Stato [Ben. 198]

Corso Cavour 21.   Tel.: 23 05 49

Hours: Monday to Friday from 9:00 AM to 2:00 PM. Tuesday and Thursday also from 3:15 PM to 5:30 PM. Saturday 9:00 AM to 12:30 PM.
The collection contains manuscripts and documents relating to the Este chapel in Ferrara, including inventories of printed music and instruments.

Biblioteca Estense e Universitaria
Music section, Palazzo dei Musei, Piazza Sant'Agostino 309.   Tel.: 22 22 48
Hours: summer: 9:00 AM to 1:00 PM and 3:00 PM to 6:00 PM.; winter: 9:30 AM to 1:00 PM and 2:00 PM to 5:00 PM. Sundays and holidays from 9:30 AM to 1:00 PM. Closed Monday, religious holidays, civic holidays and from August 15 to 30.
Facilities: microfilm reader; makes microfilm copies; all catalogs.
Description of the Collection: rare books, special collections, including the entire collection of the Este family, the choirbooks of the Obizzi collection, and the manuscripts of the Campori collection. Two thousand manuscripts, including operas, arias, sacred music. It is one of the most important music collections in all of Italy.
In the Estense Gallery, Largo Sant'Agostino 48, there are displays of instruments, rare books, and illuminated manuscripts, which are changed on a regular basis.

Museo Civico di Storia e di Arte Medievale e Moderna
Palazzo dei Musei, Piazzale Sant'Agostino 337.   Tel.: 22 67 54
Hours: 10:00 AM to 12:30 PM Tuesday to Sunday; 2:00 PM to 7:00 PM Wednesday and Friday (2:00 PM to 6:00 PM in the winter).
Description of the Collection: about 100 instruments drawn primarily from the collection of the Count Valdrighi, who gave them to the museum in the 19th century. Most of the instruments are European, but there are a few African and Asian instruments as well.

Conservatories and Schools

Liceo Musicale Orazio Vecchi
Corso Canalgrande 77.

The Business of Music

Music and Record Shops
Walter Alberti
  Via Emilia 95.   Tel.: 2 54 70

Armando Della Casa
    Via Farini 52.   Tel.: 3 13 85
Mario Fangareggi
    Via Castellaro 11.   Tel.: 2 40 47
    Via Emilia 305.   Tel.: 3 10 97
Mirando Mati
    Via Farini 6.   Tel.: 2 43 63
Pietro Messori
    Via Emilia 181.   Tel.: 2 41 01
Alfredo Pederzoli
    Via Emilia 263.   Tel.: 2 36 00
Sahara
    Via Borelli 31.   Tel.: 4 11 00

PADUA (Veneto)   (Tel. prefix: 049)

Guides and Services

Ente Provinciale per il Turismo
Riviera Mugnai 8.   Tel.: 2 50 24

Opera Houses and Concert Halls

Teatro Comunale Verdi
Via Livello 2.   Tel.: 4 28 91
Season: winter months for opera season. Concerts throughout the year.
Box Office: Tel.: 2 04 31
In 1748 a group of aristocrats promoted the construction of a theater called the
Teatro Nuovo della Nobiltà, which was finally opened in 1751. In 1846–47, it
was rebuilt under the supervision of Giuseppe Jappelli. It received its present
name in 1884.

Libraries and Museums

Biblioteca Antoniana [Ben. 233]
Musical archive, Piazza del Santo.   Tel.: 2 50 63

Hours: weekdays from 9:00 AM to noon and from 2:00 PM to 4:00 PM. Closed in August.

Credentials: apply directly to the President of Veneranda Arca del Santo.

Description of the Collection: important collection of Tartiniana, as well as manuscripts of Scarlatti, Bononcini, and other eighteenth-century composers. Contains the Oreste Ravanello bequest of seventeenth- and eighteenth-century editions.

Biblioteca del Conservatorio di Musica Cesare Pollini [Ben. 236]
Via Eremitani 6. Tel.: 4 40 87

Working collection primarily for use of students and faculty.

Biblioteca del Museo Civico [Ben. 237]
Piazza del Santo 10. Tel.: 2 31 06

Hours: Monday to Saturday in winter: 9:00 AM to 1:00 PM and 3:00 PM to 6:00 PM; summer from 9:00 AM to 1:00 PM and 3:30 PM to 6:30 PM. Annual closing July 1–15.

Credentials: identification card required.

Description of the Collection: contains illuminated choirbooks from the Benedictine abbey San Giustina di Padova, as well as some seventeenth- to nineteenth-century libretti and books of all periods. There are several spinets in the collection, as well as instruments from India.

Biblioteca Capitolare [Ben. 234]
Via Dietro al Duomo 3. Tel.: 4 20 60

Hours: weekdays by request from 10:00 AM to 1:00 PM. Apply to archivist for special permission.

Small but interesting collection including prints from the sixteenth to eighteenth centuries as well as some manuscripts. Strong in history and art.

Biblioteca del Seminario Vescovile [Ben. 239]
Via del Seminario 11. Tel.: 65 70 99

Hours: weekdays from 9:00 AM to 1:00 PM.

Although there is no separate music section, the library includes some 30,000 volumes and 250 manuscripts of musical interest. Largest Italian seminary library, it holds the music collection formerly owned by the Casa di Dio.

Biblioteca Universitaria [Ben. 235]
Via San Biagio 3. Tel.: 2 34 65

Founded in 1629, it is probably Italy's oldest university library. Contains fragments of fourteenth-century codices and liturgical music from the twelfth to the eighteenth centuries.

Conservatories and Schools

Conservatorio di Musica Cesare Pollini
Via Eremitani 6.   Tel.: 2 09 28
Founded in 1875, this is a national conservatory, subject to the same organization, regulations, and diploma-giving facilities as the Santa Cecilia in Rome (see p. 19).

Sezione Staccata per Ciechi del Conservatorio di Venezia (Separate Section of the Conservatory of Venice for the Blind)
Via Sette Martiri 33.   Tel.: 5 22 51
A special section of the Conservatory Benedetto Marcello at Venice devoted exclusively to the musical education of blind students.

Istituto L. Configliachi
Via L. Configliachi 1.
Part of the Liceo Scientifico, the Institute devotes itself to music instruction only.

Musical Landmarks

Tartiniana
Giuseppe Tartini (1692–1770) came to the University at Padua from Trieste as a student. In 1713, he eloped with one of his pupils who came of a highly placed family and had to hide in Assisi for two years, disguised as a monk. When he returned to Padua in 1715, forgiven by the Cardinal he had so offended, he was appointed to the post of first violin at the Cappella del Santo in the Basilica of Sant'Antonio. He founded a school of violin playing, and, although his services were sought by many of the leading courts of Europe, he remained loyal to Padua, bringing fame and glory to his adopted city until his death. He is buried in the church of Santa Caterina on the Via Cesare Battista, where his tombstone occupies a place of honor. There is a lifesize statue of him in the Prato della Valle, the largest square in the city.

The Business of Music

Instrument Makers

Le Ceciliana di Sinigaglia Anselmo (church organs)
      Strada Pontevigodarzere 173.

L'Organaria di Maritan and Giacon (church and chamber organs)
Strada Pelosa 3.
Guglielmo Zin & Figli (drums)
Via del Santo 7.

Music and Record Shops

Giolio Ballarin
Via Mantega 2 and Via Gozzi 8.
Tarcisio Gardoni
Via Dante.
Giordani Dischi
Corso Garibaldi 2.
Zago
Via Portello 14.

PERUGIA (Umbria)   (Tel. prefix: 075)

Guides and Services

Ente Provinciale per il Turismo
Corso Vanucci 30.   Tel.: 2 48 41

Opera Houses and Concert halls

Aula Magna dell'Università Italiana per Stranieri
Palazzo Gallenga.   Tel.: 6 43 44
Concerts sponsored by the Amici della Musica are given in this university hall.

Sala Maggiore della Galleria Nazionale dell'Umbria
Palazzo dei Priori, Corso Vanucci.   Tel.: 2 07 12
Concerts sponsored by the Amici della Musica are also given in the major hall of
the Umbrian National Gallery.

Teatro Francesco Morlacchi
Piazza Morlacchi.   Box Office Tel.: 6 12 55
Season: a season of opera in May and concert and symphonic presentations
throughout the year. Used for performances of the Sagra Musicale Umbra
(see p. 169).

Seating Capacity: 1,000.
Designed by A. Lorenzini, the Teatro Francesco Morlacchi was opened in 1871.

Libraries and Museums

Biblioteca Comunale Augusta [Ben. 264]
Palazzo Conestabile, Via delle Prome 15.   Tel.: 3 12 91
Hours: Monday to Saturday from 9:00 AM to 2:00 PM and from 4:00 PM to 7:00
  PM. Closed in October.
Although there is no separate music section, the collection includes twelfth-
and thirteenth-century *gnomi;* fourteenth- and fifteenth-century missals, motets,
and madrigals; and seventeenth-century vocal and instrumental works. Depos-
itory for works printed in the province.

Biblioteca del Conservatorio di Musica Francesco Morlacchi [Ben. 266]
Via Antonio Fratti 14.   Tel.: 6 63 13
Working library for students and faculty. Some autograph manuscripts of
Morlacchi.

Biblioteca della Badia di San Pietro [Ben. 267]
Ordine di San Benedetto, Borgo Giugno 74.   Tel.: 5 71 83
Hours: daily from 4:00 PM to 8:00 pm.
Important group of manuscripts from the eighteenth and nineteenth centuries
(operas, symphonies, etc.) and some prints.

Biblioteca Dominicini [Ben. 265]
Chiostro della Cattedrale di San Lorenzo, Piazza IV Novembre 23.
                                                             Tel.: 6 15 36
Hours: daily from 4:00 PM to 6:00 PM. Annual closing for one month in summer.
Besides some fourteenth- to sixteenth-century liturgical manuscripts, the col-
lection contains some Frescobaldi prints and some rare missals.

Conservatories and Schools

Accademia Musicale d'Italia
Via della Cupa 8.   Tel.: 5 52 91

Conservatorio di Musica Francesco Morlacchi
Via Fratti 14.   Tel.: 6 63 13
A national conservatory (see p. 20, Santa Cecilia).

Summer Schools

Università Italiana per Stranieri (Italian University for Foreigners)
Palazza Gallenga, Piazza Fortebraccio.   Tel.: 6 43 44
There are several sessions during the summer months, each featuring a different
specialty. For more specific information, write to the address above.

The Business of Music

Music and Record Shops

Ceccherini
    Piazza Repubblica 65.
Giuseppe del Bianco
    Via Fami 10.
Mangiacarne Figli
    Via Pellas 60.
Vittorio Paganini
    Via della Viola 7.
Guglielmina Tarpani
    Piazza Mattei 30.

PESARO (Marche)   (Tel. prefix: 0721)

Guides and Services

Ente Provinciale per il Turismo
Via Mazzolari 4.   Tel.: 3 14 33

Opera Houses and Concert Halls

Teatro Rossini
Piazza Albani 28.   Tel.: 3 31 84
Opened in 1818.

Libraries and Museums

Biblioteca del Conservatorio di Musica Gioacchino Rossini [Ben. 270]
Piazza Olivieri 5.   Tel.: 26 70
Hours: daily from 9:00 AM to noon and from 3:00 PM to 5:00 PM, except Saturday
    afternoon. Usually closed in August, but entry possible with special
    permission.
Description of the Collection: In addition to the Rossini manuscripts and vocal
    manuscripts of Donizetti, Morlacchi, Paisiello, etc., there is a collection of
    musical instruments in the Sezione di Strumenti Musicali Esotici della
    Biblioteca del Conservatorio. The library has a significant collection of
    string quartet parts from the early eighteenth century and opera arias
    published by Marescalchi and Barberis.

Biblioteca e Museo Oliveriana
Palazzo Almerici, Via Mazza 96.   Tel.: 3 33 44
Hours: weekdays from 10:00 AM to 12:30 PM and from 4:00 PM to 7:30 PM.
The library, founded by Annibale Olivieri and opened to the public in 1793,
contains some fifteenth-century illuminated manuscripts and other sixteenth-
and seventeenth-century works. Provincial depository.

Conservatories and Schools

Conservatorio di Musica Gioacchino Rossini
Piazza Olivieri 5.   Tel.: 3 36 70
A national conservatory organized along the same lines as the Santa Cecilia in
Rome (see p. 19).

Summer Schools

*Corsi di Perfezionamento di Canto ed Arte Scenica Indetto dall
Fondazione Rossini al Centro Rossiniano (Courses in the Perfection of
Singing and Scenic Art run by the Rossini Foundation at the Rossini
Center)*
Piazza Olivieri 5.
A special summer program in singing and scenic design for opera, sponsored by
the Rossini Foundation and held at the Rossini center of the Conservatory. For
information as to dates and course offerings, apply to the Rossini Foundation at
the address above.

Musical Organizations

Fondazione Gioacchino Rossini
Piazza Olivieri 5.   Tel.: 3 00 53
The Foundation, annexed to the Conservatory, was established in 1940 for the advancement of research and study of matters relating to Rossini. From 1946 to the present, its cultural activity has centered around national competitions, courses such as described above, scholarly congresses, support of the Rossini complete works edition, and the publication of a quarterly periodical. The Rossini Museum, housed within the Foundation, preserves autographs and mementos. United with the Centro Rossiniano di Studi, which was instituted in 1955, the entire complex represents a total Rossini resource for scholarship and performance materials.

Musical Landmarks

Rossiniana
As the reader may have already concluded, **Gioacchino Antonio Rossini** was born in Pesaro in 1792. (Unfortunately for Pesaro, he died in Paris in 1868.) Since he was educated in Bologna and made his career in Venice, Rome, and Milan until he left Italy altogether, the only memento that the town of his birth guards, aside from the names of all its musical institutions, is the place of his birth *(casa natale)* at Via Rossini 5 (Tel.: 6 44 52).
Hours: daily from 10:00 AM to noon and from 4:00 PM to 6:00 PM. Sundays from
      10:00 AM to noon only.
The house has been converted into a charming museum in which Rossini's autographs, pictures, and personal effects have been arranged.

VERONA (Veneto)   (Tel. prefix: 045)

Guides and Services

Ente Provinciale per il Turismo
Piazzetta Capreeto 4.   Tel.: 2 50 65
Information office: Via Cappello 17.   Tel.: 3 00 86

Opera Houses and Concert halls

Arena di Verona
Piazza Bra 28.   Tel.: 2 35 30
Season: from mid-July to the end of August (see p. 177).
Box Office: daily from 9:30 AM to 12:30 PM and from 3:30 PM to 7:30 PM.
Visiting Hours: summer, from 7:00 AM to 5:00 PM; winter, from 9:00 AM to 12:30
   PM and from 2:00 PM to 5:30 PM.
Seating Capacity: 25,000.
A "national institution" since 1976, this open-air Roman amphitheater was
built in the first century A.D. and is second in size only to the Coliseum in Rome.
Further, it boasts perfect acoustics, and the opera performances there are of a
very high order.

Teatro Nuovo
Corso Cavour 44.
Concerts sponsored by the Società Amici della Musica are held in this hall.

Libraries and Museums

Biblioteca Capitolare [Ben. 420]
Capitolo della Cattedrale, Piazza Duomo 13.   Tel.: 2 46 59
Hours: Monday, Wednesday, Friday, and Saturday from 10:00 AM to noon.
   Closed all of August and September.
Description of the Collection: music with other material. Includes liturgical
   manuscripts from the eighth to fourteenth centuries; manuscripts and
   prints in mensural notation from the sixteenth century originally belonging to the *maestri di cappella;* and theoretical works. There are usually about
   fifteen wind instruments on display.

Biblioteca Civica [Ben. 421]
Via Cappello 43.   Tel.: 2 16 80
Hours: Monday to Friday from 9:00 AM to noon and from 3:00 PM to 6:00 PM.
   Closed in August.
Description of the Collection: about 5,000 musical items in this diversified collec-
   tion, including sacred music, opera, libretti. Also about 2,000 books on
   history and criticism.

Biblioteca e Archivio della Società Accademia Filarmonica (Museo del Teatro Filarmonica)
Via dei Mutilati 4/1.   Tel.: 2 22 75

The Library includes operatic and instrumental works and the library of Clelia Pastori, including the singer's entire repertory. There is also a collection of approximately 60 instruments, including 16th century winds. The Society was founded in 1543. The Teatro Filarmonico was designed by Francesco Bibiena and inaugurated in 1729. It was recently reconstructed and all of its holdings returned to it.

Museo del Castelvecchio
Via Cavour.   Tel.: 2 76 34
A collection of string, keyboard, and wind instruments is on display in the castle, built in 1353 by Cangrande della Scala.

Conservatories and Schools

Centro di Perfezionamento e Avviamento Lirico Giovanni Zenatello
Villa Verde, Via Castel Felice 57.
This center annually offers a beginning course, as well as "master" training in singing, from October to June. The courses include voice placement, theory and *solfeggio,* music history, and opera history; diction, opera repertory, literary study of libretto, music analysis; concertizing, opera direction, and scenic design. Classes are held when opera is not being presented in the Arena. For more information, write to the address above.

Conservatorio di Musica F. E. Dall'Abaco
Via Abramo Massalongo 2.   Tel.: 2 28 14
A national conservatory.

The Business of Music

Music and Record Shops

Casa del Disco
    Via Nizzo.   Tel.: 2 13 47
    Via Oberdan 6.   Tel.: 2 84 91
A.L. Cherubini
    Via Pisano.   Tel.: 2 65 94
Dischi Radio Sono
    Corso P. Nuova 11.   Tel.: 2 69 59
Discofon
    Via San Nazzaro 55.   Tel.: 3 21 31

Discoteca
    Galleria Pellicciai 18.   Tel.: 59 13 13
Negocio del Disco
    Via Roma 12.   Tel.: 3 19 06
Tuttamusica
    Via Mazzini 67.   Tel.: 2 17 41

Italy, General

OPERA HOUSES AND CONCERT HALLS

Scattered throughout this musically decentralized country are some great theaters that deserve mention either because of their historical significance, architectural merit, or because they are important in the dissemination of Italian musical tradition, although not located in major urban centers. Those marked (T) are "traditional" theaters, that is, recipient of government subsidy although privately owned.

The arrangement is alphabetical according to city.

Carpi (Emilia-Romagna)

Teatro Comunale

This late-nineteenth-century theater is a member of the Associazione Teatri Emiliani Riuniti (ATER), a group of six cooperating theaters in the Emilia region. Operas are staged in one of the houses and then tour all five others, thereby broadening the repertory of each and sharing the expenses. ATER also hosts guest companies.

Caserta (Campania)

Teatro Patturelli

Opened in 1769, this was the court theater in the Royal Palace designed by L. Vanvitelli. Located 30 kilometers from Naples, the opera performances of the Primavera Casertana and concert season of the Amici della Musica are held here.

Castelfranco Veneto (Veneto)

Teatro Accademico
Inaugurated in 1745, the design of self-taught Francesco Maria Preti, a friend of the Riccati family, patrons of the city's culture, this jewel of a theater was restored in 1975 and is used for an annual festival in late August and September (see p. 163).

Cesena (Emilia-Romagna)

Teatrale Comunale Alessandro Bonci
Designed by Ghinelli and opened in 1846, this opera house with a capacity of 1,400 is regularly used for opera, theater, and concerts throughout the year. It is named for a Cesenese tenor.

Como (Lombardia)

Teatro Sociale (T)
Via Bellini 1.   Tel.: (031) 2 86 20
Designed by Fresi and opened in 1813, this theater was renovated in 1938 so that the enlarged stage could be opened onto an area in back, making it the only theater in the world where a single stage serves for both indoor and outdoor performances.

Faenza (Emilia-Romagna)

Teatro Comunale Angelo Masini
Designed by Giuseppe Pistocchi and opened in 1788. The interior retains the original decor today.

Fano (Marche)

Teatro della Fortuna
The original theater was constructed by Giacomo Torelli and inaugurated in 1677. Demolished in the first half of the nineteenth century, a new theater was constructed to the design of Luigi Poletti and inaugurated in 1863.

Fermo (Marche)

Teatro dell'Aquila
This 1,050 seat house was designed by Cosimo Morelli and opened in 1791. Today it is used primarily for opera.

Fidenza (Emilia-Romagna)

Teatro Comunale Gerolamo Magnani
Designed by the same architect who did the Teatro Regio in Parma, this theater
was opened in 1861. It is used for an opera season each October.

Foggia (Puglia)

Teatro Umberto Giordano
This house, a design of L. Oberty, was opened in the beginning of the nineteenth
century. It has fall and winter opera seasons.

Gustalia (Emilia-Romagna)

Teatro Comunale Ruggero Ruggeri
A late-eighteenth-century house. Member of ATER with an opera season from
December to March.

Jesi (Marche)

Teatro Pergolesi
One of the most celebrated houses in this area, Il Teatro Pergolesi was a project
of Francesco Maria Ciaraffoni and modified in 1791 by Cosimo Morelli. The
hall, in sober neoclassic taste, has beautiful decorations in gold stucco.

L'Aquila (Abruzze)

Teatro Comunale
Piazza del Teatro.   Tel.: 2 55 84
Season: October to May. Symphony season sponsored by the Società Acquilana
    dei Concerti. The concert season is considered both interesting and
    advanced. Occasional operatic performances.
Seating Capacity: 500.

Livorno (Toscana)

Teatro Goldoni
Designed by Cappellini and opened in 1847, this is one of Italy's largest theaters.
It has a fall opera season.

Macerata (Marche)

Teatro Lauro Rossi
Architecturally noteworthy, this house was designed by Ferdinando Bibiena, aided by his son Antonio.

Mirandola (Emilia-Romagna)

Teatro Nuovo
Member of ATER.

Novara (Piemonte)

Teatro Carlo Coccia (T)
A 900-seat, neoclassic theater designed by Oliviero and opened in 1888. Now primarily a movie theater, there is an opera season in December and January.

Piacenza (Emilia-Romagna)

Teatro Municipale Verdi (T)
Via Verdi 41.   Tel.: 2 46 31
Seating Capacity: 1,500.   Box office Tel.: 2 06 56
Season: December and January for opera.
An early-nineteenth-century theater designed by Lotario Tomba, the interior decor is by the great Sanquirico and is still greatly admired.

Pisa (Toscana)

Teatro Comunale Giuseppe Verdi (T)
The theater was designed by A. Scala and V. Michele and opened in 1867. Restored in 1935, this 800-seat theater has an opera season in March and October, with symphony concerts before and after. The building is neoclassic in style and has some of the best acoustics in Italy. A museum in the theater contains mementos and costumes of great opera singers who have appeared there in the past.

Ravenna (Emilia-Romagna)

Teatro Alighieri
Built in 1852, the work of T. and G. B. Medune, who rebuilt the Fenice in Venice, this house was completely restored in 1967. There is a fall and spring opera season.

Reggio Emilia (Emilia-Romagna)

Teatro Municipale (T)
One of the most luxuriously decorated opera houses in Italy, the white and gold interior by Girolamo Magnani was commissioned for the opening of the house in 1852. The architect was Cesare Costa. Today a member of ATER, the house features a winter concert season organized by the Famiglia Artistica Reggiana.

Rovigo (Veneto)

Teatro Sociale (T)
A theater with a seating capacity of 1,670, the Sociale has an opera season in November and December. During October there is a traditional fair featuring folklore, sports, and shows. The theater was originally constructed at the end of the seventeenth century and completely rebuilt by D. Longhi after a fire in 1904.

Sabbioneta (Lombardy)

Teatro Olimpico dello Scamozzi
Early seventeenth-century theater, the second covered theater in the world, it was completely restored several years ago and now houses performances regularly in this charming city on the outskirts of Mantua.

Spoleto (Umbria)

Teatro Caio Melisso
Small, seventeenth-century theater rebuilt between 1877 and 1880. Used extensively during the Festival of Two Worlds (see p. 174).

Teatro Nuovo Adriano Belli
A larger theater, designed by Alessandri and opened in 1864. Used for the Festival of Two Worlds (see p. 174) and also for the season of experimental theater in September with young winners of a contest sponsored by the Rome Opera.

Siracusa (Sicily)

Teatro Greco
Originally constructed in the fifth century B.C., it is one of the largest and best preserved theaters of the ancient world. The seats, hollowed out of rock, are carefully shaped for the spectators comfort. Annual opera season in June, July, and August.

Treviso (Veneto)

Teatro Comunale (T)

Small, 450-seat theater specializing in contemporary opera.

Vicenza (Veneto)

Teatro Olimpico

This is the last theater designed by the great Andrea Palladio, born in Vicenza in 1518. Commissioned by a literary society, the Accademia Olimpica, it was begun in February 1580. It is the first covered theater in the world, and the visitor is strongly advised to try to see the theater in use, no matter what is playing. It probably has the best acoustics in the world, and the stage is one of the finest in existence, featuring superimposed niches, columns, and statues, as well as three streets in perspective, painted in *trompe l'oeil* by Palladio's pupil Scammozi. There is a short musical season from September 1 to 15.

LIBRARIES AND MUSEUMS

The following, briefly described, are some of the important music collections to be found in places not already discussed. Often fine collections exist in out-of-the-way and unexpected corners, and even more often, they are inadequately cataloged. Since 1965, the Ufficio Ricerca Fondi Musicali (URFM) has been systematically cataloging all Italian music collections with manuscripts and printed works up to 1900 and libretti up to 1800. But the work goes slowly, and the majority of the Italian archives, libraries, seminaries, foundations, and museums are still relatively disorganized.

We will attempt in the pages immediately following to describe the collection in the broadest terms and supply, when possible, an address to which the interested reader may apply for further information.

The list is arranged alphabetically according to location.

Aosta (Val d'Aosta)

Biblioteca del Seminario Maggiore [Ben. 10]

Viale Xavier de Maistre 17.   Tel.: (0165) 22 49

Liturgical manuscripts from eleventh century. Codex Ao from fifteenth century.

Arezzo (Tuscany)

Biblioteca Consorziale [Ben. 13]

Palazzo Pretorio, Via dei Pileati.   Tel.: (0575) 2 28 49

Eleventh- to fifteenth-century liturgical manuscripts. Theoretical writings.

Ascoli Piceno (Marche)

Biblioteca Comunale [Ben. 14]
Palazzo Comunale, Piazza Arringo 6.   Tel.: (0736) 58 84
Illuminated choirbooks. Manuscripts of Moderati, Baglioni, etc.

Assisi (Umbria)

Archivio Musicale, Sacro Convento di San Francesco [Ben. 16]
Piazza San Francesco.   Tel.: (075) 81 22 38
Music of Franciscan masters. Printed works, treatises, performance editions of
music.

Cesena (Emilia-Romagna)

Biblioteca e Archivio di Santa Maria del Monte (Badia) [Ben. 85]
Via del Monte 999.   Tel.: (0547) 2 10 33
Sacred music; treatises; manuscripts and printed works from late eighteenth
century.

Cividale Del Friuli (Friuli-Venezia Giulia)

Museo Archeologico Nazionale [Ben. 92]
Palazzo Nordis, Piazza del Duomo 1c.   Tel.: (0432) 7 11 19
Important collection of missals, graduals, antiphonaries, etc., of thirteenth
century.

Como (Lombardy)

Archivio Musicale del Duomo [Ben. 95]
Piazza Grimoldi 5.   Tel.: (031) 26 14 86
1,000 manuscripts of seventeenth-century chapel masters. Some eighteenth-
century autographs.

Faenza (Emilia-Romagna)

Biblioteca Comunale [Ben. 110]
Sezione Musicale, Via Manfredi 14.   Tel.: (0546) 2 15 41
Libretti, church music, printed treatises. Faenza Codex from Carmelite convent
San Paolo of Ferrara. Illuminated antiphonaries. Autographs and prints.
Museo Teatrale attached to the Library has old instruments, iconography,
mementos of singers, etc.

Foggia (Puglia)

Biblioteca Provinciale [Ben. 135]
Palazzo Dogana, Piazza XX Settembre.   Tel.: (0881) 7 78 18
Collections of Antonio Nardini, Nicola Zingarelli, and Romolo Caggese.

Forli (Emilia-Romagna)

Biblioteca Comunale Aurelio Saffi [Ben. 138]
Sezione Musicale, Corso della Repubblica 72.   Tel.: (0543) 2 27 71
Manuscripts and editions of Romagna composers. Collections of Archimede
Montanelli and Carlo Piancastelli. Provincial depository.

Grottaferrata (Lazio)

Biblioteca del Monumento Nazionale della Badia Greca [Ben. 155]
Grottaferrata.   Tel.: (06) 94 53 09
Manuscripts from eleventh to fourteenth centuries important to Byzantine
studies.

L'Aquila (Abruzzi)

Biblioteca Provinciale Salvatore Tommasi [Ben. 160]
Piazza del Palazzo.   Tel.: (0862) 2 23 81
Special collections pertaining to the Abruzzi area. Listening area with discs.

Livorno (Tuscany)

Biblioteca Comunale Labronica Francesco Domenico [Ben. 162]
Villa Fabbricotti, Piazza Matteotti 19.   Tel.: (0586) 2 11 76
Bequest of baritone Delle Sedie. A Mascagni collection being made. Letters and
manuscripts of famous musicians in Autografoteca Bastogi. Collection of
instruments.

Macerata (Marche)

Biblioteca Comunale Mozzi-Borgetti [Ben. 173]
Piazza Vittorio Veneto 2.   Tel.: (0733) 24 79
Printed music in room dedicated to Domenico Silveri; manuscript music
elsewhere. Collections range from twelfth-century *Pontificale Romanum* to archive
of municipal band.

Messina (Sicily)

Biblioteca Universitaria [Ben. 182]
Sezione Musica, Via dei Verdi 71.   Tel.: (090) 1 11 83
Seventh- to twelfth-century Greek codices with Byzantine music. Also nineteenth-century works from collection of Gaetano La Corte-Cailler.

Noto (Sicily)

Biblioteca Comunale [Ben. 220]
Sezione Musicale, Via Matteo Raeli 8.
Manuscripts and printed works; discs and listening facilities.

Novara (Piedmont)

Biblioteche Riunite Civica e Negroni [Ben. 222]
Sezione Musicale, Casa Negroni, Corso Felive Cavalloti 4. Tel.: (0321) 2 30 40
Incunabula, special collections. Provincial depository.

Archivio Musicale di San Gaudenzio [Ben. 225]
Via Gaudenzio Ferrari 20.   Tel.: (0321) 2 15 02
Nineteenth-century manuscripts by church's chapel masters and others.

Orvieto (Umbria)

Archivio Musicale Biblioteca dell'Opera [Ben. 230]
Piazza del Duomo 26.   Tel.: (0763) 54 77
1,000 sacred works, including a few sixteenth-century editions and some manuscripts.

Ostiglia (Lombardy)

Biblioteca Musicale Greggiati [Ben. 232]
Palazzo del Municipio.
Late eighteenth- early nineteenth-century works. Seventeenth-century aria manuscripts. Sixteenth-century prints.

Pavia (Lombardy)

Biblioteca del Civico Instituto Musicale Franco Vittadini [Ben. 259]
Via Lazzaro Spallanzani 21.   Tel.: (0382) 3 50 47
Working music conservatory library with a large collection of band music from the music corps of the Guardia Nazionale Cittadina. Autograph scores of Zanon operas.

Pescia (Tuscany)

Biblioteca Comunale Carlo Magnini [Ben. 271]
Piazza San Stefano 1.   Tel.: (0572) 41 44
Music collection of Giovanni Pacini includes composer's own works plus 1,800 letters.

Piacenza (Emilia-Romagna)

Biblioteca del Conservatorio di Musica G. Nicolini [Ben. 275]
Via Santa Franca 35.   Tel.: (0523) 2 03 58
Eighteenth-century theoretical works. Also manuscripts and prints and nineteenth-century libretto collection. Early printed Haydn. Works of local composers.

Ravenna (Emilia-Romagna)

Museo di Antichi Strumenti Musicali
Fosso Ghiaia.
Collection of pianolas and mechanical musical instruments from the collection of industrialist Marino Marini. Fosso Ghiaia is 20 km. from Ravenna.

Rieti (Lazio)

Archivio Musicale del Duomo [Ben. 300]
Piazza Battisti.
Fragment of Senfl's *Liber* of 1520, as well as eighteenth- and nineteenth-century manuscripts.

Rimini (Emilia-Romagna)

Biblioteca Civica Alessandro Gambalunga [Ben. 301]
Palazzo Gambalunga, Via Gambalunga 27.   Tel.: (0541) 2 36 67
Sixteenth- to eighteenth-century editions, theoretical works, and a collection of letters from Boito, Leoncavallo, Ponchielli, Mascagni, Puccini, etc., addressed to Amintore Galli.

Sant'Oreste (Lazio)

Collegiata di San Lorenzo [Ben. 341]
Archivio Musicale, Palazzo Canali, Via del Podestà.
About 400 works by Innocenzo Ricci (written 1863–1915), as well as others.

Trento *(Trentino-Alto Adige)*

Biblioteca Comunale [Ben. 379]

Sezione Musicale, Via Roma 51.   Tel.: (0461) 2 68 87

About 10,000 items, including eleventh- to sixteenth-century manuscripts; fifteenth-century tablatures. Opera libretti; late eighteenth- and nineteenth-century manuscripts, especially of local composers. 2,000 works from Società Filarmonica of Trento as well as other collections.

Treviso *(Veneto)*

Biblioteca Capitolare del Duomo [Ben. 383]

Archivio Musicale, Vicolo del Duomo.

Important collection of codices, manuscripts, and rare editions of music and theory.

Museo della Casa Trevigliana

Via Canova.

Musical instruments are included in collection which consists mainly of sculpture, ceramics, furniture, glasses, and pottery.

Urbania *(Mache)*

Biblioteca Capitolare e Archivio Storico Musicale della Cattedrale di San Cristoforo [Ben. 395]

Casa Canonica, Piazza Bartolomei.

Fourteenth-century illuminated antiphonaries; later graduals and missals, psalters, and breviaries. Instrumental and sacred manuscripts of Tommasoli (nineteenth century).

Urbino *(Marche)*

Cappella del Sacramento [Ben. 398]

Archivio Musicale, Piazza Duca Federico.

Diocesan museum with illuminated choirbooks of the fifteenth century.

Vatican City *(Lazio)*

Monumenti, Musei e Gallerie Pontificie

Città del Vaticano.   Tel.: 698, ext. 3332

Hours: 9:00 AM to 1:30 PM, Monday to Saturday.

Facilities: photographic service.

Description of the Collection: Along with a library of books and musical scores, this

Vatican State Museum contains several instruments from ancient Egypt, Rome, and Etruria.

Pontifico Museo Missionario Ethnologico (Pontifical Missionary Ethnological Museum)
Città del Vaticano.   Tel.: 4714
Hours: 9:00 AM to 1:30 PM, Monday to Friday.
There are approximately 300 musical instruments, originating from Africa, Asia, Central America, and Oceania in this museum, which was founded in 1926.

CONSERVATORIES AND SCHOOLS

There are four kinds of music education institutions available in Italy today. The most prestigious by far is the national conservatory, of which there are now twenty, located in the following cities: Alessandria, Bari, Bologna, Bolzano, Cagliari, Genoa, L'Aquila, Milan, Naples, Palermo, Padua, Parma, Pesaro, Perugia, Reggio Calabria, Rome, Sassari, Trieste, Turin, and Venice. The fact that the conservatory, with its natural emphasis on the performer, is the prevailing form of musical education, is consistent with what we have observed about the essential character of Italian musical life. It is our private conviction that the average Italian opera enthusiast attends each performance in order to size up the competition; that within each opera buff there lurks a potential Caruso or a Callas manqué. This might account for the high esteem in which virtuosity and bravura are held in Italian performance and might also serve as one explanation for the dearth of amateur choral and orchestral groups—everyone is a soloist!

The second category of music education institutions is also the least numerous: the university faculty in which an advanced degree in musicology, music education, or music theory is offered. At latest count, there were thirty-two universities that offered music courses—but only two offered degrees. It continues to be a source of amazement that, given the incomparable wealth of documentation accumulated over many centuries of music-making of the highest order, that it is inevitably left to the foreign scholar to make the seminal study of the most important Italian musical phenomena.

The third division differs from the first only in degree. The "equalized institutes" (E), officially recognized by the state and, to some extent, under the jurisdiction of the Ministry of Public Instruction, came into existence for the benefit of music students who could not go to a major urban center for their education. These institutes also serve as a point of organization for local musical activities. They are now accredited (or equalized), so that the diploma they offer is the equivalent of those offered by the conservatories. The course offerings, admission requirements, and diplomas awarded will be described by each institution upon receipt of a mailed request.

Finally, there are the innumerable local music schools that dot the landscape. Each cluster of houses at a crossroad has its own beloved *Professore* who undoubtedly did study with Respighi, who does give lessons at a reasonable fee, and who may indeed call himself a *Scuola* or even a *Liceo* without a qualm.

In addition, there are summer schools of music, which have proliferated at a great rate and require neither regularity nor national standing. We mention a few of the well-established and reliable ones below.

The list that follows is arranged alphabetically by location.

Alessandria (Piedmont)

Conservatorio di Musica A. Vivaldi
Via Parma 1.   Tel.: (0131) 5 33 63
A national conservatory.

Arezzo (Tuscany)

Instituto Comunale Guido Monaco (E)
Piazzetta del Praticino 3.
Founded in 1873.

Asti (Piedmont)

Istituto Musicale Giuseppe Verdi (E)
Casa Asinari-Verasis, Via Natta 8.
Founded in 1825, the school is housed in a sixteenth-century palace in the center of the city.

Barga (Tuscany)

International Summer Course for Opera Singers
Opera Barga, Via della Fornacetta.
A summer course for young opera singers ready for professional performance. Also for theater technicians, scenery painters, costume designers, rehearsal pianists. See also p. 160.

Bolzano (Alto Adige)

Conservatorio di Musica Claudio Monteverdi
Piazza Domenicani 19.   Tel.: (0471) 2 17 64

A national conservatory with an unusually long list of course offerings. This school was known as the Liceo Musicale G. Rossini until 1940.

Cortina D'Ampezzo (Veneto)

Agosto Musicale Cortinese (Cortinese Musical August)

For information, apply to the Azienda Autonoma di Soggiorno e Turismo, Cortina D'Ampezzo. The course at this summer school runs for the month of August and features ensemble playing and seventeenth-century guitar, lute, etc.

Cuneo (Piedmont)

Civico Istituto Musicale E. Bruni (E)
Palazzo Lovera di Maria, Via Roma 37.

Foggia (Puglia)

Conservatorio Statale di Musica Umberto Giordano (E)
Piazza Vincenzo Negri 13.   Tel.: (0881) 2 36 68

Forli (Emilia-Romagna)

Istituto Musicale Angelo Masini (E)
Corso Garibaldi 30.

Gargnano (Lake of Garda)

Corsi Internazionali di Lingua e Cultura Italiana (International Course of the Italian Language and Culture)

For information apply to: Via Festa del Perdono, 20122 Milan.

For three weeks in July and three weeks in August, courses are held in this lakeside hamlet in the Villa Feltrinelli.

Grottaferrata (Lazio)

Centro Studi di Musica Bizantina (Center for Studies of Byzantine Music)

Badia Greca di Grottaferrata, Grottaferrata.   Tel.: (06) 94 53 09

Since 1968, this center for scholarly investigation has sponsored an international meeting of students and scholars in the field of Eastern Church liturgical music at regular intervals.

L'Aquila (Abruzzi)

Conservatorio di Musica A. Casella
Via dell'Annunziata 1.   Tel.: (0862) 2 21 22
A national conservatory.

Lecce (Puglia)

Liceo Musicale di Musica di Stato Tito Schipa (E)
Viale Taranto 12.   Tel.: (0832) 2 59 16
Presents a concert season in collaboration with the Accademia Salentina.

Livorno (Tuscany)

Scuola Musicale Consorziale Pietro Mascagni (E)
Via Marradi 116.

Marsala (Sicily)

Istituto Musicale Comunale G. Mule (E)
Via Teatro 2-6.

Messina (Sicily)

Istituto Musicale Arcangelo Corelli (E)
Via Laudamo 1.

Novara (Piedmont)

Civico Istituto Musicale Brera (E)
Viale Roma.

Pavia (Lombardy)

Istituto di Storia della Musica, Facoltà di Lettere e Filosofia
Università degli Studi,
Palazzo dell'Università, Strada Nuova 65.   Tel.: (0382) 2 47 64
One of the universities in Italy that offers a degree in musicology.

Civico Istituto Musicale Franco Vittadini (E)
Via Lazzaro Spallanzani 21.   Tel.: (0382) 3 50 47
School founded in 1867.

Piacenza (Emilia-Romagna)

Conservatorio di Musica G. Nicolini
Via Santa Franca 35.   Tel.: (0523) 2 03 58
A national conservatory, this institution was founded in 1839 as a *scuola comunale*, and later became an *istituto municipale*. It was named after Nicolini in 1941.

Reggio Di Calabria (Calabria)

Conservatorio di Musica F. Cilea
Via Georgia 16.   Tel.: (0965) 2 13 08
A national conservatory.

Rovigo (Veneto)

Liceo Musicale Francesco Venezze (E)
Via Cavour 17.   Tel.: (0425) 2 30 37
Building contains concert hall where local musical events are held.

Centro di Studi Musicale dell'Accademia dei Concordi di Rovigo (E)
Accademia dei Concordi, Piazza Vittorio Emanuele II 14. Tel.: (0425) 2 16 54
The center is part of the University of Padua.

Sassari (Sardinia)

Conservatorio di Musica L. Canepa
Viale Umberto 28.   Tel.: (079) 23 11 39
A national conservatory.

Sermoneta (Lazio)

Accademia Internazionale Goffredo Caetani della Provincia di Latina (Goffredo Caetani International Academy of Music).
Castello Caetani.
For information: Accademia Internazional di Musica da Camera, Monte Savello 30, Roma.
This summer school is held annually in the month of July in the Castello Caetani of Sermoneta, a town ten miles from Latina on the site of the ancient Roman city of Sulmo.

Terni (Umbria)

Istituto Musicale G. Briccialdi (E)
Via Manassei 6.   Tel.: (0744) 2 72 82
Founded in 1839 and formerly a *civica scuola di musica,* the Istituto is named for a
well-known Terni flutist.

Todi (Umbria)

Giornate Musicali Todi
Circolo Cittadino.
For information: Giornate Musicali Todi, Piazza San Salvatore in Lauro 15,
00186 Rome. A summer school with a three- to four-and-a-half-week program
in piano, chamber music, and guitar.

Trento (Alto Adige)

Corsi Estivi di Musica Sacra (Summer Courses in Sacred Music)
Seminario Maggiore Princ. Arcivescovile, Corso III Novembre 46.

Civico Istituto Musicale V. Gianferrari (E)
Via Giuseppe Verdi.

Udine (Friuli-Venezia Giulia)

Istituto Musicale Jacopo Tomadini (E)
Via Tomadini.
The school, founded in 1824, gained government recognition in 1925.

Urbino (Marche)

Corso Estivo per Stranieri (Summer Course for Foreigners)
Via Saffi 2.   Tel.: (0722) 24 30
Contemporary music is included among the courses in Italian given for the
month of August.

Varese (Lombardy)

Civico Istituto Musicale (E)
Villa Mirabello.   Tel.: (0332) 3 83 60

FESTIVALS

Adria (Rovigo)

Settembre Adriese
Associazione Pro-Loco, Ente Provinciale per il Turismo, Piazza Matteotti,
    45100 Rovigo.   Tel.: (0425) 2 28 35
Dates: September.
Musical events include an opera season at the Teatro Comunale, concerts by
Alpine choral groups, and recitals by local and international artists. The
Rassegna Nazionale Canti Popolari della Montagna (National Festival of
Mountain Folk Songs) is also part of the Adria September Festival.

Alassio (Savona)

Festival Internazionale Musiche Vocale e Strumentali Antiche
(International Festival of Old Vocal and Instrumental Music)
Azienda Autonoma di Soggiorno, Segreteria Manifestazioni, Piazza Partigiani,
    17021 Alassio.
Founded in 1965 and devoted exclusively to the performance and study of early
music.

Aosta (Val d'Aosta)

International Organ Festival
Ente Provinciale per il Turismo ed Assessorato Regionale per il Turismo,
    Piazza Chanoux 8, 11100 Aosta.   Tel.: (0165) 56 55
Dates: mid-July to mid-August.
Between six and eight concerts by internationally known organists are given
annually in the historic cathedral at Aosta. This festival was founded in 1966.
There is a competition that is part of the festivities (see p. 179).

Barga (Lucca, Tuscany)

Festival Lirico Internazionale (International Lyric Festival)
Segreteria Opera Barga, Casa Baldi, Via della Fornacetta 11, 55051 Barga
    (Lucca).
Dates: mid-July to early August.
Performance Location: Teatro dei Differenti, Via di Mezzo (capacity 400).
Box Office: at the theater. Open daily from 10:00 AM to noon and 3:30 to 6:30 PM.
    Sundays from 10:00 AM to noon.   Tel.: (0583) 71 11 or 71 53.
Opera is the main attraction at this festival, which has been in existence since

1966, but ballet and concerts are also offered. Probably due to its proximity to Lucca, the festival dedicates one work each season to Puccini and contrasts this with at least one modern work, preferably a premiere. The theater in which performances are held was opened in 1783 by authority of the Grand Duke of Tuscany. The performances are primarily by students of the International Music Course for Opera Singers (see p. 155).

Bari (Puglia)

Maggio di Bari (Bari May)
Segreteria, Ente Provinciale per il Turismo, Piazza Roma 33a, 770122 Bari.
Tel.: (080) 25 86 76
Dates: May.
Opera, ballet, drama, art, and processions in historical costume, featuring the pageant of the *Caravella.*

Batignano (Grosseto, Tuscany)

Musica nel Chiostro (Music in the Cloister)
Monastery of Santa Croce, 58041 Batignano.
Dates: late July.
Box Office: at the monastery or at Libreria Signorelli, Corso Carducci, Grosseto. Tel.: (055) 2 23 29.
A short festival, in existence since 1974, in which opera and concerts are presented in the picturesque seventeenth-century monastery of Batignano in southern Tuscany. Performances are held in the open air, using the monastery complex as background. The performers are largely British and contribute their services, living and working together in a friendly, informal atmosphere to produce an exciting theatrical experience. The village of Batignano is 12 km. outside Grosseto along the new highway to Siena.

Belluno (Veneto)

Settembre Bellunese (Belluno September)
Azienda Autonoma di Turismo, Piazza dei Martiri 27e, 32100 Belluno.
Tel.: (0437) 2 51 63
or Ente Provinciale per il Turismo, Via R. Pesaro 21, 32100 Belluno.
Tel.: (0437) 2 20 43
The opera season at the Teatro Comunale, which was opened early in the nineteenth century, is held during the September festival.

Bergamo Lombardy)

Festival Autunnale dell'Opera Lirica (Autumn Festival of Lyric Opera)
Teatro Gaetano Donizetti, Piazza Matteotti 13.   Tel.: (035) 24 96 31
Dates: October and November.
This festival has existed since 1937 and is described on page 117.

Bologna (Emilia-Romagna)

Feste Musicali a Bologna
Ente Provinciale per il Turismo, Via Marconi 45.   Tel.: (051) 23 74 14
Dates: June and July.

Bolzano (Alto Adige)

International Bolzano Spring Festival
Azienda Autonoma di Soggiorno e Turismo, Piazza Walter 28, 39100 Bol-
    zano.   Tel.: (0471) 04 71
Mailing Address: P.O. Box 452, 39100 Bolzano.
Dates: April to June.
Includes special concerts and recitals as well as artistic and sport events.

Brescia (Lombardy)

Festival Pianistico Internazionale di Brescia e Bergamo
Accademia Pianistica A. Benedetti Michelangeli, 25100 Brescia.
Dates: April to June.
Performance Locations: Teatro Grande in Brescia and the Teatro Donizetti in
    Bergamo.
Box Office: Teatro Grande, Brescia.   Tel.: (030) 5 94 48; 4 24 00
    Teatro Donizetti, Bergamo.   Tel.: (035) 24 96 31
    Information and reservations may also be obtained at the Ente Provinciale
    per il Turismo in Brescia—Tel.: (030) 4 34 18; and the Azienda Autonoma
    di Turismo in Bergamo—Tel: (035) 21 02 04.
The concerts are presented at both theaters in both cities, sometimes with slight
variations in the program. They are entirely made up of piano music, either
with chamber orchestra accompaniment or solo. The programs are usually
focussed on one particular style or period in music history (e.g., *Il Pianoforte di
Schubert e di Brahms* or *Il Pianoforte in Russia e Parigi*).

Il Rassegna Internazionale di Musica Contemporanea
See above.
This review of contemporary music takes place at the very end of the

International Piano Festival, usually during the second week in June. All information concerning locations and ticket availability is obtainable from the same sources as those listed immediately above. Differing is the nature of the programs, which include world premieres, Italian premieres, European premieres of works often featuring pianists in combination with other soloists or with chamber orchestra.

Quarta Settimana di Musica Barocco (Fourth Week of Baroque Music)

Ente per le Settimane di Musica Barocca, Biblioteca Civica Queriniana, Brescia.

Dates: one week, late in September.

Concerts, conferences, lectures, recitals of Baroque music held in such places as the Ateneo di Brescia, the Chiesa di Santa Maria della Pace (Galleria del Palazzo Colleoni), Ridotto del Teatro Grande, Sala Consiliore del Palazzo Municipale (Council Chamber of the City Hall), Chiesa dei Santi Nazaro e Celso, Chiesa dei Santi Faustino e Giovita, Chiesa di San Rocco, and the Teatro Grande. Entrance to the concerts is free.

Castelfranco (Veneto)

Festival della Musica Veneta del 1600 e 1700

Teatro Accademico, Castelfranco (Veneto).　　　　　　　　Tel.: (0423) 42039
or Clarion Music Society, Inc., 415 Lexington Avenue, New York, N.Y. 10017
　　　　　　　　　　　　　　　　　　　　　　　　　　Tel.: (212) OX 7-3862

Dates: early September.

Since its inauguration in 1975, when American conductor Newell Jenkins led the Clarion Opera Group of New York to Castelfranco to reopen that city's newly restored Teatro Accademico with three performances of *Tassilone,* written by native son Agostino Steffani, the Festival has grown remarkably. It has spread rapidly to the surrounding towns of Crema, Treviso, Asolo, and the ancient abbey at Follina in the foothills of the Dolomites. In Castelfranco, however, performances of operas are given at the 380-seat Teatro, designed in 1745 by the Venetian architect Francesco Maria Preti for his home town. When sacred works or concerts are performed, they are presented in the Duomo di Castelfranco.

Cervo (Imperia, Liguria)

Festival Internazionale di Musica da Camera (International Chamber Music Festival)

Segreteria Azienda Autonoma Soggiorno e Turismo, Via Aurelia, 18010 Cervo.
　　　　　　　　　　　　　　　　　　　　　　　　　　Tel.: (0183) 4 47 97

Date: end of July through mid-August.
Chamber music concerts by soloists and ensembles of international renown.

Como (Lombardy)

Autunno Musicale di Como
Azienda Autonoma di Soggiorno e Turismo, Piazza Cavour 33, 22100 Como.
Tel.: (031) 27 25 18
or Villa Olmo, Via Cantoni 1, 22100 Como.   Tel.: (031) 55 13 87
Date: three to five weekends in September through October.
Each weekend features one concert of contemporary music, one of sacred, and
one of chamber music; also lectures. The events are held at the Teatrino di Villa
Olmo, the Basilica di Sant'Abbondio, and the Sala Unione Industriali on
Thursday (9:00 PM), Friday (9:00 PM), Saturday (5:00 PM), Sunday (9:00 PM),
and Monday (9:00 PM).

Fano (Pesaro, Marche)

Festival of Festivals
Corte Malatestiana, 61032 Fano.
Information: Azienda Autonoma di Soggiorno, Viale Cesare Battisti 43.
Tel.: (0721) 8 25 34
Musical and theatrical events are held in July and August, including a summer
carnival and art shows.

Fiesole (Florence, Tuscany)

Estate Fiesolana (Fiesole Summer)
Azienda Autonoma di Turismo di Fiesole, Piazza Mino da Fiesole 45, 50014
    Fiesole.   Tel.: (055) 5 97 20
Dates: July and August.
Drama, ballet, and concerts presented in the Roman theater (open air).
International artists present programs that are much more adventurous and
progressive than those one can hear in nearby Florence.

Florence (Tuscany)

Incontri con la Musica (Meetings with Music)
Azienda Autonoma di Turismo, Via Tornabuoni 15, 50123 Florence.
Tel.: (055) 27 65 44
Dates: September.
Concert series performed in selected museums, palaces, cloisters, and churches,
featuring orchestral, ensemble, solo, and choral music. Sponsored by AIDEM

(Associazione Italiana per la Diffusione dell'Edducazione Musicale, see p. 61).

Maggio Musicale Fiorentino (Florence May Festival)

Teatro Comunale, Via Solferino 15, 50123 Florence.   Tel.: (055) 26 30 41

Dates: Despite its name, this major festival extends well beyond the confines of the month of May. The Festival has grown, since its establishment in 1938, to encompass two months. It usually begins in mid-May, concluding sometime in July.

Performance Locations: The wide variety of locations used for presentations of different kinds include the Teatro Comunale and the Teatro della Pergola for operas, the Basilica di San Lorenzo, Basilica di Santa Croce, and the Palazzo dei Congressi for concerts and recitals.

Box Office: Biglietteria del Teatro Comunale, Corso Italia 16.

Tel.: (055) 21 62 53

Hours: 9:00 AM to noon and 3:00 PM to 5:00 PM except on Mondays and holidays, when it is open from 9:00 AM to noon. Tickets may be purchased, when available, one half hour before performances. Information and reservations are also obtainable at the Agenzia Universalturismo, Via Speziali 7r (Tel.: (055) 21 72 41).

Accommodations: plentiful, but reservations are advisable in season.

This is one of the most international festivals in Italy. Originating in the Teatro Comunale and utilizing the orchestral forces of that opera house when possible, the festival regularly hosts opera companies from all over the world. Guest conductors and international superstars are common currency. Ballet companies from the major centers of the world appear here, and world premieres are an ordinary event. Given the intrinsic interest of its location and the convenient dates, the Maggio is the delight of tourists.

Serate Musicale Estive Fiorentine (Summer Evenings of Music in Florence)

Via Maggio 39, 50125 Florence.   Tel.: (055) 29 67 18; 29 63 19

Information also available at the Azienda Autonoma di Turismo, 15 Via Tornabuoni.

Dates: July and August, in the courtyard of the Pitti Palace.

Seating Capacity: 1,500 in the open air.

Box Office: Palazzo Pitti from 9:00 AM to noon and 3:00 PM to 6:30 PM.

Concerts by the Orchestra di Palazzo Pitti with invited guest soloists. The concerts are sponsored by AIDEM (see p. 61).

Gargonza (Arezzo, Tuscany)

Gargonza Estate (Summer in Gargonza)

Castello di Gargonza, Monte San Savino, Arezzo.   Tel.: (0575) 84 40 21

Concerts are held weekly throughout the summer. They present young Italian artists and winners of various competitions. Conferences, art exhibits, and special courses are also offered in this picturesque Tuscan hill town.

Genoa (Liguria)

Saison Lyrique de Printemps (Spring Lyric Season)
Teatro Comunale dell'Opera, Via XX Settembre 33, 16121 Genoa.
Tel.: (010) 58 02 85
Dates: April and June.
Opera, operetta, classical and contemporary theater

L'Aquila (Abruzzi)

Rassegna La Musica e le Altre Arti (Review of Music and the Other Arts)
Segreteria, Società Aquilana dei Concerti B. Baratelli, Castello Cinquecentesco,
67100 L'Aquila.   Tel.: (0862) 2 42 62; 2 03 88; 2 78 75
Dates: September.

Loreto (Ancona, Marche)

Rassegna Internazionale di Cappele Musicali (International Church Music Festival)
Ente Rassegna Musicale Nostra Signora di Loreto, Piazza Madonna, Palazzo
Apostolico, 60025 Loreto (Ancona).   Tel.: (071) 97 71 39
Dates: from the Wednesday after Easter to "Low" Sunday.
Performance Location: Teatro Comunale Loreto, Piazza Garibaldi (capacity 700).
Box Office: Tickets and schedules may be obtained at the box office of the Teatro
Comunale Loreto or from the Azienda Autonoma di Soggiorno e Turismo,
Via G. Solari 3, 60025 Loreto (Ancona). Tel.: (071) 97 71 39.
This festival of sacred music has been going on since 1961. Its concerts include choral, organ, and instrumental music as well as an exhibit of editions. There is also a very important choral competition that takes place during the festival (see p. 184).

Lucca (Tuscany)

Estate Musicale Lucchese (Lucca Musical Summer)
Associazione Musicale Lucchese, Piazza del Collegio 17.
Information: Ente Provinciale per il Turismo, Piazza Guidiccioni 2.
Tel.: (0583) 4 91 87
or Segreteria dell'Estate Musicale Lucchese, Piazza del Giglio.
Tel.: (0583) 4 61 47

Dates: July and August.

Performance Locations: Concerts are presented in the bastions of the city walls, museums, Teatro del Giglio, the fourteenth-century Villa Guinigi, Villa Oliva, the Roman amphitheater, Palazzo Mansi, and other locations of special historic and artistic interest.

Box Office: Lucca Summer Festival Office, Teatro del Giglio, Piazza del Giglio.   Tel.: (0583) 4 61 47

Season tickets and student subscriptions available at a considerably reduced rate.

Housing Accommodations: Apply to the Ente Provinciale per il Turismo at address above.

Primarily a chamber music festival, there are some symphonic programs, mostly of works by Italian musicians.

Festival Nazionale della Canzone del Vecchio e Nuova Stile (National Festival of Old and New Song)

Ente Provinciale per il Turismo, Piazza Guidiccioni 2.   Tel.: (0583) 4 91 87

Dates: early March.

Performance Location: Teatro del Giglio.

Macerata (Marche)

Stagione Lirica Macerata (Macerata Opera Season)

Stagione Lirica/Arena Sferisterio, Piazza della Libertà 18.

Dates: mid-July to mid-August.

Performance Location: the Arena Sferisterio, a neoclassical arena that seats 10,000. Presents a short opera season of two or three works at most, performed in a highly dramatic outdoor setting.

Milan (Lombardy)

Teatro alla Scala Summer Season

Via Filodrammatici 2, 20124 Milan.   Tel.: (02) 80 70 41

The regular La Scala season runs through June. During the summer, there are occasional opera performances in the open air, given in the courtyard of the Castello Sforzesco and in the piazza at the Fiera Campionaria. For precise information, apply to the administration at the address above.

Monreale (Palermo, Sicily)

Settimana di Monreale di Musica Sacra, Liturgica, et Spirituale (Liturgical and Spiritual Music Week)

Segreteria AAT of Palermo and Monreale, Villa Igiea, 90100 Palermo.

Tel.: (091) 25 32 05

Dates: variable; usually ten days in September or October.

Box Office: Azienda di Turismo, Villa Igiea, from 9:00 AM to 1:00 PM Monday through Saturday.

Organ recitals, oratorios, and concerts of liturgical music held in the Duomo of Monreale (seats 1,800) and in a Byzantine cloister.

Montepulciano (Siena, Tuscany)

Cantiere Internationale d'Arte (International Art Workshop)

Montepulciano (Siena). Tel.: (0578) 7 71 88; 7 70 80

Dates: one week in August.

A new experimental festival established in 1976 by Hans Werner Hense and Giuseppe di Leva in which performances are combined with master classes. During the first year, there were classes in guitar, in mime, in composition. Performances take place in the Teatro Poliziano, the local elementary school, the Tempio di San Biagio, the Palazzo Ricci, and the Piazza Grande (town square). During the week of the Cantiere, sixteen events are scheduled, averaging two a day. All services are donated, thereby keeping prices, both on an individual and subscription basis, very low.

Naples (Campania)

Autunno Musicale Napoletano (Neapolitan Musical Autumn)

RAI, Viale Marconi 5, 80125 Naples. Tel.: (081) 39 16 27

Dates: October to Nobember.

Annual series of operas and concerts; established in 1958. Scarlatti Orchestra participates. Usually there is a theme around which the festival is organized.

Luglio Musicale (Musical July)

RAI, Viale Marconi 5, 80125 Naples. Tel.: (081) 38 16 27

Information: Segreteria, Azienda Autonoma di Cura Soggiorno e Turismo, Palazzo Reale.

Organized by the RAI-TV, the Azienda Autonoma, and the Associazione A. Scarlatti, this festival features opera performed at the Palazzo Capodimonte.

Estate Musicale Napoletana di Teatro di San Carlo (Neapolitan Summer Music at the San Carlo)

Teatro di San Carlo, Via Vittorio Emanuele III.

Tel.: (081) 39 07 45; 39 38 27

Dates: July and August.

Summer season of opera and ballet held in the open air at the Arena Flegrea on the Mostra d'Oltremare exhibition grounds. There are also summer concerts given in the Nuovo Teatro all'Aperto.

Palermo (Sicily)

Festival di Palermo
Teatro Massimo, Piazza G. Verdi, 90128 Palermo.
Tel.: (091) 24 74 54; 21 06 72
Dates: July and August.
Since its inception in 1965, this festival has been presenting opera, ballet, drama, and concerts at the Teatro del Parco di Villa Castelnuovo, Viale del Fante 78b, Palermo.

Settimana Internazionale Nuova Musica (International Week of Contemporary Music)
Azienda Autonoma di Turismo di Palermo e Monreale, Villa Igiea, 90100 Palermo.   Tel.: (091) 23 32 05
Dates: autumn.
A series of concerts dedicated to contemporary music, in which the musical and literary avant-garde participate.

Perugia (Umbria)

Sagra Musicale Umbria (Umbrian Sacred Music Festival)
Mailing Address: P.O. Box 341, 06100 Perugia.
Information: Segreteria, Associazione Sagra Musicale Umbria, Palazzo dei Priori.   Tel.: (075) 2 23 41; 2 13 74
Dates: end of September into October. About two weeks.
Box Office: Piazza Morlacchi, weekdays and holidays. Also ticket agency of the Ufficio CIT, Corso Vannucci 2. Evening events begin at 9:15, as a rule.
Concerts for soloist, choir, and orchestra, for vocal and instrumental ensembles; choral concerts, opera, spirituals, oratorios, biblical ballet. Established in 1938, this peregrinating festival takes place, for the most part, at the Teatro Morlacchi in the city of Perugia. However, there are also scheduled performances in Assisi, Foligno, Città di Castello, Gualdo Tadino, Gubbio, Narni, Nocera Umbra, Norcia, Orvieto, Sangemini, Terni, and Todi. Each festival has a specific theme, such as "faith as manifested in music."

Pisa (Tuscany)

Primavera Musicale (Pisa Musical Spring)
Ente Provinciale per il Turismo, Lungarno Mediceo 42.   Tel.: (050) 2 03 51

Dates: May to June.
Featuring organ recitals at the Chiesa Nazionale dei Cavalieri di Santo Stefano.

Positano (Salerno, Campania)

*Festival Internazionale di Musica da Camera, Musica d'Estate
(International Chamber Music Festival, Music of Summer)*
Positalta Associazione Artistico-Culturale, 84017 Positano.
Tel.: (089) 87 53 81
Dates: first two weeks in September.
Classical ballet and chamber music concerts are given at the Palazzo Murat,
which seats 500.

Il Piccolo Festival di Positano

Azienda Autonoma Soggiorno e Turismo Positano, Via del Saracino 2, 84017
    Positano.   Tel.: (089) 87 50 65
Dates: end of June and early July.
Box Office: Hotel Sirenuse, Tel.: (089) 87 50 01; Hotel Buca di Bacco, Tel.:
    (089) 87 50 04; and Teatro Estivo.
A festival of theater and theater music, plus chamber music and solo recitals
held in the Teatro Estivo, the Chiesa Madre, and Nuova, as well as the Buca di
Bacco, a hotel. During the festival, the center of town is designated a zone of
silence.

Prato (Florence, Tuscany)

Sagra Musicale Pratese (Sacred Music at Prato)

Segreteria, Azienda Autonoma di Turismo, Via Cairoli 48, 50047 Prato
    (Florence).   Tel.: (055) 2 41 12
Dates: September.
A series of symphonic concerts and solo recitals featuring music of a liturgical
nature. The festival has been in existence since 1966.

Ravello (Salerno, Campania)

Festival Musicale di Ravello

Azienda Autonoma di Turismo, Piazza Archivescovado, 84010 Ravello;
    Tel.: (081) 7 10 14
    or Ente Provinciale per il Turismo, Piazza Ferrovia, 84010 Ravello.
Dates: July.
Founded in 1953, this charming festival features a series of chamber and
symphonic concerts in open air at the Giardini di Villa Rufolo.

Ravenna (Emilia-Romagna)

Festival Internazionale di Musica d'Organo (International Festival of Organ Music)
Azienda Autonoma di Soggiorno e Turismo, Via Salara 8–12, 43100
Ravenna.   Tel.: (0522) 2 50 17
Dates: July into August.
Box Office: Tickets are on sale from end of June. The program is available by
May 15th. Seat reservations may be obtained from the Azienda at the
address above. Telephone reservations held only until 6:30 on the evening
of the concert.
Solo organ recitals are held in the octagonal-shaped interior of the Basilica di
San Vitale. An annual event since 1961, this festival traditionally invites the
greatest organists from all over the world to perform programs of a highly varied
nature.

Rimini (Forlì, Emilia-Romagna)

Sagra Musicale al Tempio Malatestiano (Sacred Music at the Malatestiano Temple)
Comune di Rimini and Azienda Autonoma di Soggiorno in collaboration with
the Associazione Teatri Emilia-Romagna (ATER).
Segreteria, Azienda Autonoma di Soggiorno, Parco Indipendenza 2.
                                                              Tel.: (0541) 2 45 11
Dates: one week in August or early September.
Box Office: Tempio Malatestiano, Rimini; Tel.: (0541) 5 12 22. Reservations
may also be made through Neg. Torsani, Corso d'Augusto, Rimini;
                                                              Tel.: 2 43 37
Dress: Ladies must wear dress suitable to a house of religion.
Music festival featuring choral, symphonic, and chamber music with young,
international performers from as many as twenty countries presenting greatly
varied programs. Events are presented in the Tempio Malatestiano, a magnificent Renaissance construction of the second half of the fifteenth century; the
Sala dell'Arengo, a concert hall in a Romanesque-Gothic building of the early
thirteenth century; and the Teatro Novelli. During the course of the week-long
festival, concerts are also presented at nearby Santarcangelo (in the Pieve di San
Michele Arcangelo) and in San Leo (in the Duomo di San Leo). Since its
establishment in 1950, this annual event has attracted an increasingly large
number of faithful attendants. The surroundings are superb.

Rome (Lazio)

Caracalla—Summer Opera Season
Via della Termi di Caracalla.   Tel.: (06) 57 83 00
Dates: July and August
Begun in 1937 as an experiment with one opera, there are now about forty
performances of opera every summer. Due to the ideal nature of the setting, *Aida*
always occupies at least half of the season's schedule. Three to six other operas
are usually presented, employing conductors, principals, chorus, orchestra, and
ballet of the Rome Opera. (see pp. 9–10).
    The Baths of Caracalla were built in 206 A.D. and represent the largest
architectural complex in the city. Open to visitors in the summer daily from
9:00 AM to 6:30 PM; in the winter from 9:00 AM to 4:00 PM.

*Festival di Polifonia Vocale Classica (Festival of Classical Vocal
Polyphony)*
Sponsored by the Organizzazione Romana Sviluppo Arte Musicale (ORSAM),
Aula Magna dell'Ateneo Antoniano, Viale Manzoni 1.
Dates: two weeks from the end of April into May.
Programs organized with the cooperation of UNCI (Unione Nazionale Corali
Italiane) are devoted to medieval and renaissance music.

*Festival Internazionale di Clavicembalo (International Harpsichord
Festival)*
Associazione Musicale Romana, Via dei Banchi Vecchi 61, 00186 Rome.
                                                                Tel.: (06) 65 68 41
Dates: one week in April or May.
A series of concerts presented at the Basilica di Santa Cecilia, Piazza Santa
Cecilia, Trastevere, featuring outstanding harpsichordists in solo concerts and
with chamber orchestras. The recitals take place at 9:00 PM. The festival has
been in existence since 1969.

*Festival Internazionale di Organo (International Festival of Organ
Music)*
Associazione Musicale Romana, Via dei Banchi Vecchi 61, 00186 Rome.
                                                                Tel.: (06) 65 68 41
Dates: mid- to late September.
Ten festival concerts in ten different Roman churches featuring historical
organs. Each year the festival is devoted to the organ works of two different
composers and the soloists are drawn from all over the world. Founded in 1968,
the festival has presented recitals in such churches as Chiesa del Gesù, Chiesa
dei Santi Cosma e Damano, Chiesa di San Carlo al Corso, Basilica di Santa
Cecilia in Trastevere, Chiesa di Santa Maria della Mercede, Chiesa di Santa
Maria in Aracoeli. Concerts begin at 9:30 PM.

Festival Internazionale Latino di Musica da Camera (International Latin Festival of Chamber Music)
Piazza di Monte Savello 30, Rome 00186.
Dates: late June into August.
Series of chamber music concerts held in the historical castles, churches, and towns surrounding Rome.

Nuova Consonanze (New Sound)
Associazione per la Musica Contemporanea, Piazza Firenze 24, 00186 Rome.
Tel.: (06) 56 28 25
Dates: end of October, early November for five days.
This festival of contemporary music, which consists of as many as seventeen sessions held in as few as five days, is located primarily in the hall of the Academy of Santa Cecilia and in other concert places such as the Aula Magna Scuola Germanica, and the Galleria Marlborough.

Rovigo (Veneto)

Festival Internazionale di Musiche Medioevali, Rinascimentali e Barocche (International Festival of Medieval, Renaissance and Baroque Music)
Segreteria, Centro Studi Musicali, Accademia dei Concordi, Piazza Vittorio Emanuele II 14, 45100 Rovigo. Tel.: (0425) 2 16 54
Dates: August and September.
A very elegant little festival specializing in old music played on old instruments in the Palazzo dell'Accademia dei Concordi, designed by Sante Baseggio in the early nineteenth century.

Salerno (Campania)

Festival Musicale Salerno
Ente Provinciale per il Turismo, Via Velia 15. Tel.: (089) 32 84 02; 32 07 93
Dates: mid-July to mid-August.
Orchestra of young American-trained professionals giving chamber and symphony concerts, indoors and outdoors in Salerno, Amalfi, Ravello, and Paestum.

Sermoneta (Latina, Lazio)

Festival Internazionale di Musica da Camera (International Festival of Chamber Music)
Accademia Internazionale di Musica Roffredo Caetani, Castello Caetani di Sermoneta, (Latina) 04010.
Dates: June and July.

Series of chamber music concerts held in the Castello Caetani of Sermoneta and in nearby towns in conjunction with the courses at the International Academy of Music.

Siena (Tuscany)

Settimane Musicale Senese (Sienese Musical Weeks)

Segreteria, Fondazione Accademia Musicale Chigiana, Via di Città 89, 53100 Siena. Tel.: (0577) 4 70 51

Dates: one week or more at the end of August or beginning of September at the end of the summer session of the Accademia Musicale Chigiana (see p. 102).

Box Office: Segreteria Ente Autonomo Settimane Musicali Sienese, Piazza del Campo, Tel.: (0577) 2 05 51
or Cortile del Palazzo Comunale, Tel.: (0577) 2 19 17
Hours: 10:00 AM to 12:30 PM and 4:00 PM to 7:00 PM daily during festival.
Customary Dress: dark suits and conventional dress welcomed.

Concerts include contemporary premieres, music of all centuries, especially chamber works presented by visiting artists, orchestras, choral groups, etc. The events are held in the Palazzo Chigi Saraceni; Sala dei Concerti, which seats about 500; in the Teatro Comunale dei Rinnuovati; or the Palazzo Publico, Sala del Mappamondo. Founded 1944.

Spoleto (Umbria)

Festival dei Due Mondi (Festival of Two Worlds)

Via Guistolo 10, 06049 Spoleto. Tel.: (0743) 28 10
Information: Spoleto Festival Foundation, 119 West 57th Street, New York, N.Y. 10019. Cable address: FESPOLETO; Tel.: (212) 582-2746
or Festival dei Due Mondi, Via Margutta 17, 00187 Rome.
Tel.: (06) 68 67 62.

Dates: two to three weeks, late June to early July.
Performance Locations: Teatro Nuovo (capacity 900), Teatro Caio Melisso (capacity 500), San Niccolò Cloister and the Piazza del Duomo.
Box Office: Mail orders should be addressed to the Teatro Nuovo, Spoleto. From March 15th on, tickets may be obtained at the American Express office in the Piazza di Spagna 38, Rome; from the Agenzia CIT, Azienda del Turismo, Piazza della Libertà 7, Spoleto; and from the Messaggerie Musicali, Via del Corso 123, Rome. During the Festival, the box office at the Teatro Nuovo and the Teatro Melisso in Spoleto are open from 9:00 AM to 1:00 PM and from 3:30 PM to 7:30 PM daily. Tickets for the concerts in the piazza and for the chamber music concerts in the Six-O-Clock Theater are sold only on the day of the performance at the Melisso Theater.

Customary Dress: ordinary and casual dress except for opening night, when black tie is obligatory.

Housing Information: extremely limited and somewhat medieval. Apply to the Azienda Autonoma di Cura, Soggiorno e Turismo, Piazza della Libertà 7, 06049 Spoleto.

This world-famous festival, founded by Gian Carlo Menotti in 1958 and the realization of his life-long dream, is generally considered the testing ground for the up and coming talent of Europe and America. It is part of the enormous attraction of the Festival that the entire town becomes involved in it for its entire duration. Art exhibits line the streets; chamber music concerts take place in the open air; the various performance sites are used for ballets, concerts, opera, drama, folk singing. The range of performances may best be demonstrated by mentioning some of the recent attractions: the London Royal Ballet, the McClain Family Blue Grass Singers, the Westminster Choir, the ETC Company of La Mama, the Chorus of the Accademia of Santa Cecilia, and the Noa Eshkol Dance Company from Israel.

Stresa (Novara, Piedmont)

Settimane Musicali di Stresa (Stresa Musical Weeks)
Palazzo dei Congressi, 28049 Stresa (Lago Maggiore);

Tel.: (0323) 3 10 95; 3 04 59

or Via R. Bonghi 4, 28049 Stresa.

Dates: late August or early September for approximately three weeks.

Box Office: Prior to the end of May, reservations may be made through the mail to the address above. After the month of May, the box office will be open on weekdays from 9:00 AM to 12:30 PM and from 3:00 PM to 7:30 PM; on holidays only from 9:00 AM to noon. After the first of August, the box office will remain open for the full day, even on holidays. During performance days, the box office closes at 6:30 PM and reopens at 8:00 PM. Evening concerts begin at 9:15 PM generally. Concert subscriptions are available.

A series of musical events featuring symphony orchestras, chamber ensembles, internationally known soloists, and, most especially, competition winners from all over the world, this festival has been in existence since 1962. Concerts are held at the Teatro del Palazzo dei Congressi, the Villa della Azalee (Parco del Grand Hotel et des Iles Borromees), and the Chiesa di Sant'Ambrogio, depending on the nature of the event.

Syracuse (Sicily)

Stagione dell'Opera Siracusa (Opera Festival of Syracuse)
Enti Provinciale per il Turismo, Corso Gelone 92C, Siracusa.

Tel.: (0931) 2 67 07

Dates: June and July.

The ancient Roman amphitheater, an imposing structure dating from the third to fourth centuries, is the setting for an annual summer festival of opera. Three or four operas are produced each season and done in repertory.

Taormina (Messina, Sicily)

Estate Musicale di Taormina (International Summer Music Festival)

Centro Internazionale Studi Musicali (CISM), Segreteria, Hotel Jolly Diodoro,
  Taormina   Tel.: (090) 37 51
Dates: two weeks in August.
Box Office: Azienda Autonoma Soggiorno e Turismo di Taormina, Palazza Cor-
  vaia.   Tel.: (090) 32 43
  Subscriptions are available at a reduced rate.

A series of concerts begun in 1962 and held in conjunction with music courses and competitions. The public events are held at the Roman-Greek Theater, the Sala Congressi of the Jolly Hotel Diodoro, and the Cattedrale, depending on the nature of the event.

Venice (Veneto)

Festival Internazionale di Musica Contemporanea della Biennale di Venezia (International Festival of Contemporary Music of the Biennale of Venice)

Segreteria, Ente Autonomo, La Biennale, Ca' Giustinian, Venice.
Dates: early September for one week.

Musical events include operas and concerts in their first Italian performances. Celebrated conductors of worldwide importance perform with Italian as well as foreign orchestras. Events are held at La Fenice Theater, public gardens, and other sites. There is a tendency to be inbred in this festival. Composers, critics, editors, publishers, local students determinedly avant-garde.

La Fenice Summer Opera Festival

Campo San Fantin 2519, 30124 Venice.   Tel.: (041) 2 51 91; 2 44 73
Dates: June to August.

Open-air season held in the courtyard of the Palazzo Ducale with occasional performances in one of the two open-air theaters, Piccolo Teatro and Teatro Verde on the Isola San Giorgio. *Otello,* when it is performed, is done at the Doge's Palace. The Fenice itself is also a frequent site for an opera production in the special summer series. Despite the name, symphonic concerts are presented intermittently.

Verona (Veneto)

Festival dell'Opera Lirica (Festival of Lyric Opera)
Ente Autonomo Arena di Verona, Piazza Bra' 28, 37100 Verona.

Tel.: (045) 3 86 71; 2 22 65; 2 35 20.

Dates: mid-July to mid-August.

Box Office: Tickets may be reserved ahead by money order reaching Verona from mid-January to eight days before a weekend performance. (Address: Ente Arena, Biglietteria, Verona.) You may claim your tickets at Gate 5 of the Arena upon presentation of a voucher or a postal receipt. The box office is open weekdays after June 1 from 9:30 AM to 12:30 PM and from 3:30 PM to 7:00 PM. No standing room. Opening night is the most expensive, and concert or ballet evenings are less expensive than opera.

Since 1923 this festival has been presenting two or three operas each season, repeated for one month. The Roman amphitheater, which was built in the second half of the first century and is astonishingly well-preserved, is the setting for this fascinating series. In addition to the operas and at least one ballet, there are occasional concerts featuring international artists. Since the amphitheater seats 20,000 comfortably, the kinds of presentations suitable for it are very limited. The stage, upon which as many as 3,000 people may be massed for a crowd scene, is longer than a city block and as high as a five-story building. Maria Callas, Placido Domingo, and Richard Tucker all made their Italian debuts at the Arena.

The Arena di Verona, elliptical in shape, is located at the center of the city and is very accessible from every point. Since its inception, the Arena Festival has presented well over 700 performances of 50 operas. Most of them are Italian and a good percentage of those are by Verdi, the favored composer here. Tradition calls for the public to light small candles during the overture and sometimes as many as 10,000 are lit at one time—a stunning sight! The acoustics of the Arena are magnificent. Related events in the many churches, cloisters, and palaces in the area are held during the period of the Arena Festival.

Estate Teatrale Veronese (Veronese Summer Theater)
Piazza Bra' 28, 37100 Verona.

Tel.: (045) 2 35 20

Dates: immediately after or immediately before the Arena di Verona season for one month.

A varied program of cinema, ballet, drama, church concerts, chamber music, electronic concerts, jazz festival, and art exhibits takes place in the following locations: Teatro Romano, Cortile di Castelvecchio, Teatro Filarmonico, Cinema Filarmonico, and various churches, depending on the event.

Viterbo (Lazio)

Festival Barocco (Baroque Festival)
Ente Provinciale per il Turismo di Viterbo, Piazzale dei Caduti 16.

Tel.: (0761) 3 47 95

Dates: two weeks in early August.

Featured in this festival, which has been taking place annually since 1973, are operas, concert works, and programs of religious music of the Baroque period. The IVth Festival Barocca (1976), for example, was prepared with the collaboration of the Accademia Barocca of Rome and included Caldara's *Ifigenia in Aulide* (1718), Galuppi's *Il Filosofo di Campagna* (1754), based on the Goldoni comedy, chamber music by Vivaldi, Bach, Telemann, Vecchi, and Monteverdi, and sacred music by Pergolesi. Concerts are given in old churches and cloisters such as the Basilica di Santa Maria della Quercia (fifteenth century), Chiesa di San Sistro (begun in the ninth century, enlarged in the twelfth, and reconstructed after World War II), Basilica di San Francesco (thirteenth century, restored in 1953), and the Chiesa di Santa Maria della Verità (twelfth century). For operas, a small open-air theater has been erected in the Nymphaeum of the seventeenth-century Villa Lante at Bagnaia, a sixteenth-century Italian garden 4 kilometers outside of Viterbo.

Performances generally begin at 9:00 PM.

COMPETITIONS

The competitions listed below are, as far as we know, of international standing, aiming at a very high level of professionalism, and offering substantial rewards. We have included those already well-established—or bidding fair to become important—regular events without restriction upon entrants based on national origin. Where precise information has not been available or was of a highly variable nature, we have tried to provide an exact address to which the interested applicant may apply.

Alessandria (Piedmont)

Concorso Internazionale di Chitarra Classica Città di Alessandria (International Competition of Classic Guitar)
Dates: held annually in October.

Awards: first prize: 500,000 lire; second prize: 300,000 lire; third prize: 200,000 lire.

Deadline: end of August.

For information apply to: Istituto Musicale Antonio Vivaldi, Via Parma 1, 15100 Alessandria.

Ancona (Marche)

Festival Nazionale di Chitarra (National Guitar Festival)
Dates: annually held sometime in October.
Awards: diploma first class in each of three categories: A, B, and C.
Deadline: mid-September.
For information apply to: Via Redipuglia 65, 60100 Ancona.

Aosta (Val d'Aosta)

Premio Valle d'Aosta (Aosta Valley Prize)
Dates: annual, July into August, during International Organ Festival (see p. 160).
For information apply to: Assessorato al Turismo ed alle Belle Arti, Segreteria del Concorsi d'Organo, Regione Autonome Valle d'Aosta, 11101 Aosta.

Arezzo (Tuscany)

Concorso Polifonico Internazionale Guido d'Arezzo (International Choral Competition)
Dates: four to five days annually at the end of August.
Eligibility: amateur choruses in five different categories according to the size of the chorus and the sex of its members.
Awards: from 500,000 lire to 150,000 lire, according to the category. Total awards amount to more than three million lire.
Deadline: April 15.
For information apply to: Concorso Polifonico, Piazza Vasari 6, 52100 Arezzo.
This competition, one of the most important in Italy, has been in existence since 1953, when it was established by the Friends of Music of Arezzo. A brochure is published every year, in which details of the categories are outlined, as well as the names of past winners and the fixed program in each category for the next year. Each year there is an obligatory piece, a piece from a multiple-choice list, and one free choice to be performed by contestants. The competition, which has stimulated choral singing throughout Italy, is held at the Teatro Petrarca.

Bagnacavallo (Ravenna, Emilia-Romagna)

Concorso Nazionale Giovani Liutar Città di Bagnacavallo (National Young Violinmakers Competition)
Dates: held annually in late September or early October.
Awards: diploma of honor.
Eligibility: for young violinmakers, with special emphasis on Italians, in order to stimulate the ancient craft.

Deadline: early September.
For information apply to: Segreteria del Commune, 48012 Bagnacavallo.

Bardolino (Verona, Veneto)

Concorso Internazionale di Pianoforte e Canto (Festival of Romantic Music)
Dates: four to five days annually in early June or July.
Age Limit: 32 years old.
Awards: 400,000 lire. The piano and singing competition alternates annually as part of the Festival of Romantic Music.
For information apply to: Segreteria Interfestival, Azienda Soggiorno e Turismo, 37011 Bardolino.

Bergamo (Lombardy)

Concorso Vittorio Carrara di Composizione per Organo o Armonio (The Vittorio Carrara Competition for Compositions for Organ or Harmonium)
Awards: first prize: 100,000 lire.
For information apply to: Casa Musicale Carrara, Via Ambrogio da Calepio 4, 24100 Bergamo.

Bolzano (Alto-Adige)

Concorso Pianistico Internazionale Ferrucio Busoni (Ferrucio Busoni International Piano Competition)
Dates: end of August or beginning of September annually for two weeks.
Age Limit: 15 to 32.
Awards: Prix Busoni, 1,000,000 lire and concert engagements; second prize, 500,000 lire; third prize, 400,000 lire; fifth prize, 200,000 lire.
Deadline: June 30.
For information apply to: Secretariat du Concours, Conservatorio C. Monteverdi, Piazza Domenicani 19, 39100 Bolzano.
The competition, established in 1949, actually lasts a good deal longer than the two weeks allotted to the trials. There is at least one week devoted to qualifying tests before the trials begin. The prize winner gives a recital to mark the end of the festivities. Past winners of this distinguished competition have included Michael Ponti (1964) and Garrick Ohlsson (1966).

Busseto (Emilia-Romagna)

Concorso Internazionale per la Ricerca di Voci Verdiane (International Voice Contest for Verdian Voices)

Dates: annually in June or July for four to five days.

Age Limit: under 32 for sopranos and tenors; under 35 for mezzo-sopranos, contraltos, baritones, and basses.

Eligibility: Singers are eligible who have never sung a leading role in a major opera-house production of a Verdi opera. Three Verdi arias must be sung from memory.

Awards: a total of 2,500,000 lire; also medals, diplomas, etc., and an opportunity for finalists to participate in the autumn opera season in Busseto.

For information apply to: Segreteria del Concorso di Busseto, Via Edmondo de Amicis 40, 20123 Milan.

Caltanissetta (Sicily)

Concorso Pianistico Nazionale Premio Marisa Cancelliere (National Piano Competition, Marisa Cancelliere Prize)

Dates: annual competition.

Awards: 100,000 lire.

For information apply to: Segreteria Amici della Musica, Via Mon. Guttadauria 10, 93100 Caltanissetta.

Carpi (Modena, Emilia-Romagna)

Concorso Nazionale Pianistico Città di Carpi (City of Carpi National Piano Competition)

Dates: biennial, alternating with competition listed below. Occurs at the end of May.

Deadline: April.

Awards: vertical Zimmerman piano and 500,000 lire.

For information apply to: Sezione Scuola Communale, Piazzale Re Astolfo 2, 41012 Carpi.

Concorso Nazionale di Violino Città di Carpi (City of Carpi National Violin Competition)

Dates: biennial. Alternates with competition above, but held in October.

Deadline: September 15.

For information apply to: address above.

Cava De'Tirreni (Salerno, Campania)

Concorso Internazionale di Musica Ritmo-sinfonia (International Competition of Rhythmic Symphonic Music)

Dates: annually in August.

Awards: first prize, 1,000,000 lire; second prize, 500,000 lire; third prize, 200,000 lire.

For information apply to: Social Tennis Club, 84013 Cava de'Tirreni (sponsor); or Segreteria, AAST, Corso Vittorio Emanuele 95, 84100 Salerno; or Azienda Soggiorno e Turismo, Corso Umberto I 277, 84013 Cava de'Tirreni.

Enna (Sicily)

Concorso Internazionale per Pianisti e Cantanti Lirici F. P. Neglia (F. P. Neglia International Competition for Pianists and Lyric Singers)
Dates: annually during the month of July.
Age Limit: 35 years old for pianists and male singers; 32 for female singers.
Awards: first prize, 250,000 lire; second prize, 175,000 lire; third prize, 125,000 lire.
Deadline: June.
For information apply to: Sindaco di Enna, 94100 Enna; or Assessorato Pubblica Istruzione, 94100 Enna.

Florence (Tuscany)

Concorso Internazionale di Violincello Gaspar Cassadò (Gaspar Cassadò International Cello Competition)
Dates: biennially in odd-numbered years.
Age Limit: up to 31 years of age.
Awards: first prize, 1,500,000 lire plus performance with the orchestra of the Maggio Musicale in Florence; other performances throughout Italy. Second to fourth prizes total 2,300,000 lire.
Deadline: March of even-numbered years.
For information apply to: Maggio Musicale Fiorentino, Teatro Communale, Via Solferino 15, 50123 Florence.

Concorso Internazionale per Giovani Direttori d'Orchestra (International Contest for Young Orchestra Conductors)
Dates: annually held in June. Founded in 1964.
Age Limit: under 35.
Awards: first prize, 1,000,000 lire and a concert; second prize, 500,000 lire; third prize, 200,000 lire.
For information apply to: Concorso AIDEM, Via Maggio 39, 50125 Florence.

Forte Dei Marmi (Lucca, Tuscany)

Festival Internazionale del Duo Strumentale (International Instrumental Duet Festival)
Dates: held annually for three days in mid-September.
Awards: for a composition for two instruments, first prize, 500,000 lire; second prize, 300,000 lire; third prize, 200,000 lire.

Deadline: August 30.
For information apply to: Palazzo Communale, 55042 Forte dei Marmi.

Genoa (Liguria)

Concorso Internazionale di Violino Niccolò Paganini (Niccolò Paganini International Violin Competition)
Dates: held annually early in October.
Age Limits: under 35.
Awards: first prize, 3,000,000 lire plus concert; second prize, 1,250,000 lire; third prize, 800,000 lire; fourth, fifth, and sixth prizes, 500,000, 300,000, and 200,000 lire respectively.
Deadline: middle to late July.
For information apply to: Segreteria di Concorso, Comune di Genova, Palazzo Tursi, Via Garibaldi 9, 16124 Genoa.
The trials are held in the Istituto Musicale Paganini, in the Palazzo della Merediana, Salita di San Francesco 4. An international jury judges the performances, and the closing concerts are held at the Margherita Theater. The winner gives a concert at the Palazzo Tursi, using the violin that Paganini bequeathed to his hometown, the "Guarnieri del Gesù."

Imola (Bologna, Emilia-Romagna)

Concorso Nazionale Pianistico Giovanissimi Concertisti (National Piano Competition for Young Concert Artists)
Dates: held annually in early September for two to three days.
Deadline: August 21.
Awards: an upright piano and the funds to give two concerts.
For information apply to: Auditorium Cassa di Risparmio, Via le Rivata 6, 40026 Imola.

Concorso Nazionale di Violino Giovanissimi Concertisti (National Violin Competitions for Young Concert Artists)
Awards: a Galimberti violin and funds to give two concerts.
All other details as for National Piano Competition above.

La Spezia (Liguria)

Concorsi Nazionali Allievi Pianisti (National Competition for Student Pianists)
Dates: annually in early May.
Deadline: mid-April.
For information apply to: ENAL Provinciale, Via le Mazzini 47, 19100 La Spezia.

Lonigo (Vicenza, Veneto)

Concorso Internazionale per Cantanti Lirici (International Competition for Lyric Singing)
Dates: three to four days annually in early June.
Age Limits: 28 years old, sopranos and tenors; 30 years old, mezzo-sopranos, baritones, and basses.
Awards: first prize, 1,250,000 lire.
Deadline: end of March.
For information apply to: Teatro Comunale di Lonigo or Segreteria, Comune di Lonigo, 36045 Lonigo.

Loreto (Ancona, Marche)

Concorso Internazionale di Composizione Sacra (International Competition for Sacred Compositions)
Dates: annual.
For information apply to: Segreteria Ente Rassegne Musicali N. S. di Loreto, Palazzo Apostolico, Piazza Madonna, 60025 Loreto (Ancona).

Rassegna Internazionale di Cappelle Musicali [Rassegna Lauretano] (International Review of Music Chapels)
Dates: annually from the Wednesday after Easter to Low Sunday. Competition of choral groups.
Eligibility: four different categories of choirs are eligible: equal voices (men only); equal voices (boys only); both with from twelve to twenty-four singers; unequal voices (STTB and SATB) of not more than fifty singers.
Awards: diploma of participation and medals.
Compensation: free board and lodging for members of competing choral groups.
Deadline: October 31 of preceding year. Tape recordings should be sent with application.
For information apply to: Segreteria Ente Rassegne Musicali N. S. di Loreto, Palazzo Apostolico, Piazza Madonna, 60025 Loreto (Ancona).
Eight compositions are required in performance, all of sacred nature and two of which must have organ accompaniment. One Gregorian piece is required. Combined choirs perform a pontifical mass at the end of the festival.

Lucca (Tuscany)

Concorso Internazionale di Canto G. Puccini (Puccini International Singing Competition)
Dates: held annually for three days in June.
Award: 800,000 lire.

Deadline: May.
For information apply to: Giacomo Puccini Foundation, Palazzo Orsetti, Lucca.

Milan (Lombardy)

Concorso Internazionale Città di Milano per Una Composizione Sinfonica (City of Milan International Competition for a Symphonic Work)

Dates: annual. Winner announced in February.
Eligibility: Orchestral compositions submitted must be unpublished and of fifteen to forty-five minutes' duration.
Deadline: end of September.
For information apply to: Teatro alla Scala, Via Filodrammatici 2, 20121 Milan.
The competition is organized by the city of Milan in cooperation with La Scala.

Concorso Internazionale di Canto Gaetano Donizetti (Donizetti International Singing Competition)

Dates: irregularly in late October.
Age Limit: two sections: one for singers under 40 and the other for anyone who intends to begin or continue to study singing.
Deadline: beginning of October.
For information apply to: Famiglia Artistica Milanese, Piazza Cavour 2, 20121 Milan.

Concorso Internazionale di Composizione Sinfonica F. Ballo (Ballo International Competition in Symphonic Composition)

Dates: held biennially in late October.
Awards: first prize is 500,000 lire.
Deadline: beginning of October.
For information apply to: Segreteria, Ente Pomeriggi Musicali, Corso Matteotti 20, 20121 Milan.
Competition organized in collaboration with the RAI.

Premio Dino Ciani (Dino Ciani Prize)

Dates: This international competition for young pianists is held annually for ten days in June.
Age Limit: open to pianists under 21 years of age.
Awards: first prize: 3,000,000 lire, a public recital, a concert with the Teatro alla Scala Orchestra, engagements at the festivals of Spoleto, Brescia and Bergamo, Stresa, and many other solo appearances; second prize: 1,500,000 lire, five concerts under the auspices of Jeunesses Musicales, three concerts in the Lombardy region; third prize: 1,000,000 lire, five concerts with the

Jeunesses Musicales, and two concerts in the Lombardy region; fourth prize: 500,000 lire and two concerts in the Lombardy Region.
Deadline: March 1.
For information apply to: Premio Dino Ciani, Teatro alla Scala, Via Filodrammatici 2, 20121 Milan.

Concorso Internazionale per la Conquista della Chitarra Classica (Classical Guitar Competition)

Dates: held annually for two days in mid-June. Founded in 1966.
Age Limit: In the four categories, there are sections for different age groups and one special division for duos. The categories include those under 13 and those over 18.
Awards: first prize, a concert with the orchestra of the RAI. Other minor prizes.
For information apply to: Comitato Organizzatore Accademia della Chitarra Classica, Viale Marche 31, 20125 Milan.

Concorso Nazionale di Composizione per Orchestra da Camera Premio Angelicum (Angelicum Prize. National Competition for Chamber Music Composition.)

Dates: biennially in September.
Eligibility: chamber orchestra composition, maximum duration twenty minutes. No age limits. International contestants welcome.
Awards: first prize: 800,000 lire, performance, and publication. Second prize: 300,000 lire.
For information apply to: Segreteria, Angelicum dei Frati Minori, Piazza Sant'Angelo 2, 20121 Milan.

Concorso Nazionale Giovani Cantanti Lirici (National Competition for Young Singers)

Dates: held annually in May.
Deadline: end of April.
For information apply to: Segreteria, As.Li.Co., Via Mazzini 7, 20123 Milan.

Concorso Ricordi per una Composizione per Orchestra (Ricordi Competition for an Orchestral Composition)

Award: first prize, 300,000 lire.
For information apply to: Segreteria Casa Ricordi, Via Berchet 2, 20121 Milan.

Premio Internazionale di Composizione Musicale Teatrale Guido Valcarenghi (The Guido Valcarenghi International Prize for Theatrical Musical Composition)

Dates: triennial. Next prize awarded in 1979, etc.

Awards: first prize of 1,000,000 lire given in memory of the late head of the house of Ricordi.

Eligibility: a piece of operatic music, chamber opera, or dramatic oratorio that has never been published.

Deadline: A copy of the music must be submitted by registered mail no later than March 31 of the year before presentation of award.

For information apply to: Ufficio di Rappresentanza della Direzione Generale della Società Autori e Editori, Foro Bonoparte 18, 20121 Milan.

Montecchio Maggiore (Vicenza, Veneto)

Concorso Internazionale Flautistico (International Flute Competition)
Dates: held annually the first week in August.

Age Limit: under 35 years of age.

Awards: first prize of 1,000,000 lire plus a concert engagement for the following season.

For information apply to: Giornate Musicali, Piazza San Salvatore in Lauro 15, 00186 Rome.

Montichiari (Brescia, Lombardy)

Concorso Nazionale Giovani Cantanti Lirici (National Competition for Young Lyric Singers)
Dates: held biennially in June.

Award: 600,000 lire.

Deadline: end of May.

For information apply to: Ente Manifestazioni Fieristiche, Comune di Montichiari, 25018 Montichiari.

Monza (Milan, Lombardy)

Concorso Pianistico Internazionale Claudio Monteverdi (Claudio Monteverdi International Piano Competition)
Dates: held irregularly at the end of September.

Awards: first prize, 400,000 lire; second prize, 300,000 lire; third prize, 200,000 lire.

Deadline: end of August.

For information apply to: Sezione Musicale Università Populare, Rina Sala Gallo, Via Missori 14, 20052 Monza.

Naples (Campania)

Concorso Internazionale Alfredo Casella di Pianoforte e Composizione (Alfredo Casella International Competition in Piano and Composition)
Dates: held biennially in even-numbered years for one week in mid-April.
Age Limit: for pianists, from 18 to 32; for composers, no age limit.
Awards: total awards of 1,500,000 lire. Also silver cup, diploma, gold medal, etc., and for the winning composition, publication.
Deadline: March 15th in even-numbered years.
For information apply to: Segreteria Concorso Casella, Via San Pasquale a Chiaia 62, 80122 Naples.

Concorso Internazionale di Violini della Fondazione Alberto Curci (The Alberto Curci Foundation International Violin Competition)
Dates: held biennially in odd-numbered years in November or December.
Age Limit: 32 years.
Awards: first prize, 2,000,000 lire; second prize, 800,000 lire; third prize, 400,000 lire.
Deadline: end of August in odd-numbered years.
For information apply to: Fondazione A. Curci, Via Nardones 8, 80132 Naples.

Concorso Nazionale di Canto per Giovani Cantanti Lirici (National Contest for Young Lyric Singers)
Dates: held annually in January.
Awards: first prize, 300,000 lire; second prize, 250,000 lire; third prize, 200,000 lire.
For information apply to: Teatro San Carlo, Via Vittorio Emmanuele III, 80132 Naples.

Concorso Nazionale di Composizione F. M. Napolitano (Napolitano National Composition Competition)
Dates: biennial.
Awards: 500,000 lire.
Deadline: end of November.
For information apply to: Via Tarsia 23, 80135 Naples.

Concorso Nazionale per un Opera Lirica Fondazione A. Curci (Curci Foundation National Competition for a Lyric Opera)
Dates: held biennially in May.
Awards: 3,000,000 lire.
Deadline: April of competition year.
For information apply to: Fondazione Curci, Via Nardones 8, 80132 Naples.

Novara (Piedmont)

Premio Guido Cantelli. Concorso Internazionale per Giovani Direttori d'Orchestra (Guido Cantelli Prize. International Competition for Young Conductors)

Dates: held annually for one week in the middle of July at the Teatro alla Scala, Milan.

Age Limit: under 32 years of age.

Requirements: presentation of a program not exceeding one hour and forty minutes in duration.

Awards: first prize: 2,000,000 lire and a diploma with gold medal. Also the right to conduct a concert at La Scala with the winner of the International Dino Ciani Pianists Competition (see p. 185). The concert is to be repeated at Novara on the occasion of the prize-giving. Second prize and third prize will consist of medals of vermeil and silver, respectively.

Deadline: end of May.

For information apply to: Ente Provinciale per il Turismo, Corso Cavour 2, 28100 Novara.

Probably the most prestigious conductors' competition in Italy, this is named after the gifted Novarese conductor, who died suddenly at the height of his career. The orchestra for the elimination rounds, as well as for the final performance, is that of the Teatro alla Scala. The jury is composed of renowned Italian as well as foreign musicians.

Orvieto (Umbria)

Premio Città di Orvieto (City of Orvieto Prize)

Dates: held annually at the beginning of September.

Eligibility: Contestants must be inscribed in the Corso di Perfezionamento Musicale.

Awards: 1,000,000 lire and a public recital.

For information apply to: Orvieto Festival, c/o Ornella Cogliolo, Via del Babuino 79, 00167 Rome.

Osimo (Ancona, Marche)

Concorso Coppa Pianisti d'Italia (Italian Pianist Cup Competition)

Dates: held annually in late September at the Palazzo Campana in Osimo, concluding at the Teatro La Nuova Fenice.

Age Limit: under 25 years of age.

Awards: The winner of category G, soloists between the ages of 10 and 25, wins a baby grand piano. Other prizes, in all other categories (four hands, two pianos, etc.) receive diplomas of the first, second, and third class.

Deadline: September 1.
For information apply to: Ente Manifestazioni Artistiche, Piazza Dante 7, 60027 Osimo.

Palermo (Sicily)

Concorso Internazionale di Canto (International Singing Competition)
Dates: annual.
Deadline: April 30.
For information apply to: Centro di Avviamento al Teatro Lirico, Teatro del Parco di Villa Castelnuovo, Viale del Fante 70b, 90146 Palermo.

Parma (Emilia-Romagna)

Concorso Internazionale Giovani Cantanti Lirici Premio G. Verdi (G. Verdi Prize, International Competition for Young Opera Singers)
Dates: held annually in mid-October at the Teatro Regio, Parma. Preliminaries are held for about three weeks in July.
Age Limit: 18 to 35.
Awards: first prize, 500,000 lire; second prize, 200,000 lire; third prize, 100,000 lire, and minor prizes.
Deadline: June 30.
For information apply to: Società Corale Parmense G. Verdi, Vicolo Asdente 1, 53100 Parma.

Pisa (Tuscany)

Concorso Internazionale d'Organo Azzolino B. della Ciaia (International Organ Contest)
Dates: biennial. Held in even-numbered years, between September and December.
Age Limit: 31 years of age.
Awards: first prize, 150,000 lire; second prize, 100,000 lire; third prize, 50,000 lire, and other minor prizes.
Deadline: July 15th, even-numbered years.
For information apply to: Segreteria Ente Provinciale del Turismo, Lungarno Mediceo 57, 56100 Pisa.

Ravenna (Emilia-Romagna)

Concorso Internazionale di Organo (International Organ Competition)
Dates: annual.

Awards: first prize, 500,000 lire; second prize, 300,000 lire; third prize, 200,000 lire.

For information apply to: Azienda Autonoma di Soggiorno e Turismo, 48100 Ravenna.

Recanati (Macerata, Marche)

Rassegna Internazionale per Giovani Fisarmonicisti e Chitarristi (International Review of Young Harmonium Players and Guitarists)
Dates: held annually for three days in mid- to late April.
Awards: diplomas in all categories.
Deadline: April 10.
For information apply to: Azienda Autonoma de Soggiorno e Turismo, Piazza Leopardi, 62019 Recanati.

Reggio Nell'Emilia (Emilia-Romagna)

Concorso Internazionale di Canto Premio Achille Peri (International Singing Contest: Achille Peri Prize)
Dates: held annually in late spring or early summer.
Age Limit: none.
Awards: first prize, 200,000 lire; second and third prizes, 100,000 lire. Winners are occasionally invited to take part in one of the performances put on by the ATER (see p. 125).
Deadline: May 15.
For information apply to: Teatro Municipale, 42100 Reggio nell'Emilia.

Rome (Lazio)

Concorso Internazionale di Chitarra Fernando Sor (Fernando Sor International Guitar Competition)
Dates: held annually for four days in May.
Age Limit: 32.
Awards: first prize, 500,000 lire and a gold medal; second prize, 300,000 lire; third prize, 200,000 lire.
For information apply to: Segreteria del Concorso Internazionale di Chitarra F. Sor, Via Flaminia 118, Rome.

Concorso Internazionale di Composizione (International Composition Contest)
Dates: annual.
Awards: a total of 7,600,000 lire distributed in six categories as follows:
    1. One-act opera: 1,000,000 to 3,000,000 lire;

2. Orchestra music with or without soloist: 1,000,000 to 3,000,000 lire;
3. Instrumental and/or vocal music for 36-member orchestra: 600,000 to 1,000,000 lire;
4. Instrumental music for eleven players: 600,000 to 1,000,000 lire;
5. Religious music for orchestra or organ: 500,000 to 1,000,000 lire;
6. Electronic or computer music: 600,000 to 1,000,000 lire.

Eligibility: Entries in categories 2 through 6 may have been published at least three years before the competition. Entries in category 1 may not have been published at all.

Deadline: January 31.

For information apply to: SIMC (Segreteria del Concorso), Piazza Buenos Aires 20, 00198 Rome.

This important competition is sponsored by La Società Italiana Musicale Contemporanea (SIMC) in collaboration with RAI (Radiotelevisione Italiana), as well as the Fenice in Venice, the tourist agency of Perugia, and La Sagra Musicale Umbra, the Accademia Musicale Romana, and Ricordi as well as Suvini-Zerboni.

Concorso Internazionale di Essecuzione per Quartetto d'Archi (International Competition for String Quartet Performance)

Dates: held annually for ten days in late September.

Age Limit: No member of the quartet may be over 40 as of September 1.

Awards: first prize, 2,000,000 lire; second prize, 1,000,000 lire.

For information apply to: Segreteria, Fondazione Carlo Jachino, Conservatorio di Musica Santa Cecilia, Via dei Greci 18, 00187 Rome.

Concorso Internazionale di Musica Sacra (International Competition of Sacred Music)

Dates: held annually in May.

Awards: first prize, 1,000,000 lire and performance of the composition at the International Festival of Taormina.

Deadline: April 30.

Eligibility: The work submitted must be of a definitely sacred nature, either in text or program.

For information apply to: L'Oratorio di S. Filippi Neri, Via del Governo Vecchio 134, 00186 Rome.

Concorso Internazionale per Computer Music

Dates: held annually in February.

Awards: 1,000,000 lire for a program using the computer in musical performance or composition.

Deadline: February.

Eligibility: single people or groups, Italian or foreign.

For information apply to: Segreterio del Concorso, Piazza Buenos Aires 20, 00198 Rome. Sponsored by SIMC in collaboration with Il Centro Nazionale Universitario di Calcalo Elettronico (CNUCE) di Pisa.

Concorso Internazionale per Direttori d'Orchestra Arturo Toscanini (Arturo Toscanini International Orchestra Conductors' Competition)
Date: annual. Mid-September to early October.
Age Limit: under 38.
Awards: first prize, 1,000,000 lire.
Deadline: July 15.
For information apply to: Conservatorio di Musica Santa Cecilia, Via dei Greci 15, 00187 Rome.

Concorso Internazionale per Direttori d'Orchestra (International Symphony Orchestra Conductors' Competition)
Dates: triennial in May or June. Held in 1977.
Age Limit: 35 as of May 1st, year of competition.
Awards: first prize, 2,000,000 lire and invitation to conduct a subscription concert at the Accademia Nazionale di Santa Cecilia. Second prize, 1,000,000 lire.
Deadline: between the end of January and the end of February, year of competition.
For information apply to: Segreteria dell'Accademia Nazionale di Santa Cecilia, Via Vittoria 6, 00187 Rome.

Concorso Nazionale di Composizione per Solisti di Fisarmonica V. Melocchi
Dates: held annually in April.
Awards: first prize, 250,000 lire; second prize, 150,000 lire.
Deadline: end of March.
For information apply to: UNIFA, Via Caltagirone 6, 00182 Rome.

Concorso Nazionale per un'Opera Lirica in Un Atto (National Competition for a Lyric Opera in One Act)
Awards: 1,500,000 lire.
Deadline: January 31.
For information apply to: Cassa Nazionale Assistenzie Musicisti, Via Vicenza 52, 00185 Rome.

Concorso Nazionale per Interpreti di Musica Contemporanea (National Competition for Contemporary Music Interpretation)
Dates: held annually, December 14–18.
Awards: first prize, 400,000 lire; second prize, 300,000 lire; third prize, 200,000 lire.

Deadline: November 15.
For information apply to: Via di Villa Patrizi 14, 00161 Rome.

Concorso Nazionale di Composizione per Complessi (National Competition for Ensemble Composition)

Dates: held annually in May.
Awards: first prize, 200,000 lire; second prize, 100,000 lire.
Deadline: April.
For information apply to: Corali Polifonoci, USCI, Via Caltagirone 6, 00182 Rome.

Rassegna Nazionale Giovani Concertisti (Meeting of Young Artists)

Dates: held annually in early December.
Awards: first prize, 300,000 lire; second prize, 150,000 lire.
Eligibility: pianists, violinists, cellists, singers, chamber groups.
For information apply to: Cassa Nazionale Assistenze Musicisti, Via Vicenza 52, 00185 Rome.

Rovereto (Trentino-Alto Adige)

Concorso Internazionale di Composizione per Due Pianoforti Riccardo Zandonai (Riccardo Zandonai International Two-piano Competition)

Dates: held annually at the end of June.
Awards: first prize, 500,000 lire and performance at Rovereto by the Canino and Ballistra two-piano team the following season.
Eligibility: composition for two pianos between five and ten minutes long which has never been published and never performed.
Deadline: mid-June.
For information apply to: Azienda Autonoma del Turismo, Corso Rossini 33, 38068 Rovereto.

San Remo (Imperia)

Rassegna Internazionale Gino Marinuzzi per Giovani Direttori d'Orchestra e Compositori (Gino Marinuzzi International Competition for Young Orchestra Conductors and Composers)

Dates: held annually in the spring: conductors, even years; composers, odd years.
Age Limit: for conductors and composers who have not yet reached thirty years of age by the 10th of March, the year of competition. No national or sex restriction.
Awards: first prize, 1,500,000 lire; second prize, 800,000 lire; third prize, 500,000 lire plus plentiful performance opportunities.

Deadline: March 10.
For information apply to: Amministrazione Comunale, Rassegna Internazionale
Gino Marinuzzi, 18038 San Remo.

Taormina (Sicily)

Concorso Internazionale di Composizione per Orchestra (International Competition for Orchestral Composition)
Dates: held annually from August 9 to 23.
Awards: 1,500,000 lire.
Deadline: May 15.
For information apply to: CISM, Via Santa Lucia 25, 00165 Rome.

Concorso Internazionale Pianistico Petrof (Petrof International Piano Competition)
Dates: held annually for ten days in early August.
Age Limit: 15 to 32 years.
Awards: first to tenth prizes, ranging from a Petrof grand piano, gold medal,
    250,000 lire, a concert with orchestra, and a recording made in Prague
    (first prize) to a diploma of merit. All finalists are reimbursed for their
    trip.
For information apply to: Azienda Soggiorno e Turismo, Taormina; or the
    Segreteria CISM, Hotel Jolly Diodoro, Taormina.

Premio Mozart (Mozart Prize)
Awards: 1,000,000 lire and gold medal to the best student of Mozart
    interpretation in the summer course of the Estate Musicale di Taormina
    (see p. 176).

Teramo (Abruzzi)

Concorso per Orchestra da Camera (Chamber Orchestra Competition)
Dates: held annually in July.
Eligibility: Any group is eligible, from the smallest string ensemble to large
    wind, percussion, or mixed group.
Deadline: beginning of June.
For information apply to: Ente del Turismo, Via Nazario Sauro 80, 64100
    Teramo.

Terni (Umbria)

Concorso Internazionale Pianistico Alessandro Casagrande (Alessandro Casagrande International Piano Competition)

Dates: held annually in late June for three to four days.
Age Limit: for pianists 32 and under.
Awards: first prize, 1,500,000 lire plus a concert; second prize, 700,000 lire; third prize, 350,000 lire; plus other minor prizes.
For information apply to: Segreterio, Comune di Terni, 05100 Terni.

Treviso (Veneto)

Concorso Nazionale di Esecuzione Pianistica, Premio Città di Treviso (City of Treviso Prize, National Competition of Piano Performance)
Dates: held annually in November.
Awards: first prize, 600,000 lire; second prize, 400,000 lire; third prize, 250,000 lire.
Deadline: October 15.
For information apply to: ENAL, Via Roma (Galleria Altinia), 21100 Treviso.

Trieste (Friuli-Venezia Giulia)

Concorso Internazionale di Composizione Sinfonica, Premio Città di Trieste (City of Trieste Prize, International Symphonic Composition Competition)
Dates: held annually in the fall. Sponsored by the Tartini Conservatory.
Eligibility: No age limits. Symphonic work, with or without soloists, never before published or performed.
Awards: first prize, 2,000,000 lire and public performance; second prize, 750,000 lire and public performance; third prize, 250,000 lire and public performance.
Deadline: early October.
For information apply to: Segreterio, Premio Città di Trieste, Palazzo Municipale, Piazza dell'Unità d'Italia 4, 34100 Trieste.

Turin (Piedmont)

Concorso Nazionale di Musica (National Music Competition)
Dates: held biennially in late May.
Eligibility: open to chamber ensembles.
Awards: first prize, 500,000 lire; second, 250,000 lire.
Deadline: end of April, year of competition.
For information apply to: Circolo degli Artisti, Via Bogino 9, 10123 Turin.

Vercelli (Piedmont)

Concorso Internazionale di Musica e Danza Gian Battista Viotti (G. B. Viotti International Music and Dance Competition)

Dates: held annually from October through early December. Competitions in different categories are held at different times.

Age Limits: for performers under 35 years of age. No age limit for composers.

Awards: Awards differ according to categories. Awards total 8,000,000 lire. Cash plus publication for composition. Cash plus performance for soloists.

Deadline: September or October, according to category.

For information apply to: Società del Quartetto, Casella Postale 127, 13100 Vercelli.

PERIODICALS

One might surmise that, in a country like Italy, where the most important musical product is opera—a spectator sport—there would not be an active market for words *about* music. Nevertheless, there are literally dozens of magazines, published with a fair degree of regularity, devoted entirely to musical subjects. Granted that many of them concern the super-world of rock, many are of a specialized and professional nature, and some are regional in all respects including dialect; this situation notwithstanding, we are able to prepare a list of periodicals with intrinsic interest for the musical amateur, provided he understands Italian. Wherever possible, we have provided the information necessary for the reader to obtain particulars concerning subscription rates and publication schedules. As a general rule, the visitor to Italy will find most of the popular periodicals on newsstands and most of the more esoteric ones in the music shops of the major cities.

Agimus

Notiziario musicale per i giovani (Music news for the young).
Via dei Greci 18, 00187 Rome.
Six times a year.

Almanacco della Canzone e del Cinema (Almanac of song and film)

Editrice VIP, Via del Babuino 181, 00187 Rome.
Monthly.

Angelicum Santandrea

Piazza San Angelo 2, Milan.
Bimonthly.
Recordings: news and reviews.

L'Approdo Musicale

Edizioni ERI, RAI Radiotelevisione Italiana, Via del Babuino 9, 00187 Rome.

Armonia di Voci

Editrice Elle di Ci, 10096 Leumann (Turin).
Bimonthly.

Big (1) della Canzone

Via Treviso 33, 00161 Rome.
Monthly.

Bollettino Ceciliano

Via della Scrofa 70, 00186 Rome.
Bimonthly.
Official organ of the Associazione Italiana Santa Cecilia per la Musica Sacra.

Bollettino del Centro Rossiniano di Studi

Fondazione Gioacchino Rossini, Piazza Olivieri 5, Pesaro.
Quarterly.
Devoted to scholarly articles on Rossini and also lists Rossini events throughout
the world.

Bollettino Notiziario Editoriale Musicale

Pucci e Florio, 80055 Proctici (Naples).
Semiannual.

Caecilia

Via Amrogio Calepio 4, 24100 Bergamo.
Semiannual.

Canto dell'Assemblea

Centro Catechistico Salesiano, Libreria Dottrina Christiana, 10086 Leumann
(Turin).
Quarterly.
Journal of sacred music.

Cappella Sistina

Via della Dataria 94, Rome.
Quarterly.

Carrara

Edizione Musicali Carrara, Via Calepio 4, Bergamo.
Monthly.
Free house journal concerning sacred music.

Celebriano

Revista mensile di musica per la liturgia (Monthly journal of liturgical music).
Casa Editrice Musicali Carrara, Via Calepio 4, Bergamo.
Monthly.

Chigiana

Casa Editrice Leo S. Olschki, Casella Postale 66, 50100 Florence.
Annual.
Publication of the Accademia Musicale Chigiana, Siena.

Collage

Revista internazionale di nuova musica e arti visiva contemporanee (International review of new music and contemporary visual arts).
Casa Editrice Denaro, Via Margueda 177, Palermo.
Semiannual.
Text in English, French, German, Italian, and Spanish.

Il Convegno Musicale

Revista di storia della musica (Review of music history).
Corso Fiume 16, Turin.
Three times a year.

Corriere del Teatro

Corso Vittorio Emanuele 1, Milan.
Six times a year.

D.I.—Discografia Internazionale

Piazzale Loreto 9, 20131 Milan.
Weekly.

Disclub

Piazza San Marco 11, 50121 Florence.
Bimonthly.

Il Disco

Via Milano 46, Lomagna.
Bimonthly.

Discosette

Via Monte Faraone 6, 00141 Rome.

Discoteca Alta Fedeltà

Revista di dischi e musica e alta fedeltà (Review of discs, music, and high
    fidelity).
Esperto S.P.A., Via Martignoni 1, 20124 Milan.
Monthly.
Contains information about current records, artists, special features, and pop
releases. Also technical information about equipment.

L'Eco della Musica

Ufficio Stampa EKO, Casella Postale 7, Recanati.
Bimonthly.

Educazione Musicale

Rassegna trimestrale degli insegnanti di musica (Quarterly review for music
    teachers).
Casa Editrice Angelicum, Piazza Sant'Angelo 2, 20121 Milan.
Quarterly.
Official journal of the Centro Didattico Nazionale Istruzione Artistica.

EKO Club

Revista degli Amici della Musica (Review of the Friends of Music).
Via G. B. Pagano 70, Rome.
Monthly.

Fiori dell'Organo

Revista di musica sacra (Sacred music review).
Casa Musicale Edizioni Carrara, Via Ambrogio Calepio 4, Bergamo.
Monthly.

Fronimo

Revista trimestrale di chitarra e liuto (Quarterly guitar and lute review).
Edizione Suvini Zerboni, Via M. F. Quintiliano 40, 20138 Milan.
Quarterly.

Guida della Musica Leggera (Light Music Guide)

Via Somalia 5, 00199 Rome.
Annual.

Harmonia

Via Guglielmo Massala 83–85, 50154 Florence.
Monthly.

Internazionale Teatro dell'Opera

Via San Gottardo 7, 25100 Brescia.
Bimonthly.

Italcanto

Galleria del Corso 4, 20122 Milan.
Irregular.

Jazz di Ieri e di Oggi (Jazz of Yesterday and Today)

G. Ingoglia, Via Gluck 59, Milan.
Monthly.

Jazzland

Via Pacini 20, 20131 Milan.
Monthly.

Jucunda Laudatio (Joyful Praise)

Rassegna di musica antica (Journal of old music).
Editioni Southern Music S.R.L., Piazzetta Pattari 2, Milan.
Quarterly.
Articles on liturgical music, theory, and practical performance matters. Sponsored by the Fondazione Cini, Venice.

Lirica d'Oggi

Via Verdi 2, 20121 Milan.
Monthly.

Lirica nel Mondo

Casella Postale 7246, 00100 Rome.
Monthly.

Madia l'Amici dell'Arte

Associazione Amici dell'Arte, Fiuri Porta Bazzano 3, L'Aquila.
Bimonthly.

Maestri dell'Organo (Masters of the Organ)

Via Calepio 4, 24100 Bergamo.
Bimonthly.

Magnifici Delle 7 Note

A. Bellinvia, Via Grey 24, 38066 Riva del Garda (Trento).
Quarterly.

Metronomo

Via Baracchini 2, 20123 Milan.
Semiannual.

Il Mondo della Musica

Via della Fonte di Fauno 5, 00153 Rome.
Bimonthly.

Mondo Lirico

Periodico internazionale di attualità lirica (International magazine of lyrical
    events).
Via Nizza 66, 00198 Rome.
Irregular.

Mondomusica

Rassegna del disco e della musica leggera (Review of records and light music).
Via Colombo 24, Canicatti.
Monthly.

Musica d'Oggi (Today's Music)

Rassegna di vita e cultura musicale (Review of musical life and culture).
Edizioni Ricordi, Via Berchet 2, 20121 Milan.
House organ.

Musica e Dischi (Music and Records)

Via Carducci 8, 20123 Milan.
Monthly.
An international musical review.

Musica Jazz

Rassegna mensile d'informazione e critica musicale (Monthly review of music
information and criticism).
Messaggerie Musicali, Via Quintiliano 4, 20138 Milan.
Monthly.
Indexed. Back issues available.

Musicalia

Rivista internazionale di musica (International music review).
Via dei Franzone 6–1, 16145 Genoa.
Quarterly.
Specializes in twentieth-century music, featuring interviews with conductors
and soloists, feature articles in three languages on important composers with
lists of works, discographies, etc. Read by lay public as well as professionals.
Record reviews. Concert reviews and reprints of interest.

Musica Minima

Via G. Negri 8, 20123 Milan.
Bimonthly.

Musica & Nastri (Music and Tapes)

Via Carducci 8, 20123 Milan.

Musica Sacra

Rivista di musica sacra (Sacred music review).
Casa Editrice Musicale Carrara, Via Calepio 4, 24100 Bergamo.
Bimonthly.

Musicae Sacrae Ministerium

Consociato Internazionalis Musicae Sacrae, Piazza Sant'Agostino 20/A, 00786
Rome.
Quarterly.
Editions in English, French, German, Spanish, and Italian. Sacred music only.

Musica Università

Periodico quindicinale di cultura e informazioni musicali (fortnightly review of culture and music information).
Casella Postale 7181, 00100 Rome.
Fortnightly.

Musicalbrande

Colan a Musical diz Brande, Corso Palermo 11, Turin.
Quarterly.
Text in Italian and Piemontais.

Musicisti

Via Palestro 56, 00187 Rome.

Noi Tutti (All of Us)

Piazza Orsini 14, 82100 Milan.
Monthly.

Nuova Rivista Musicale Italiana (New Italian Music Review)

Trimestrale di cultura e informazione musicale (Quarterly culture and music information review).
Edizioni RAI—Radiotelevisione Italiana, Via del Babuino 51, 00187 Rome.
Quarterly.
Articles, book, music, and record reviews.

Oggi in Discoteca

Via Cesare Pratico 21, 00041 Albano Laziale (Rome).
Bimonthly.

L'Opera

Rassegna internazionale del teatro lirico (International review of lyric theater).
Editorial Fenerete, Via Beruto 7, 20131 Milan.
Quarterly.
A magazine dedicated to the international lyric theater. Text mainly in Italian, with some articles in English, French, German, and Spanish.

L'Organista

Casa Editrice Musicale Carrara, Via Calepio 4, 24100 Bergamo.
Bimonthly.

L'Organo

Rivista di cultura organaria e organistica (Review of organs and organists).
Casa Editrice Patron, Via Badini, 40127 Bologna.
Semiannual.
Summaries in Italian, French, English, and German. Back issues available.

Pentagramma

Via Bolzano 32, Rome.
Monthly.
Tabloid format.

Psalterium

Rivista internazionale di musica sacra (International review of sacred music).
Edizioni Casimiri, Via Santa Caterina de Siena 61, Rome.
Bimonthly.

Quaderni della Rassegna Musicale

Giulio Einaudi, Via Umberto Biancamano, Turin.
Irregular.

Rassegna Melodrammatica

Corriere de musica (music news).
Corso Porta Romana 80, Milan.
Semimonthly.
Opera journal.

Rassegna Musicale Curci

Periodico di cultura e attualità musicali (Cultural and musical events periodical).
Edizioni Curci, Galleria del Corso 4, 20122 Milan.
Quarterly.
Free house organ.

Risveglio Bandistico

A music review published by ANBIMA (see p. 26) and the Center for the Diffusion of Music Cultures.
Via Marianna Dionigi 43, 00193 Rome.
Bimonthly.

Rivista Italiana di Musicologia (Italian Musicological Review)

Casa Editrice Leo S. Olschki, Viuzzo del Pozzetti 6, Viale Europe, 50126
  Florence.
Semiannual.
Official journal of the Italian Musicological Society.

La Scala

Rivista dell'Opera.
Editoriale Delvino, Corso Monforte 16, Milan.
Eleven times a year.
House organ of La Scala.

Schola e Assemblea

Rivista musicale sacra (Review of sacred music).
Casa Musicale Edizioni Carrara, Via Ambrogio da Calepio 4, 24100 Bergamo.

Lo Spettatore Musicale (The Musical Spectacle)

Via Nizza 45, 00198 Rome.
Bimonthly.

Strumenti e Musica (Instruments and Music)

Via Redipuglia 65, 60100 Ancona.
Monthly.

Studi Musicali

Casa Editrice Leo S. Olschki, Casella Postale 66, 50100 Florence.
Semiannual.
Student periodical of the Accademia di Santa Cecilia.

Verdi

Bolletino dell'Istituto di Studi Verdiani (Bulletin of the Institute for Verdi
  Studies).
Strada della Repubblica 57, 43100 Parma.
Irregular.
Text in English, German, Italian, and other languages.

$e\mathscr{A}$ppendix

Several organizations with offices in New York City and others with offices abroad can be of service to those intending to spend several months or a year studying in Europe. They include the following:

Institute of International Education
809 United Nations Plaza, New York, N.Y. 10017   Tel: (212) 883-8200

Council on International Educational Exchange'
777 United Nations Plaza, New York, N.Y. 10017   Tel: (212) 661-0310
(Paris address of the CIEE: 49 rue Pierre Charron, Paris VIII)

Institute for American Universities (under the suspices of)
University of Aix-Marseille, 27 place de l'Université, 13, Aix-en-Provence, France.

Some organizations can provide assistance in locating employment abroad. These include:

International School Services, Educational Staffing Program
392 Fifth Avenue, New York, N.Y. 10018

American Association of Colleges for Teacher Education
Associate Secretary for International Relations
One Dupont Circle, Suite 610, Washington, D.C. 20036

U.S. Government, Committee on International Exchange of Persons
Senior Fulbright-Hays Program
2101 Constitution Avenue, N.W., Washington, D.C. 20418

Recruitment and Source Development Staff, Office of Personnel and Training
U.S. Information Agency, Washington, D.C. 20547

Finally, two additional organizations that can help you if you intend to stay abroad for a considerable length of time:

Sabbatical Year in Europe
265 Maple Avenue, Morton, Pa. 19070

This organization provides information on special rates for sabbatical flights, establishes contacts with Europeans who are willing to advise you on your sabbatical, and helps make available an exchange of apartments for its members.

Vacation Exchange Club
663 Fifth Avenue, New York, N.Y. 10036.
This group helps to arrange an exchange of homes or apartments for those who need it.

It is advisable when writing to any of these organizations to state your reasons for going abroad and to ask for practical as well as professional advice for your visit. In the United States, send along a stamped, self-addressed envelope. When writing to foreign organizations, send an International Reply Coupon, available at most local post offices. This added courtesy should assure you a more prompt reply.

For additional information on living in various countries of Europe during a sabbatical year, consult *Shoestring Sabbatical,* edited by Harold E. Taussig (Philadelphia, Pa.: Westminster Press, 1971).

Reference Books for the Student or Scholar Going Abroad

European Library Directory: A Geographical and Bibliographical Guide. Richard C. Lewanski, Florence: Olschki, 1968.
Fellowship Guide for Western Europe, published by the Council of European Studies, 213 Social Sciences Building, University of Pittsburgh, Pittsburgh, Pa. 15213
   The *Fellowship Guide* is intended for American graduate students, faculty, and researchers in the social sciences and humanities who need funds for study or research in Western Europe. Included is information about those fellowships that permit an extended stay abroad (usually one academic year), either in residence at a specific foreign university or for independent research.
Guide to Study in Europe. Shirley Herman. New York: Four Winds Press. 1969.

Handbook on International Study for U.S. Nationals. New York: Institute of International Education.
International Library Directory: A World Directory of Libraries, 3rd ed. A. P. Wales. London: The A. P. Wales Organization, 1969-70.
Performing Arts Libraries and Museums of the World. André Veinstein, Paris: Editions du CNRS, 1967.
Study Abroad. Paris: United Nations, Educational, Scientific and Cultural Organization, 1969.
Subject Collections in European Libraries: A Directory and Bibliographical Guide. Richard C. Lewanski. New York: Bowker, 1965.
Youth Travel Abroad: What to Know Before You Go. This pamphlet is issued by the State Department and is designed to help young Americans abroad. It is available for 20 cents from the U.S. Government Printing Office, Washington, D.C. 20402.

Additional Information for Student Travelers

A *Student Travelpack* put together by the Council on International Educational Exchange includes information on discounts available to students, intra-European charter flights, youth fares, student tours, etc. It can be obtained free from the Council at 777 United Nations Plaza, New York, N.Y. 10017

The Council also issues to eligible students, at a cost of $2.00, the *International Student Identity Card* (for college undergraduates and graduate students) and the *International Scholar Identity Card* (for high school and other nonuniversity students). These are accepted throughout Western Europe for discounts on intra-European air, train, and bus travel, low-cost tours, student lodgings, and meals in student restaurants. Several cities will give student rates for concerts and opera performances if one presents an I.S.I.D. card, although this does not apply to all theaters in those cities. Museums often give discounts too. The cards are valid from October 1 of one year to December 31 of the following year.

The Student Air Travel Association
British Student Travel Centre, Suite 1602, 80 Fifth Avenue, New York, N.Y. 10011   Tel: (212) 243-9114

This organization operates student charter flights. For information, write to the above address.

International Student Exchange
Europa House, University of Illinois, 802 West Oregon, Urbana, Ill. 61801
                                                          Tel: (217) 344-5863

This organization arranges study trips in Europe.

Internationaler Jugendaustausch—und Besucherdienst
Lennestrasse 1, D 53 Bonn, Germany

This organization provides information about vacation language courses which combine language instruction and tours of Germany.

Council on Intercultural Relations
3 South Prospect Avenue, Park Ridge, Ill. 60068
Director: Mr. Paul F. Koutny
Austrian Branch: Bindergasse 5-9, A-1090 Vienna IX, Austria   Tel: 34 33 60

This organization sponsors the Undergraduate Program at the Vienna International Music Center, which offers American college students a music study program for a semester or the entire year. The Council also makes special arrangements for faculty on sabbatical to do research in Vienna. In addition, it co-sponsors with the American Choral Directors Association the Vienna Symposium for American Choral Directors (held in June and August). For further information, write to above addresses.

The Institute of European Studies
The John Hancock Center, 875 North Michigan Avenue, Chicago, Ill. 60611
Tel: (312) 944-1750

The Institute offers American college students a variety of programs in six European cities: Durham, Freiburg, Madrid, Nantes, Paris, and Vienna. The Institute offers its own courses taught in many fields by European professors, but it also encourages students to take regular European university courses for which they have satisfactory preparation. Only the Vienna and Nantes programs offer courses in music. The Extension Division of the Institute provides services for a complete range of tours, workshops, and professional programs for the American musician—students and professionals alike. In addition, the Institute sponsors music festivals from time to time. For complete information, write to the above address.

International Institute for Humanistic Studies
3718 Dumbarton Street, Houston, Tex. 77025

This institute sponsors master courses in music in Vienna and Salzburg from the end of May through the end of June. The Piano Master Course was given in 1973 by Paul Badura-Skoda, Jorge Demus, Viola Thern, and Eva Badura-Skoda; the faculty of the Seminar in Baroque Performance Practices included Nikolaus Harnoncourt, Alice Harnoncourt, Christoph Wolff, and Herbert Tachezi.

Certificates of attendance will be awarded all persons successfully participating in the piano course and performance practices seminar. A limited number of scholarships is available. Undergraduate and graduate students are eligible. Pianists who wish to apply for a scholarship must send a tape by April 1. For further information, write to the above address.

International Postal Abbreviations for European Countries (For Intra-European Mail Only)
    These abbreviations are to be used *only* when writing from one European country to another. For example, when writing to the Palais des Beaux-Arts in Brussels from Paris, the address of the Palais should be: 23 rue Ravenstein, B-1000 Bruxelles. (The "B" stands for Belgium.) When writing to the Palais from Brussels or anywhere else in Belgium, the address is simply 23 rue Ravenstein, 1000 Bruxelles. (The "B" is unnecessary within the country.) However, when writing from the United States to Belgium, be sure that the address has Belgium *as well as* 1000 Bruxelles indicated on the envelope.

Austria = A
Belgium = B
Denmark = DK
Finland = SF
France = F
Germany = D
Great Britain = GB
Italy = I
Netherlands = NL
Norway = N
Sweden = S
Switzerland = CH

Index